An Illustrated History of
SCOTLAND

JARROLD
PUBLISHING

Eilean Donan Castle, Wester Ross

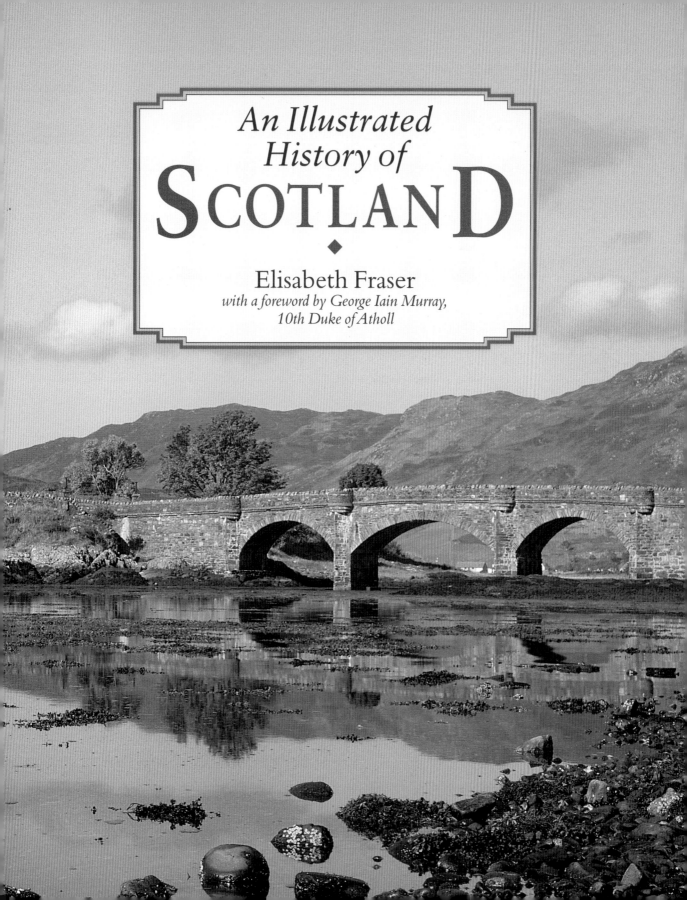

An Illustrated
History of
SCOTLAND
◆

Elisabeth Fraser
with a foreword by George Iain Murray,
10th Duke of Atholl

Acknowledgements

I would like to thank the many people who have helped me in the compilation of this work, in particular: Dr J N G Ritchie, Dr D Breeze, Pat Dishon, Francis Thompson, J MacKenzie and Mae MacLeod and also to the following for their help and assistance: the National Trust for Scotland; Historic Scotland; Burns Heritage Centre, Alloway; Old Town Mill, Burns Interpretation Centre, Dumfries; Glamis Castle; Dunvegan Castle; Scone Palace; Blair Castle; the North Assynt Estate; Sabhal Mor Ostaig-Gaelic College, Skye; Dualchos Museum, Skye; Lochalsh District Council; Pluscarden Abbey; the David Livingstone Centre; the John Muir Trust; the Carnegie Trust; the National Galleries of Scotland; Glasgow Museums; Aberdeen Art Gallery; Mary Evans Picture Library; Provost Skene's House, Aberdeen; the Edinburgh Reference Library; the Edinburgh Library; the National Library of Scotland; the Edinburgh Festival Office; the Royal Botanic Garden, Edinburgh; the Botanic Garden, Glasgow and the Scottish Tourist Board. I would also like to thank Miss Joan Matthews of C J Brown, Son & Co., Bob Taylor, Geoffrey Sutton and the many people who have given me encouragement to persevere, as well as invaluable assistance and helpful suggestions and without whom I could not have managed.

Over the last 30 years I have visited nearly every place that I have mentioned in this book and this gave me a unique opportunity to gather information from the many places of interest, historical sites, libraries, museums and information centres to be found all over Scotland. Finally, I would like to express my special gratitude to Edward Averill, William Dolby, Norman Atkinson and Kathleen Cook for their painstaking efforts in helping me through so much of the text. Also to my publishers, Jarrold Publishing, in particular Antony Jarrold and Donald Greig, and the many people whose efforts have made this book possible, especially Therese Duriez, Bridget Lely, James Hopkin, Stuart McLaren, Ellen Moorcraft and Steve Plackett.

An Illustrated History of Scotland

Designed and produced by Jarrold Publishing, Whitefriars, Norwich NR3 1TR

Copyright © 1997 Jarrold Publishing
Text © 1997 Jarrold Publishing
Photographs © Jarrold Publishing, except for those detailed on page 189

ISBN 0-7117-0856-8

Printed and bound in Scotland by Cambus Litho Ltd, East Kilbride and Hunter & Foulis Ltd, Edinburgh.

Contents

Maps

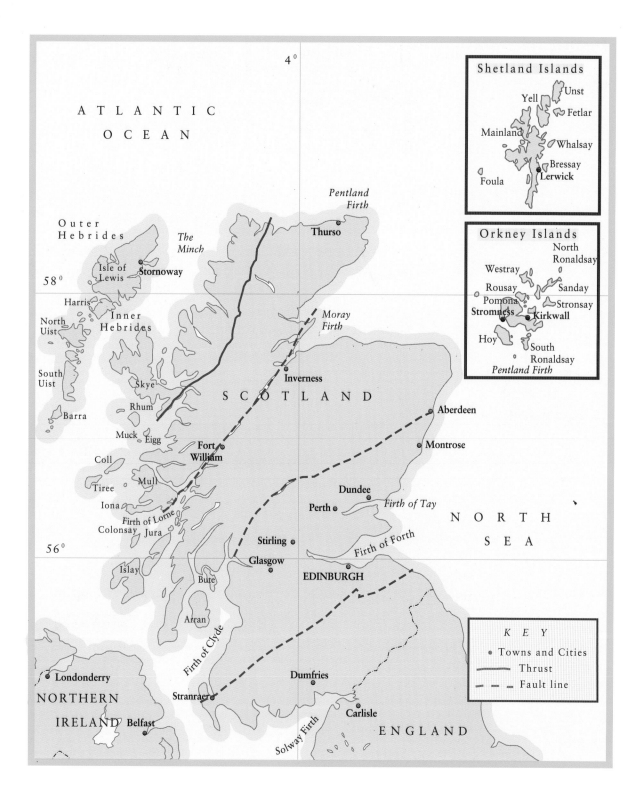

4°

ATLANTIC
OCEAN

Shetland Islands

Yell   Unst
          Fetlar
Mainland
          Whalsay
          Bressay
Foula   **Lerwick**

*Pentland
Firth*

Thurso

Outer
Hebrides

*The
Minch*

Isle of
Lewis   **Stornoway**

58°

Harris

North
Uist

Inner
Hebrides

*Moray
Firth*

Orkney Islands

North
Ronaldsay
Westray
Rousay   Sanday
Pomona   Stronsay
Stromness **Kirkwall**

Hoy   South
           Ronaldsay
Pentland Firth

South
Uist

Skye

Rhum

Barra

Muck Eigg

Coll

Tiree Mull

Iona
Firth of Lorne
Colonsay Jura

Islay

Bute

Arran

Inverness

S C O T L A N D

Aberdeen

Montrose

**Fort
William**

Dundee
Perth *Firth of Tay*

Stirling
Glasgow

EDINBURGH

Firth of Forth

N O R T H

S E A

Londonderry

NORTHERN

IRELAND **Belfast**

Firth of Clyde

Stranraer

Dumfries

Carlisle

Solway Firth

E N G L A N D

56°

K E Y

● Towns and Cities
── Thrust
- - - Fault line

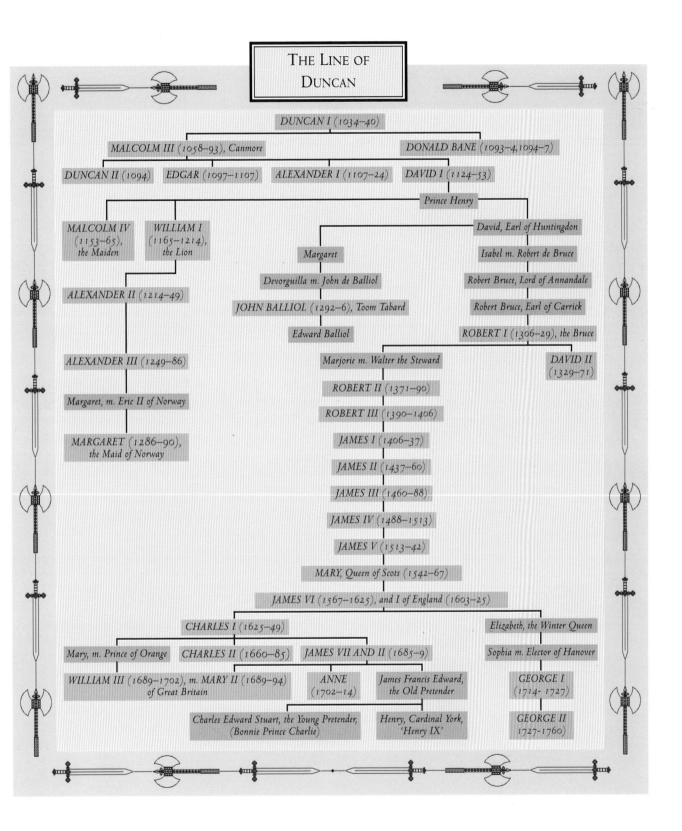

THE LINE OF
DUNCAN

DUNCAN I (1034–40)

MALCOLM III (1058–93), Canmore

DONALD BANE (1093–4, 1094–7)

DUNCAN II (1094)   EDGAR (1097–1107)   ALEXANDER I (1107–24)   DAVID I (1124–53)

Prince Henry

MALCOLM IV (1153–65), the Maiden   WILLIAM I (1165–1214), the Lion

David, Earl of Huntingdon

Margaret

Isabel m. Robert de Bruce

Devorguilla m. John de Balliol

Robert Bruce, Lord of Annandale

ALEXANDER II (1214–49)

JOHN BALLIOL (1292–6), Toom Tabard

Robert Bruce, Earl of Carrick

Edward Balliol

ROBERT I (1306–29), the Bruce

ALEXANDER III (1249–86)

Marjorie m. Walter the Steward

DAVID II (1329–71)

Margaret, m. Eric II of Norway

ROBERT II (1371–90)

MARGARET (1286–90), the Maid of Norway

ROBERT III (1390–1406)

JAMES I (1406–37)

JAMES II (1437–60)

JAMES III (1460–88)

JAMES IV (1488–1513)

JAMES V (1513–42)

MARY, Queen of Scots (1542–67)

JAMES VI (1567–1625), and I of England (1603–25)

CHARLES I (1625–49)

Elizabeth, the Winter Queen

Mary, m. Prince of Orange   CHARLES II (1660–85)   JAMES VII AND II (1685–9)

Sophia m. Elector of Hanover

WILLIAM III (1689–1702), m. MARY II (1689–94) of Great Britain   ANNE (1702–14)   James Francis Edward, the Old Pretender

GEORGE I (1714–1727)

Charles Edward Stuart, the Young Pretender, (Bonnie Prince Charlie)   Henry, Cardinal York, 'Henry IX'

GEORGE II 1727–1760

Foreword

It is indeed a great honour to be asked to write a foreword to *An Illustrated History of Scotland*. This book fills the need for an accessible account of the events which have shaped the Scottish nation, for within these pages lie all the people, places and great moments in history for which Scotland is justly renowned. Many of these places I have the privilege of being associated with in my capacity as President of the National Trust for Scotland, an organisation which has contributed so much to the preservation of this country's magnificent heritage.

From prehistoric days to twentieth-century discussion, this is a comprehensive look at a country known the world over for the friendliness of its spirit and warmness of its welcome, traditional and enduring qualities which stem from the past but are rooted in the present.

Athole

Sadly, the 10th Duke of Atholl died before this book was published. It is dedicated to his memory.

Left: *piper at Blair Castle, Perthshire,*
the ancient seat of the Dukes of Atholl

Out of the mists of time

Observing Scotland's natural beauty makes you wonder how the contours of its varied landscapes were formed, and how they moulded the characters and lives of the people who lived there long ago. Upheavals of immense magnitude produced the grandeur to be found in so many parts of the country, and it has taken hundreds of millions of years for the land to assume its present form. Extremes of temperature, volcanic eruptions and earthquakes all contributed in creating such breathtaking scenery. Some 10,000 to 11,000 years BC there was a massive glaciation which proved to be the last significant event to play its part in forming the Scottish landscape.

Slowly the land took shape as it responded to the pressure of the elements and, when the ice melted, new contours were revealed. On the resulting debris, small shrubs and grasslands came into being and these were followed by birch and hazel trees, precursors of the great forests of oak and pine that eventually came to cloak the landscape.

As the ice melted, the sea level rose, causing first Ireland and then the British mainland to be separated from the continental land mass, and resulting in the formation of the North Sea.

Faults in the earth's surface produced distinct structural divisions, or geographical areas, in the land that is now Scotland. The Highland Boundary Fault Line was formed about four million years ago by the splitting and folding of the earth's crust, and lies diagonally from south-west (Firth of Clyde) to north-east (Stonehaven), roughly separating the Highlands to the north from the Lowlands to the south. Divisions were also formed by the Moine Thrust, running from the extreme north-western Highlands (Loch Eriboll, sea loch) to the south-west Highlands (Sound of Sleat, South Skye); the Great Glen Fault Line, running from the Moray Firth (by Inverness) to the sea loch, Loch Linnhe (by Fort William); and the Southern Upland Fault Line, separating England from Scotland and lying diagonally across the land from the Solway Firth in the south-west to Berwick-on-Tweed in the north-east. All these fault lines helped to make Scotland geographically and geologically unique.

THE HIGHLANDS

North-west of the Highland Boundary Fault Line, an area of startling beauty gradually emerged. Rugged and often boggy, this land became covered with dense forests, interspersed with extensive stretches of water that linked meandering rivers and deep gorges. Awesome mountain ranges gave way to unfathomable lochs where primitive creatures lurked. Sea lochs penetrated far inland through wild untouched country.

The varied coastline, with its isolated islands often shrouded in mist, sometimes reveals sharp receding cliffs – rocky and imposing. Waterfalls cascade down

Left: *'cup and ring' marked stone outcrop, c. 1800BC*
Right: *the tranquil waters of Loch Linnhe, near Fort William, at the western end of the Great Glen Fault Line*

the face of the rock into the turbulent sea below. These rocky shorelines occasionally open out into beautiful golden beaches extending for miles. Remote sheltered bays are backed by fertile lands that once stretched into virgin forests teeming with wildlife.

THE LOWLANDS

To the south-east of the Highland Boundary Fault Line, the Lowlands were also covered with forests and with wild coastal areas, but the land was generally richer and more suitable for settlement. On the eastern and western sides of the country, the sea ventured inland to form wide passages where strong currents and tides met the major rivers; these became known as 'firths'. On the eastern side lie the Firth of Tay and the Firth of Forth; on the western side, the Firth of Clyde and the Solway Firth.

Top right: *the dramatic rocky shoreline at Kilt Rock waterfall, near Staffin on the Trotternish Peninsula, Isle of Skye*
Above: *Scott's View, near Melrose, in The Borders*
Right: *Ardessie Falls, near Little Loch Broom, in the Highland region*

Right: *the carefully constructed interior of Unstan Chambered Cairn on Orkney*

The hills in the Lowlands were formed at the same time as the mountains of the Highlands but, being of a different rock formation, are not so high or rugged. The glens alternated with wide open areas that became densely forested, while the rivers which ran between the hills formed deep gorges or waterfalls, or flowed gently on through rich fertile lands.

These Lowlands – especially on the western coast, where the seas are dotted with many small islands – enticed early settlers. In those far-off days the weather was somewhat warmer than it is today, but the environmental distinctions between the Lowlands and the Highlands had widely differing effects upon the lives of the people who ventured to live there.

PREHISTORIC MONUMENTS

No one really knows for certain who the first people to reach Scotland were, although it is known that settlers came to the country several thousand years after the last Ice Age and lived around the coast, by the rivers and on some of the surrounding islands. They followed a nomadic way of life, hunting and fishing to sustain themselves. The Provost Skene House Museum in Aberdeen reports that there were settlers in the Aberdeen area 8000 years ago, while the *Skye Data Atlas* reports that there were people living on the Island of Rhum at about the same time. In Morton, in Fife and elsewhere in Scotland there is evidence of other early prehistoric communities.

Ronald Hutton, in his book *The Pagan Religions of the Ancient British Isles*, maintains that human beings were living on these isles before the last Ice Age. Axes have been found in the south of Scotland which substantiate this, and it is known that several branches of the ancient Celtic race roamed in tribes all over Europe thousands of years ago.

The earliest ancient monuments go back to about 6000 BC, but the construction of many of them remains an enigma. As they bear close similarities to other monuments found across Europe, the ruins reveal a link between the tribes inhabiting Scotland and those of neighbouring countries.

Chambered cairns

Examples of chambered cairns or burial sites have been found in many parts of Scotland, mostly dating back between 5000 and 6000 years. Their construction was ordered and careful. For example, the huge kerbstones found at the entrance of some of the cairns have been shaped to fit a passageway leading to the burial chambers. The extraordinary chambered cairn at Maes Howe on Orkney is the largest in Scotland, and is believed to have had a royal connection.

Standing stones or stone henges

Perhaps the most fascinating ruins are the massive standing stones, or henges, found in the area of burial cairns, such as the standing stones of Callanish, which are situated around the shores of Loch Roag on the Isle of Lewis in the Western Isles, and date back to about 3000 BC. The site was deeply buried in peat when it was first excavated in the middle of the last century, and some of the stones have been repositioned. The monument takes the form of a circle of thirteen standing stones with a taller central monolith. A double line of stones to the north forms an avenue which leads to a very small chambered cairn near the

centre of the circle. This cairn dates from a later period but was built in accordance with the overall layout. There are also single lines of stones to the east, south and west which make the site resemble a cross. It has been suggested that all the stones are aligned to mark astronomical movements of the sun, moon and stars. The Callanish Circle is similar to those found at Stonehenge in England and Carnac in Brittany.

The stone circle at Maes Howe in the Orkney Isles is found some distance away from the cairn. The Ring of Brogar, which is regarded as the finest standing stone circle in Orkney, lies nearby above the Harray Loch (not far from Stromness), and is of roughly the same period as Maes Howe. At one time it was believed to have comprised of 60 standing stones in a 2-acre (0.8-hectare) site, but now there are only a few stones left. Nevertheless, they still form a perfect circle, 340ft (103.6m) across, inside a rock-cut ditch. To the south-east is the huge outlying Comet Stone, so called in the eighteenth century because the Ring of Brogar was considered to be the Temple of the Sun.

Nearby, across the narrow isthmus, is the circle or henge of Stenness, thought to represent the Temple of the Moon because of its crescent shape. Of the Stenness Circle only four of the original twelve stones remain, one of which is over 15ft (4.6m) high.

Brochs

One of the most interesting prehistoric monuments found in Scotland is the broch. These towers, built of drystone and with one entrance, were a unique architectural invention found mostly in the northern area of Scotland and dating back to before 1000 BC. Their hollow wall construction was designed to allow the builders to achieve as great a height as possible without adding disproportionately to the weight. The walls were joined by long stones to strengthen them, and the area between the two walls was used for living in and for stairs to the top of the tower. Brochs are usually 9–11ft (2.–3.m) in internal diameter, about 15–16ft (4–5m) thick and around 30–40ft (9–12m) high. They are often weathered away at the top, giving the impression that they could have been much higher originally. The finest example is the Broch of Mousa, which stands on a raised rocky stretch on the shoreline of Mousa, one of the Shetland Isles.

PREHISTORIC VILLAGES

Jarlshof

One of Scotland's greatest archaeological sites is found close to the airport in the Shetland Isles. Discovered in 1890 after a winter's storm, when the wind exposed a site dating from neolithic times to the Norse era, it was christened Jarlshof – the name Sir Walter Scott

EARLY CULTURE IN SCOTLAND

The Celtic tribes came over to the British Isles in the centuries before Christ. They had already successfully dominated large areas of Europe, and built strongholds in Scotland to secure their position. The Celtic language was a common link between the different Celts who once occupied Brittany in France and parts of England, Wales, Scotland and Ireland.

Celtic peoples were often associated with a ritualistic form of faith organised by the Druids, their religious leaders, who possibly guided Celtic kings in matters of government.

The Celts had a deep appreciation of nature and a considerable knowledge of how to till the land and rear cattle. They were also cultured and artistic, creating intricate and delicate motifs which are still copied today.

The Ring of Brogar, an early gathering place on Orkney

gave to the sixteenth-century mansion house on the site. Some of the early historic finds almost certainly date back 3500 to 4000 years, and archaeologists believe that beneath the existing ruins lie other remains from an even earlier period.

One of the most interesting discoveries in Jarlshof was a Norse farmstead, which constitutes one of the largest settlements of Vikings to have been discovered, and which suggests that they had set up a community in the same area as earlier settlers. The Jarlshof ruins also contain one of the best preserved wheelhouses, or round-house complexes, so called because the ground plan resembles a spoked wheel.

Skara Brae

Another exceptionally interesting prehistoric village was found at Skara Brae in Orkney. The ten houses which made up the settlement were exposed after a savage storm in 1850, and when archaeologists excavated them, they discovered an almost perfectly preserved village which had been buried beneath sand for nearly 4000 years. People appear to have lived there continuously for 600 years. There are only one or two similar sites in the whole of Europe. The structure of the village shows that people settled there as a community in interconnected stone houses, and the size of the complex indicates that the land was good for cultivation, allowing the inhabitants to prosper.

Right: *arrowheads found at Skara Brae in Orkney*
Left: *a round-house at Jarlshof in the Shetland Isles*

In the footsteps of the Romans

By the first century AD, the Romans had achieved domination over the Mediterranean basin and surrounding lands. At the dawn of the Christian era, during the reign of Augustus, they had already established a powerful empire, the might of which had not been seen since the time of Alexander the Great, four centuries earlier.

INVASION

The Romans occupied southern Britain for over three and a half centuries and during this time the native tribes were influenced by Roman culture and began to develop into communities. The Romans also invaded the Lowlands of northern Britain (now Scotland) and at times occupied territory there. However, this area never really became part of the Roman Empire, its inhabitants remained outside Roman jurisdiction and their own ancient customs prevailed.

If it had not been for the remarkable Roman historian, Tacitus, who wrote a meticulous account of this period, the early history of Scotland would not have been recorded. During AD 79–84, he produced *The Life of Julius Agricola*. Agricola was Tacitus' father-in-law and the first Roman general to invade Scotland. There were other Roman records of the times, but none dealt so directly with the events that took place in Scotland.

Julius Caesar had made an expedition to Britain in 55 BC and invaded the land with a considerable force, yet he had returned to Rome without conquering the people. It was not until AD 43 that the fourth Emperor, Claudius, through his general, Aulus Plautius, successfully invaded the British Isles. Riding at the head of a prodigious force, Claudius was determined to conquer Britain and add prestige and glory to his new status as emperor. The island inhabitants were incapable of defending themselves against the power of Rome. The invading army was strong, united and disciplined, whereas the people living on the British Isles were of many different races, divided into diverse tribes, and spoke a variety of dialects.

The Romans regarded the people native to southern Britain as barbarians, but the ancient Britons had more advanced procedures for governing themselves than the Romans appreciated. Indeed, in AD 61 Queen Boadicea, who came from the area now known as Norfolk and Suffolk, severely weakened the Roman occupation. However, Claudius considered the country conquered, and he returned to Rome in triumph.

CNAEUS JULIUS AGRICOLA

In AD 78, General Julius Agricola, a Roman senator born in Gaul, was sent by the Emperor Vespasian to govern Britain. He was appointed to continue the process of Romanising the southern Britons.

Left: *bust of Julius Caesar*
Right: *Scotland at the time of the Romans*

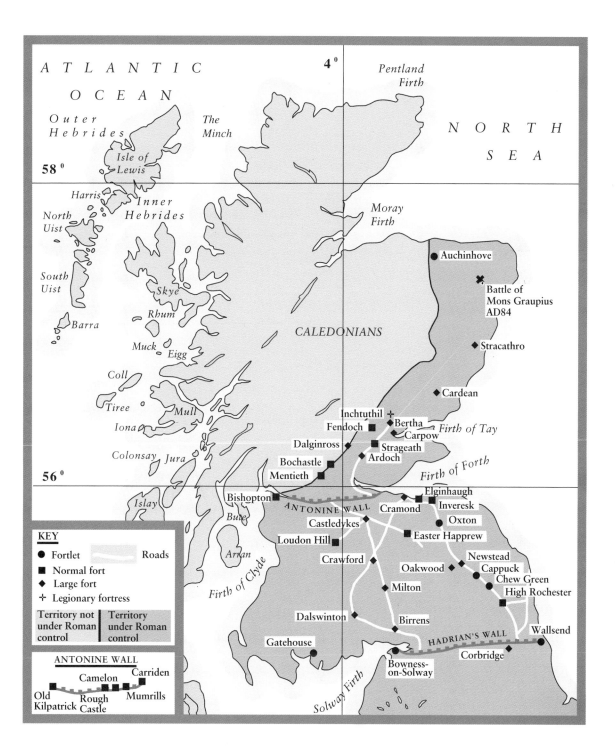

ATLANTIC
OCEAN

*Outer
Hebrides*

*The
Minch*

4⁰

*Pentland
Firth*

N O R T H

S E A

58⁰

*Isle of
Lewis*

Harris

*Inner
Hebrides*

*North
Uist*

*Moray
Firth*

*South
Uist*

Barra

Skye

Rhum

Muck
Eigg

Coll

Tiree

Iona

Mull

Colonsay
Jura

56⁰

Islay

Bute

Arran

Firth of Clyde

CALEDONIANS

● Auchinhove

✕

Battle of
Mons Graupius
AD84

◆ Stracathro

◆ Cardean

Inchtuthil ✢
Fendoch   ◆ Bertha
■   Carpow
Dalginross ◆   *Firth of Tay*
■ Strageath
Bochastle   ◆ Ardoch
Mentieth ■

Bishopton ■   Elginhaugh ■
        ANTONINE WALL Inveresk ◆
Castledykes Cramond ◆ ● Oxton
◆   ■ Easter Happrew
Loudon Hill ■
Crawford ◆   Oakwood ◆ Newstead ◆
                           Cappuck ◆
Milton ◆   Chew Green ●
                  High Rochester ■
Dalswinton ◆   Birrens ◆
                      HADRIAN'S WALL Wallsend ●
Gatehouse ●
Bowness-   Corbridge ◆
on-Solway

Firth of Forth

Solway Firth

KEY

● Fortlet
■ Normal fort
◆ Large fort
✢ Legionary fortress

| Territory not under Roman control | Territory under Roman control |

ANTONINE WALL
                    Carriden
      Camelon
Old   Mumrills
Kilpatrick Rough
            Castle

In the meantime, the Britons of the north, whom the Romans called Caledonians, became aware that south Britain was occupied by an army of powerful fighting men from across the seas. Being descended from an early Celtic race, the north Britons were not afraid to combat the invaders.

The imperialist Romans were, however, intent upon conquering the whole of Britain. Excavations in Annandale suggest that there had been an earlier attempt by the invaders to push their way into northern Britain which had reached as far as Carlisle. There is also evidence that Roman forts and camps were established throughout the area now known as the Borders, and in the Dumfries and Galloway area.

In AD 79–80, Agricola assembled a large army, but the further north he went, the more difficult it was for him to manoeuvre, as the terrain became mountainous and forested. He also found that although the tactics of the northern Britons were no real threat to his men, they were a constant source of aggravation.

Each time Agricola advanced northward he took a different route, engineering a number of roads and forts as he advanced. The first route took him as far as Elginhaugh (near Dalkeith), where he set up a fort well equipped with cook-houses and camping areas. Once the Romans were properly established, Agricola marched from Elginhaugh to attack the northern Britons. From AD 79–84 he proceeded to conquer one

Above: *bronze head of the Emperor Hadrian*
Right: *one of the regularly positioned mile-castles, or fortified positions, on Hadrian's Wall*

Unique Roman defensive pits at Rough Castle by the Antonine Wall, near Falkirk

tribe after another, building forts as he did so, in a line running between the Firth of Forth and the Firth of Clyde. He left soldiers behind to defend these forts and supervise the conquered tribes. After two years, all the tribes south of the Firths of Forth and Clyde were under Roman authority. For a while, these Lowland tribes coexisted with the Romans without any major problems, and even began to trade with their new rulers.

Once Agricola had control of the Lowlands of northern Britain, he made several attempts to conquer the tribes further north. Sending a fleet to explore the western coasts, he founded a base at Carpow on the Tay estuary to supply the Roman soldiers with rations of corn, oil and wine. He made an advance through Strathallan, Strathearn and Strathmore to the permanent forts built at Ardoch and Stracathro. The large military complex at Ardoch, near Dunblane, was one of the Romans' best-fortified encampments in Britain and was one of the most impressive forts in the whole Roman Empire. It comprised an annexe, a watch-tower and six overlapping marching camps, and was constantly improved and enlarged. Other fortifications in the area included that of the Fendoch in the Sma' Glen and a fortified settlement at Comrie built in the period AD 80–8. Agricola also established a

camp at Auchinhove (by Keith, Banffshire), which was once thought to be the northernmost Roman camp in the Empire, but aerial photography has since shown that there were camps much further north, along the Moray coast.

Agricola tried several times to advance further into the Highlands. Finally, using Stracathro fort as a base, he made one more concerted attempt. The Caledonians put up fierce resistance, but were not strong enough to repel the highly disciplined Roman army. Agricola was victorious, beating the Caledonians at the Battle of Mons Graupius in AD 83.

However, the Roman victory was short-lived. When winter came they had little choice but to withdraw their 10,000 men and auxiliaries. Having come so near to establishing complete control of Scotland, Agricola was recalled to Rome by the Emperor Domitian in the winter of AD 84.

HADRIAN'S WALL

After Agricola's recall to Rome, all the vanquished Lowland tribes became restless. At one time it was thought that they had managed to free themselves from the Romans by their own efforts, but it now seems that the invading forces were needed elsewhere, so the freedom of the Lowland tribes of northern Britain was more of a gift than a victory.

Forty years after Agricola had returned to Rome, the Emperor Hadrian came over, determined to conquer the rest of the isles of Britain. He built what became known as Hadrian's Wall, which runs from Wallsend in the east to Bowness-on-Solway in the west, over a distance of 73 miles (117km). The wall failed to deter the northern Britons though, for it has been established that at least one raiding party of 180 Caledonians managed to cross the partition.

THE ANTONINE WALL

Hadrian died in AD 138, some years after returning to Rome. He was succeeded by the Emperor Antoninus Pius who, on receiving reports that the Caledonians were continually attacking the southern Britons, sent one of his trusted generals, Quintus Lollius Urbicus, to bring order to that corner of his empire. Urbicus followed Antoninus' command to build a strong wall of defence as a frontier.

This magnificent Roman wall was named the Antonine Wall, after the Emperor. At one time it was thought to have been built between the rows of forts that Agricola had erected, but is now believed to have followed a different line. There were between sixteen and nineteen forts to house the many hundreds of soldiers who manned the entire length of the wall, which, at 37 miles (60km) long, was about half the length of Hadrian's Wall. Some of the forts had signal towers, one of the best remaining examples being at Rough Castle, near Falkirk. Parts of the wall are visible on Mumrills near Laurieston, by Falkirk.

The Antonine Wall was started in around AD 142 and is thought to have been completed six years later. This masterpiece of architectural engineering was built from east to west, running from Bo'ness on the

Firth of Forth to Old Kilpatrick on the River Clyde. Near the end of the wall, close to Old Kilpatrick, Urbicus laid a bridge across the Duntocher Burn. In 1772, Lord Blantyre had a plaque attached to the bridge which ascribed the honour of its creation to Quintus Lollius Urbicus.

The Antonine Wall was almost 12ft (3m) high, resting upon a base of earth and stone 14ft (4m) wide, with a distance of 2–4 miles (3–6km) between the forts. On the north side was a deep ditch to deter the Caledonians and, on the south, a broad road which enabled the Roman soldiers to keep watch as they marched between forts.

The Antonine Wall was finally abandoned in about AD 165 and, sadly, neither this magnificent wall nor the road adjacent withstood the test of time. Many centuries later, its remains became known locally as Graham's or Gavin's Dyke, or the Devil's Dyke, because people could not believe that it had originally been constructed by man.

SEPTIMIUS SEVERUS

A detail of the Septimius Severus Arch in the Forum in Rome, showing Septimius Severus with a prisoner

The Romans found that even the Antonine Wall did not stop the fearless Caledonians from constantly invading the lands of the Lowlanders. During this time there appears to have been a general uprising of the many tribes of north Britain, who were putting up a united front against the Romans. So threatening were the Caledonians that finally, in AD 208–11, Septimius Severus, the Roman Emperor, came to Britain with his two sons to silence them.

Severus made York his headquarters and, like Agricola before him, used Ardoch, Stracathro and other forts in northern Britain to assemble a large army. The Roman base at Carpow was used to access ships bringing supplies. Faced with this mighty and disciplined force, the Caledonians did well to remember the lesson they had gained from their encounters with Agricola: it was unwise to meet the Romans head-on in battle. They cunningly followed the invaders as they marched northwards, making frequent and unexpected attacks at every opportunity. This tactic ensured the death of many Romans, with the loss of only a small number of Caledonians.

Severus and his army reached as far as the Moray Firth. They had been fighting for nearly four years, penetrating further into the Highlands of Scotland than any other Roman army. Severus felt he had achieved his purpose in restraining the rebellious northern Britons and had shown them the strength and power of the Roman Empire. In poor health, and reluctant to face another winter in north Britain, he ordered his soldiers to return to the Lowlands. As he retreated, the Caledonians continued to harry his army – some sources report that 50,000 Roman soldiers lost their lives during these campaigns.

CONSTANTIUS

In AD 306 the Emperor Constantius, with his son, the future Emperor Constantine, tried to attack the Caledonians again, but this time the Picts and the

A coin of the Emperor Constantius

Scots joined forces in an attempt to push the Romans out of northern Britain. Had it not been for the Caledonians, there is no doubt that history would have been very different. The Britons of the north were now openly on the offensive.

In AD 367, the Caledonians joined forces with the Lowlanders once more in a concerted effort to move south against the Romans, who had to bring in reinforcements from mainland Europe.

ROMAN INFLUENCES ON BRITAIN

The final downfall of the Roman Empire came on 24 August AD 410, when Rome was overrun by barbarian tribes. Forty thousand slaves from within the city rose up against their masters, and unbelievable horrors were perpetrated following the capitulation of the Empire.

The fall of Rome had an enormous impact upon the areas of Europe that had been under Roman rule. More than three and a half centuries had passed since Julius Caesar had first set foot in the 'green and fertile lands' of the British Isles, and Roman influences had changed the course of the islands' history profoundly and irreversibly.

In many ways, the Roman occupation was of great benefit to Britain. The people they conquered learnt how to build roads, construct better and stronger buildings, and establish the rule of law – though Roman rule was still enforced rule. Northern Britain largely escaped Roman domination and never truly became a part of the empire, but Roman culture still left its mark there. The presence of the Romans had made the native people aware of the great benefits to be gained from working together rather than remaining in isolated tribes.

Forming a nation

There is no record of what happened to the people of northern Britain for 150 years after the Romans left, though Tacitus' account states that a large variety of tribes, speaking different, though similar languages, had occupied the whole of Britain in AD 43. These tribes were descendants of the Celtic Indo-Aryan people who had spread across Europe after the last Ice Age.

When the Roman Senator Agricola came to northern Britain in the first century AD, there were three Celtic-speaking peoples living in the British Isles: the Picts in the Highlands, the Britons around the west coast of what is now England, and the Scots, who had migrated from Ireland to Argyll. They had travelled to the British Isles between 500 and 700 years before. Other earlier Celtic races had established settlements throughout Europe and had at one time formed a very powerful community.

THE BEGINNING OF CHRISTIANITY

Christianity came to Britain during the Roman occupation, but British Christians remained isolated from the rest of Europe, and the Celtic Christians began to organise their own Church.

Most historical knowledge of Scotland between the fourth and eighth centuries AD is provided by the Venerable Bede (AD *c.* 673–735) in his great work, *The Ecclesiastical History of the English People*. A scholar and a historian, Bede spent most of his life in the monastery at Jarrow, Northumberland.

The earliest known Christian missionary was St Ninian, who was born by the shores of the Solway Firth, the son of a chieftain from the tribes of the Britons. He spent much of his early life studying and is believed to have lived in Rome for some time, where he learnt about the teachings of Jesus in greater depth. On his return from Gaul in Ireland, he settled down near Whithorn in Wigtownshire to begin his missionary work and, in about AD 400, built the

Top left: *a stained glass window at Iona Abbey depicting St Columba*
Left: *St Columba, founder of Christianity in Scotland*
Right: Christ, *from the* Gospel of St Matthew *in the beautifully illuminated* Book of Kells

PICTISH SCULPTURED STONES

The Picts left behind many upright carved stones with messages which are still being deciphered. These interesting relics are found all over Scotland. Four of them, the Aberlemno stones, depict everyday scenes from Pictish life.

The Glamis Pictish Stone is in the front garden of the Manse of St Fergus' Kirk at Glamis in Angus. This remarkable Pictish stone dates back to the early eighth century and has earlier carvings incised on its west side, representing the serpent, salmon and mirror. The prominent Celtic cross is entangled with serpentine creatures. On the east side is a centaur holding an axe in each hand, a deer's head, two warriors bearing axes, a cauldron with two legs projecting from the pot, and a hunting beast.

Sueno's Stone is one of the most exquisitely carved examples of Celtic art surviving in Scotland. Found buried underground in the eighteenth century, it is now positioned on the outskirts of Forres on the Moray coast. The stone is over 20ft (6m) high and is the tallest surviving cross-slab in Scotland. There is a huge elaborately carved ring-head cross on the front face, and on the back there appears to be a battle scene, depicting cavalry as well as foot soldiers, and the severed heads of the vanquished. Various explanations of this scene have been suggested; one possibility is that it represents the defeat of the Picts by the Scots in the mid-ninth century. This fascinating stone is now encased in glass to save it from further weathering.

Many other Pictish stones can be found along the Moray coastal area and in Caithness.

One of the four stones at Aberlemno

church of Candida Casa ('shining white building'), using limestone and plaster. Ninian drew many loyal men to him to share his missionary work and monastic life, and often travelled great distances to spread the Gospels to the people. He was described by the Venerable Bede as 'a most reverend Bishop'.

St Columba is universally known as the founder of Christianity in Scotland. Born of royal blood in AD 521 in Ireland, or Scotia as it was then called, he was responsible for converting many to Christianity. In AD 563, Columba, with twelve monks, settled on the Isle of Iona, off the coast of the Isle of Mull. Here he constructed his first Celtic church, using clay and wood, and established a monastic community.

The reputation of the community was soon widespread and it came to be recognised in Europe as an outstanding missionary centre and place of learning. Consequently, Iona became a sacred isle where kings of Scotland and Norway were buried.

Legend has it that St Regulus (or Rule), who may also have been the Irish St Riagail, a contemporary of St Columba, brought the relics of St Andrew from the East (possibly from Patras, where St Andrew had been crucified on a saltire or diagonal cross), to Muckross or Kilrimont in Scotland. When Regulus landed, a vision of the Apostle was revealed to the King of the Picts, Angus MacFergus, promising him victory over his enemy. In gratitude, Angus dedicated Kilrimont to the relics of St Andrew, and the settlement took the name of St Andrews. St Andrew was later adopted as the patron saint of Scotland and his saltire has become the national symbol. His relics were probably laid to rest in the church named after him, and the magnificent sarcophagus which still survives in St Andrews Cathedral was possibly fashioned for his body. A Celtic Culdee monastery, also established at St Andrews, survived until the thirteenth century (the name 'Culdee' is derived from the Gaelic *Cele Dei* – 'friends of God').

Another Celtic saint of the early eighth century, also from Ireland, was St Fergus (Fergusianus), who introduced Christianity in the area from Caithness to

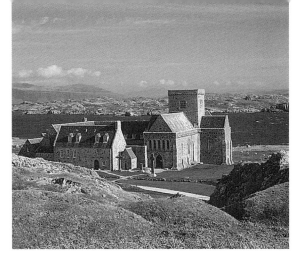

the Moray Firth, and founded several churches. His teachings were widely known and he became Bishop of the Picts, taking part in the Council of Rome in AD 721. He is also associated with Glamis, in Angus, and is said to have died in a cave near the well which lies just within the grounds of Glamis Castle. Recently the minister of St Fergus' Kirk initiated a group effort to create a 'wild garden' around the well in remembrance of St Fergus and the Picts' well known love of nature. A Pictish stone standing outside the manse shows that this site was an important Celtic shrine.

THE PICTS

The Venerable Bede also wrote of the various tribes that had been found by the Romans in Scotland. He referred to the kingdoms of the Picts, the Scots, the Britons and the Angles. The largest kingdom belonged to the Picts, who were descendants of the first settlers in Scotland.

An early reference to the Picts was made by the Roman writer, Eumenius, in the fourth century BC, and the name was possibly derived from the ancient Celtic word, *Priteni*. Alternatively, the Roman soldiers may have named the Picts from the Latin *Picti*, 'the painted ones', for there are reports that the Picts daubed their bodies with pictures of animals when

Above: Iona Abbey, the home of Christianity in Scotland
Right: St Andrew the Apostle with his saltire, the national symbol of Scotland

going to war. The Picts ruled Scotland north of the Forth (with the sole exception of Argyll, which was Scots territory) from the third century until they were usurped by Kenneth MacAlpin in AD 843. Even so, MacAlpin was styled 'Rex Pictorum' on his death, and the title 'King of the Picts' was used until AD 904–5. The Picts were referred to as Caledonians by the Romans, Tacitus and Agricola, and by Ptolemy.

There were two sub-kingdoms: the southern Picts ruled the area of Fife, Perth and Angus; and the northern Picts, based around the Moray Firth, commanded the Highlands and the Western Isles, as well as Moray and Aberdeen. The ravages of the Norsemen reduced this northern territory considerably, and while the Scots' houses of Angus and Gowrie took over southern Pictland, the Lorne house moved up the Great Glen and settled in Moray in the

mid-ninth century. Eventually, the Picts were completely supplanted as rulers by the Scots, through a combination of intermarriage and the use of force.

Columba meets the King of the Picts

Past experience rendered the Picts suspicious of any religion that did not comply with their own rituals. Columba knew this, and, in undertaking a journey which was to lay the foundations of Scotland as a nation, he planned his approach to the King of the northern Picts with extreme care.

The well-fortified Pictish palace of King Bruide lay to the north of the Great Glen. Columba was able to travel nearly all the way by boat, accompanied by a few of his trusted brethren.

Sailing from Iona to the Firth of Lorne, they rested near Oban and then continued past the Isle of Lismore on their way through to Loch Linnhe. After that, they passed through Loch Lochy and Loch Ness, finding overland paths between the lochs. At last they arrived at the Moray Firth, where they came upon the palace of King Bruide.

When St Columba and his brethren saw that the gates of the palace were locked, the saint prayed earnestly and repeatedly made the sign of the cross over them. He waited patiently and suddenly they opened before him. Much astonished by this miracle, King Bruide invited the visitors into his palace, where St Columba spent many weeks as a guest. Gradually they became friends, as Bruide, determined to understand more about Christianity, questioned St Columba closely about his beliefs.

THE SCOTS

The Scots were the second most important group of people living in Scotland at this time. Their ancient kingdom, Dalriada, derived its name from their home in Antrim, Northern Ireland. In AD 500, there was a strong link between the Irish Scots and the Argyll

BOOK OF KELLS

Manuscripts of vellum (parchment) provide evidence of a 'golden age' of faith, culture and learning in Ireland, which also embraced Scotland.

The individual scribes of the Celtic Church devoted themselves to spreading the Word of God through their illuminated manuscripts.

Many of the artistic works of the monks were inspired by St Columba. The most beautiful of all the volumes is the *Book of Kells*, which was probably written in Columba's monastery on Iona during the eighth and ninth centuries. This manuscript book, inscribed in Latin, contains copies of the four Gospels.

Virgin and Child with angels from the eighth-century illuminated manuscript, the Book of Kells

BOOK OF DEER

A priceless manuscript was discovered in one of Columba's monasteries in the village of Old Deer, Aberdeenshire. Known as the *Book of Deer*, it is believed to have been produced in the ninth century.

This manuscript contains the whole of the *Gospel of St John* and portions of the other three Gospels, all exquisitely written in Latin. In the margins, written in the eleventh century in Gaelic, is a reference to the foundation of the monastery at Deer. The illustrations are created in an unusual design and the artistry is outstanding. A painting of St Ninian is also contained in the book.

Glasgow Cathedral
*by Myles Birket Foster
(1825–99):
'The Cathedral of
St Mungo'*

Scots because the same king, Fergus, ruled over both kingdoms. His royal palace is thought to have been close to the fortification of Dunadd that was perched on a rocky crag, 4 miles (6km) north of Lochgilphead. The Antrium Dal Riata tribe came over to Argyll from Ireland in about AD 400, led by Fergus. They kept their ancient name for Ireland, Scotia, which is how Scotland acquired its name.

Like the Irish, they spoke the Gaelic language and gained a foothold in the country, north of the Firths of Forth and Clyde. Ambitious and demanding, they increased their territory whenever they could.

However, the Vikings from Scandinavia, who had landed in Scotland before the Romans had left England, were causing such terror that Kenneth I, 36th King of Dalriada, moved his kingdom to Scone, away from the vulnerable coast. The Scots claimed to have brought with them the Stone of Destiny, upon which they crowned all their kings.

When Christianity was adopted by the Picts and the Scots, the people of both kingdoms looked upon Iona as the home of their faith. Indeed, it was because Columba had founded a place of learning in Iona that his disciples were to play such an important part in establishing Christianity in Scotland.

THE BRITONS

The third kingdom straddled the areas now known as Strathclyde in Scotland and Cumbria in north-west England. When the Romans invaded the British Isles, they derived the name of Britannia or Britain from the many Britons living in Wales and throughout the coastal areas of what is now western England. The Britons belonged to the same original Celtic culture as the Scots, their language being similar to that of the people who later lived in Wales. Their monarch lived in Dumbarton, or Alcluyd as it was then called, meaning 'Fortress of the Britons'. They also had a settlement at Traprain Law.

At the same time as St Columba was preaching the Christian faith to Iona, another missionary living in northern Britain was bringing the gospels of Jesus to the Britons. He was known as Mungo, meaning 'dearest beloved', but his real name was Kentigern, or 'chief lord'. Glasgow became the main centre for Mungo, and today it is sometimes styled 'the city of St Mungo' and its cathedral is known as the 'Cathedral of St Mungo'.

The Britons accepted Christianity more readily than the Picts or the Angles, possibly hoping to use

religion to re-establish themselves after persecution by the Angles, who had forced them westwards to the Firth of Clyde and northwards beyond Edinburgh.

THE ANGLES

The other kingdom in Scotland was that of the fierce and warlike Angles. The name originates from the people of Angul, a district of Holstein, so called because of its angular shape. They were Germanic, coming from the banks of the River Elbe, and eventually settled in the British Isles, forming the kingdoms of Northumbria, Mercia and Anglia in the land area stretching from the Humber to the Forth. Later, their name was given to all the people of England.

The Angles had originally been invited to the British Isles as mercenary soldiers by the Romans to help them keep order in their occupied countries. In AD 547 the Angles were ruled by King Ida, whose kingdom, Bernicia, or the 'country of the Braes',

stretched from the Tees as far as the Firth of Forth. They later merged with the Germanic Saxons and eventually the Anglo-Saxon invasion of the British Isles confined the Celtic peoples to Cornwall, Wales and Scotland.

The Angles of Bernicia, or the Lothians as it was later known, were the only non-Christians left in northern Britain during the late sixth century. A missionary, St Aidan, was sent from Iona some 40 years after the death of St Columba to preach the Christian faith to them. He built a monastery on Holy Island off the coast of Northumberland.

Soon after Aidan died, Cuthbert, a shepherd, had a vision whilst tending his sheep on the Lammermuir Hills. He saw angels descending and then carrying St Aidan back up to heaven. Cuthbert took this as a sign for him to preach the Christian faith to the Angles, and he spent the rest of his life devoted to this work. Known as the greatest missionary of his time, St Cuthbert was later called the 'Apostle of Lothian'. Many churches have been named after him, and he has always been particularly respected in the Edinburgh area.

DIFFERENCES IN THE CHURCH

The Celtic Church had become separated from Europe during the Dark Ages and had remodelled itself upon the early Desert Fathers. There were many isolated cells of individual holy men around whom monastic communities often formed. The Celtic Church had no central or local organisation, nor a hierarchy like that of the Roman Church, in which the Pope was

Left: *St Cuthbert on Farne Island*
Right: *the east face of St Martin's Cross, which stands near Iona Abbey*

recognised as the head. The lay preachers of the Celtic Church acted completely independently of the Pope. St Columba and St Aidan both belonged to this Irish-Celtic Church.

Bede wrote appreciatively of the Lindisfarne Celtic monks who originated from Ireland:

The whole care of those preachers was to serve God, not the world; to feed the soul, and not the belly. If any priest happened to come into a village, the inhabitants flocked together to hear from him the word of life; for the priest and clergy went to the villages only to preach, to baptise, and to visit the sick: in brief, to care for souls.

Meanwhile, monks who were following the rule of St Benedict, which had been established in the sixth century, were starting to attract converted Christians with their centres of learning and disciplined religious rites and routines. Consequently a growing number of new converts sought to join a permanent religious organisation. The hierarchy of the Roman Church provided exactly what they needed: a strong, authoritarian structure offering religious security together with disciplined practices.

The Roman Church was stronger than the Celtic Church, partly because of its organised structure, but also because the three most important countries in Europe – Italy, France and Germany – had been part of the Roman Empire and, like England, had come under the influence of the Roman Church. Shortly after the death of St Cuthbert, the Celtic Church began to withdraw from Scotland, even from Iona, and was replaced by the Roman Church.

UNITING THE FOUR KINGDOMS

Now that the Scots, Picts, Britons and Angles had all been converted to Christianity, unification of the four kingdoms became a possibility, though the Angles remained a warring tribe.

Finally, a Pictish king, Bruide, could no longer accept Anglian domination. He gathered a great force to attack King Ecgfrith of Northumbria, and lured the Angles into a trap at Dunnichen Hill (by Forfar in Angus) where they were forced to fight. The bloody battle took place at 3 o'clock in the afternoon of 20 May AD 685. The Picts knew the land and so avoided the pitfalls, and the trapped Northumbrians were defeated.

Following this defeat, Ecgfrith's tyranny was ended, although he retained his kingdom. The battle was a major landmark in the formation of the Scottish nation. If King Bruide had not been victorious, the four kingdoms would probably have come under the rule of the Angles and merged with the Anglo-Saxons in England. A carved stone slab at Kirkton, Aberlemno marks the events of the battle, and a cairn was erected at Dunnichen in 1985 to commemorate the 1300th anniversary of this decisive encounter.

In AD 843 the King of the Scots, Kenneth MacAlpin, the 36th King of Dalriada, became King of the Scots and the Picts. This gave him greater power than the Britons and the Angles combined. He became determined to defeat the Angles totally, but died after six abortive attempts.

It was another 175 years before the Angles were finally conquered. King Malcolm of Scotia assembled a massive army and crossed the River Forth, marching into Lothian. Immediately prior to this, a comet had appeared in the sky for 30 days, and the Angles considered this a bad omen. Their fears were justified, for Malcolm routed them in the Battle of Carham in 1018, and became ruler of the Angles.

Another key event occurred that same year when King Owen of the Britons died without an heir. By a fortunate coincidence, the rightful heir was Malcolm's grandson, Duncan, who, because of previous marriages between the royal houses of Scotia and the Britons, was able to unite the four kingdoms under one throne. Scotland was established as a nation.

Scotland as a nation

Although Scotland had finally become a single nation, there were still many problems to be addressed. Most of those ruled by Malcolm II had been at war with each other for centuries. The northern Scots, who lived in the Moray coastal area, were descended from the Lorne Scots and they continued to lay claim to the Scottish throne. Indeed, their demands did not end until the child of the last claimant had her brains dashed out against the market cross in Forfar in 1230.

MARAUDERS

The Norsemen, or Vikings, from Norway created further difficulty for King Malcolm by continually sending raiding parties to Scottish shores, as they had done since long before northern Britain became a united kingdom. Warlike and cruel, with an adventurous spirit, they were imbued with a strange glamour despite the devastation they caused. Their galleys were shaped like dragons, with the head at the bow and the tail at the stern. To gain as much speed as possible they had 30 oarsmen on each side of each galley, as well as a square sail. When Vikings landed, they would plunder whatever they could, whether it was property, food, or the inhabitants themselves. The people living along the coastal areas of Scotland so feared the Vikings that the churches would give out the special prayer: 'God save us from the Norsemen.'

In AD 794–6 the Vikings raided the sacred island of Iona, stealing the monks' precious works of art and burning their records and manuscripts. They also burned down the church built by St Columba.

By about the mid-ninth century the Norsemen, no longer content with quick raids, became bolder and set out to conquer the land they had previously invaded. The King of Norway, Harold the Fair-haired (or Fine-haired), led a fleet of ships to the Isles of Orkney and Shetland, and soon ruled there. Later, he advanced into mainland Scotland and took possession of Caithness and Sutherland. Not satisfied by this, he invaded the Western Isles and completely overpowered them; the Norsemen were to remain in power there for more than 350 years. It became clear that the Scots would not be able to live in peace until they were free of these vicious invaders.

Other difficulties arose within Britain, from the English. In many ways these proved to be harder to overcome than the threat of the Norsemen. Even before the Romans came to Britain, there had been constant battles between the different English tribes. The main problem during Malcolm's reign was that the Scots felt that Northumberland, Westmorland and Cumberland belonged to them whilst the English strongly believed that the Lothians was their territory. In fact, the English were adamant that the whole of Scotland belonged to them, and felt that these northern men should be their vassals.

Left: *the emblem of William the Lion and Scotland*
Right: *a dramatic, if historically fanciful depiction of Viking raiders*

DUNCAN (1034–40)

On Malcolm's death in 1034, Duncan became king, the second to rule all Scotland. He was a weaker man than his grandfather, Malcolm II, with less understanding of the vulnerability of his position. The northern Scots, ever on the watch to snatch the throne, took advantage of this weakness. Macbeth, chief of this powerful race, harboured a claim to the throne through his mother. He fought tenaciously, and finally managed to kill Duncan in 1040, becoming King of Scotland in his place.

MACBETH (1040–57)

When Macbeth became King of Scotland, he was respected for his strong and powerful leadership. He reigned for 17 years, and though he did not rule over the Western Isles or the Orkneys, he maintained good relations with them. He managed to keep order in Scotland because he had a well-trained army on hand to enforce his decisions. He lived in a fortified castle at Dunsinane (or Dunsinnan), north of Perth, and dealt

T. Hall sculp.

MACBETH.

with administration from a seat of justice at Lawton, 2 miles (3km) further north. He kept many of his warriors in readiness at Forteviot, south of Perth.

Malcolm Canmore, who was the illegitimate son of King Duncan by the daughter of the miller of Forteviot, raised an army of Scots and English supporters against Macbeth, and fought a victorious battle in 1057 at Lumphanan, in Aberdeenshire. Macbeth and his stepson, Lulach, were killed.

SHAKESPEARE'S MACBETH

The interplay between Macbeth and Duncan is the subject of Shakespeare's famous Scottish play. His version of Macbeth's story deliberately mixes fact with fable. Apparently using Holinshed's *Chronicles of Scottish History* as a historical source, Shakespeare locates the action of his-

play at Birnam Hill, Perthshire, whereas the events actually occurred at Forres. Likewise, Macbeth is given the title of Thane of Glamis, but neither Cawdor nor Glamis were known to be thanages in the eleventh century.

Tradition, embellished by Shakespeare's poetic licence, asserts that Macbeth later moved to Dunsinane Hill in order to be nearer

the witches' stone where he could consult the witch who was able to predict his future. In the play, Macbeth even dies at Dunsinane, which was not the case. Shakespeare weaves so many famous Scottish places into his version that it is hard to avoid confusion at times – in fact, the setting and story of Macbeth have come to be regarded as almost more real than history itself.

MARGARET, QUEEN OF MALCOLM III

Margaret, the much-loved queen of Malcolm III, was Anglo-Hungarian by birth and had travelled widely in Europe. When she came to Scotland she was determined to change the way of life at the court, transforming fashions in both clothes and standards of behaviour: the nobles were given individual drinking cups and forbidden to fight or get drunk; spiced meats and French wines were introduced, as were fine clothes; and dancing and ballad-singing were also encouraged.

Margaret did much to help the poor, giving them food, shelter and clothing, and received the full support of her husband, who allowed her to use his wealth as she thought fit. She was also active in persuading foreign merchants to trade with Scotland. She instigated a programme of repairs for the royal palaces, and rich cloth was imported for the tables and walls.

Margaret made many changes to the wooden castle that stood on the site of the present Edinburgh Castle. Known as the Maidens' or Virgins' Castle, because maidens of royal blood were supposed to reside there, this ancient Celtic castle dominated the surrounding area. It may have been used as a royal residence before, but there is no evidence confirming its status as such until Malcolm and Margaret's reign; even then, their main home was at Dunfermline. The restored remains of St Margaret's eleventh-century chapel, the oldest

St Margaret's Chapel, Edinburgh

building in Edinburgh, still stand on the summit of the Castle Rock.

Margaret was deeply religious and eager to promote the Church, endeavouring to bring the Celtic Church and her own Roman Church closer together. She also helped to set up new monasteries and encouraged pilgrimages by paying for ferries across the Forth to carry pilgrims journeying to St Andrew's shrine at Kilrimont (later renamed St Andrews).

She restored the abbey at Iona and brought the first Benedictine monks to Scotland to found the Abbey of Dunfermline in 1074. The remains of her church were found beneath the Romanesque church which superseded it. After Margaret's death, David I, her son, continued to build and enlarge the church – the second dedication was in 1150. Margaret herself was later canonised.

MALCOLM III (1058–93)

The reign of Malcolm III, or Canmore, as he was known, began the rule of the house of Canmore, which was to preside over Scotland for more than two centuries. During Malcolm's enforced exile at the English court of Edward the Confessor, he had met Edgar the Atheling, Edward's great-nephew, who was later dethroned when William the Norman conquered England. Edgar now came to Scotland to find refuge at Malcolm's court, bringing his two sisters and his mother. Malcolm married Margaret, the eldest sister, who became his second wife, and they lived in Dunfermline, which was then the capital of Scotland.

Wars were a constant pastime for the early Scots, and Malcolm III, angered by the English, felt he owned much of the ground they occupied in Northumberland and Cumberland. In 1093, he decided to invade England for the fifth time. Margaret was very ill in Edinburgh Castle and pleaded with him not to go, but Malcolm would not listen. Not long after the fighting had commenced, Malcolm was killed at Alnwick. Four days later, Margaret, lying on her deathbed, received the news of her husband's death from her son, Edgar, and died almost immediately.

Very soon after Malcolm's demise, Edinburgh Castle was surrounded by Highlanders employed by Donald Bane, Malcolm III's brother, who intended to capture the fortress, enabling him to become king, and condemn his nephews, Margaret's sons, either to prison or to death. The brothers were trapped. They had to take their mother's body to Dunfermline to be buried. In their hour of despair came a miracle. By some freak of fortune or nature, a heavy white mist descended upon the castle and was so dense that Margaret's sons were able to creep away with their mother's body, unseen by the Highlanders. The brothers buried their mother in Dunfermline Abbey and then made their escape to France.

Malcolm had ruled for 35 years, but the stability he had given Scotland quickly disappeared after his death. A succession of different kings followed. Donald Bane became king, but the Crown was taken from him by Malcolm's son, Duncan II. The next year Duncan II was killed and Donald became king again. Three years later, Edgar, another of Malcolm's sons, took the Crown from Donald and ruled for nine years. When Edgar died, the kingdom passed to his brother, Alexander I, although southern Scotland was ruled by Alexander's younger brother, David.

DAVID I (1124–53)

David I was the youngest son of Margaret and Malcolm III. No one expected him to become king, but his reign proved to be one of the most outstanding in the history of Scotland.

After escaping from his uncle, Donald Bane, David was sent to live at the court of Henry I of England and therefore became familiar with English and Norman ways. Henry treated him well, giving him the Honour of Huntingdon and arranging a marriage for him to a widow, the heiress of the vast Northumberland estates. David was now in a much more powerful position, especially after Henry appointed him ruler of Cumbria.

As Earl of Huntingdon, David had to swear an oath of loyalty to the English king, and when he returned to Scotland to succeed Alexander, he brought with him powerful Anglo-Norman influences which would eventually transform Scottish society.

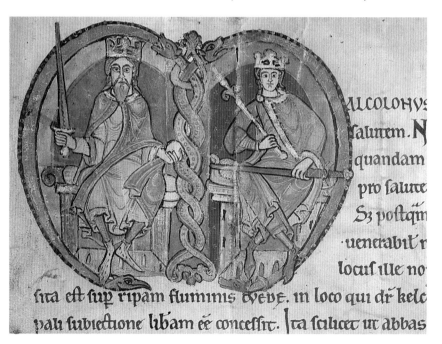

Above: *David I*
Right: *David I and Malcolm IV, from the illuminated Charter of Kelso Abbey (1159)*

MONASTIC LIFE

Most of the abbeys were guarded by thick, high walls. To gain entrance you had to pass through a huge arched gateway like that at St Andrews. This led into a large court-yard where there were workshops, granaries, smithies, bakeries and many other rooms.

A further wall, with several arched gateways, divided the monks' private quarters. The cloisters, where only the monks were allowed, led to the inner sanctum where they lived. Within this area there were usually a fine library, magnificent chapel, refectory and kitchens, the monks' sleeping quarters and usually a hospital.

Work

The abbey was a self-contained social unit. Some monks worked in various parts of the monastery; a few spent all day in study or prayer.

There were gardeners, tailors, workmen of every kind, all under the monks' supervision. The abbey also included lay brothers who had taken religious vows but did not have as many choir duties or studies to fulfill as the monks. They looked after the monks, cooking, cleaning and washing for them, and were also expected to take part in other activities besides praying and meditating.

Schooling was available for the children of the nobility. In addition, an abbey would have a guest house, run by the lay brothers under the supervision of their superiors, which provided food for the poor.

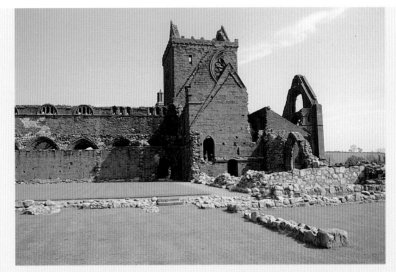

The ruins of Sweetheart Abbey

Farming

The monks were excellent farmers and managed their estates well. The land received by the abbeys from kings or nobles often had to be culti-vated from a wilderness. The monks showed the tenants how to till the land in order to gain the best results from it and, in turn, the tenants directed the slaves.

Other farms were rented to the tenants, who supplied the monasteries with crops and livestock. The monks also reared sheep, sending the wool to foreign lands in exchange for other goods; thus helping to promote over-seas trade.

Salt

If a monastery was near the sea, salt would be produced by heating sea water; if there were coal seams close by, the slaves from the monastery would be organised to extract coal from the mines for use in heating the sea water.

Justice

The abbeys even dealt with the administration of justice, through courts which were held there to deal with any troublesome criminals. The abbot or prior was the supreme ruler of his domain and his influence was widespread, for good or ill depending on his integrity. If the abbot was a leader of sound character, the result was a thriving community.

Building

The largest Scottish abbeys were founded during the medieval era, in the twelfth century. Sweetheart, which was completed in 1273, was the last abbey of comparable magnitude to be constructed.

In Aberdeen in 1413, Franciscan monks, known as the Grey Friars, built the stone churches of Tolbooth and St Nicholas on Guestrow, the principal street in the city at that time.

FEUDALISM

David imposed the Anglo-Norman feudal system of land ownership in order to give his country structural unity. He rewarded the Anglo-Norman barons who had assisted him by granting them land, thus binding them to him and strengthening the power of the monarchy.

David also built castles on his lands, with a sheriff in each one to control the area and assume the roles of tax collector, royal law officer and judge. All David's castles were placed at vantage points, for protection in case the nobles grew too powerful and attempted to overthrow him. This strategy helped to safeguard the kings of Scotland in the centuries ahead.

The feudal system, which was widespread in Europe, put the king in a strong position. The laws were hierarchical and no one dared to exceed his station or disobey his superior in rank. The king relied on loyal noblemen, who were his vassals, to protect him and his kingdom. With this obligation came the grant of land which gave the nobles absolute power over the lives of those living there.

Earls, lairds and tenants-in-chief

Under the feudal system, barons who held land directly from the king were drawn into his service by taking an oath, promising to serve the king. The land was rent-free, given through an agreement written on a charter. The amount of land depended largely on how much the king trusted the baron. The feudal system demanded the utmost loyalty, and if the king did not keep strictly to the feudal laws, he could easily lose his throne.

The oath

The vassal or nobleman was brought into the presence of the king to swear his allegiance. At this very solemn occasion all the earls of the land were grouped around the king to receive the new earl. Taking the hand of the king, the vassal would fall to his knees, swearing a life-long oath of allegiance to his monarch and country. The king would then ask him to rise and, as a pledge of faith, would kiss his subject on the lips. The vassal also swore to produce fully armed troops with their own rations to fight for the king when requested. If the king was taken prisoner, the vassals were expected to fight to gain his release.

Lesser-barons

The lesser-vassals served under the barons in rather the same way as the barons served their king. For this, the lesser-vassals were given land by the barons, together with a certain amount of freedom, and in return were expected to serve the barons with the utmost loyalty and engage in military service as knights.

Free-tenants

The free-tenants rented land from the barons or lesser-barons, paying with money or produce such as cattle or wood. The free-tenants did have some freedom, but were obliged to work for the lord on his land at his command. Also, in the event of war, tenants would have to go with the nobleman and fight alongside him, providing their own food and weapons.

Although the free-tenant was entitled to change his place of work, leaving one nobleman to become a free-tenant for another was risky. The power structure of the feudal system was practically absolute, and unconstrained by law. Few men were brave

enough to make any effort to change their position.

Serfs or slaves

Below the free-tenants were the serfs who were, in effect, slaves, bought and sold like cattle. They were tied to the land on which they were born and could not marry without the lord's permission. If they ran away and were caught, they were returned to their masters and could be flogged without mercy. The slaves' sustenance was usually leftovers, and if food was in short supply, they would be the first to go hungry.

Close to a castle or great house, there would be a hamlet, or small village, which belonged to the lord, with houses built of wood and occupied by the workers. The fertile lands around the castle were farmed by the workers to supply the castle with produce. They received shelter and food in return for their intense labours.

Life at the very bottom of the feudal ladder was hard and without hope. Feudalism's insistence on total obedience from all subjects inevitably made it a very cruel system. However, it did offer some compensation for the poor, in the form of protection from warring bands of greedy neighbours.

The nobleman's court

The nobleman had powers to hold courts of law and inflict punishments on all those who lived on his lands. Punishments were varied and much depended upon the crime committed and the mood of the nobleman at the time of the trial. Trials by ordeal were a common method for dealing with criminal offences.

One way of settling a dispute was for the accused to challenge his accuser to a duel. Whoever won would be vindicated. Another method was to plunge the naked hand and arm of the accused into boiling water, or to force them to take hold of a red-hot iron. If the skin healed within a certain time, the accused was judged innocent of the charge. Eventually, these inhumane practices were replaced by fairer ones.

The nobleman's castle

If the land that a noble had been given was without a castle, he would immediately set about building one. Usually the chosen site would be near the mouth of a river, at the head of a loch, on an island in the middle of a loch, or upon a hill; often castles were constructed on the site of old forts.

Norman castles were in the 'motte and bailey' style, and more than 200 of them were built in Scotland during the twelfth century. The bailey (wooden fence) formed an outer barrier, with a space inside before the inner castle itself. The motte, or mound, which could be real or man-made, was usually protected by a moat or dyke spanned by a drawbridge which could be raised at a moment's notice to quickly secure the castle when under seige. Huge iron and wooden gates were another formidable deterrent to attackers.

Eilean Donan Castle

Eilean Donan is one of the most picturesque Scottish castles. Situated on a promontory near Dornie in Wester Ross, it commands the entrance of the sea loch, Loch Duich. Completely restored in the 1930s, the original castle was built in the thirteenth century, on the site of an ancient fort, as a defence against Viking raiders.

Norman influences

David I's aristocratic Norman friends were soon holding most of the important positions within the Church and State. David gave them lands as well, which meant they gained all the privileges of land ownership: authority over every aspect of the lives of those living on their land. Thus a new French-speaking Norman aristocracy became established in Scotland, organising the country in a similar way to England. In the Lowlands, the old Celtic concepts of tribe and kinship were replaced by the new feudal system of laws and regulations.

David's reign was remarkable for enhancing the prestige of the monarch. He maintained order, overcoming all his enemies, including the troublesome northern Scots from the Moray Firth. This was achieved because of the support from the Normans, who helped him to establish royal burghs and shires and a system of control that brought people together. Trade, especially, benefited from these improvements.

Abbeys

The need for abbeys arose during the very early days of Christianity. A number of dedicated holy men who lived alone in the deserts of Egypt and Syria decided it was better to live together than in isolation, as the disciplined life of a community was more conducive to prayer and meditation. Alexandria was the centre of Christian thought at that time, but the holy men chose not to live there, as they felt the distractions of the town interfered with their contemplative lives. They established religious communities elsewhere which later developed into monasteries.

The concepts of individual salvation and communal monastery living were reconciled by a written constitution which has endured to the present day – the code or rule given by St Benedict, written around AD 529. This code, though brief, deals with every aspect of monastic life and was adopted by monastic communities throughout Europe.

Like his mother, David was deeply religious and founded more than twelve abbeys, including those at Kelso, Cambuskenneth, Melrose, Jedburgh, Holyrood, Dundrennan, Kinloss and Newbattle. Although many of them are now in ruins, it is still possible to envisage the outstanding architecture of these magnificent buildings as it once was.

The abbeys were all supported by the feudal system. The king assigned lands to the abbey and in return gained protection and spiritual support from the abbots, monks and clergy. It was a mutual arrangement which enabled the monks to take part in a communal life of meditation and prayer, but also let them lead varied and useful lives and enjoy all the privileges that a grant of land yielded.

MALCOLM IV (1153–65)

After David died, he was succeeded by Malcolm IV, who was known as the 'Maiden' because he never married. The eldest grandson of David, Malcolm was only 11 years old when he came to the throne. His succession was disputed and there were several rebellions during his reign, but it was in fact at this time that the first references were made in written charters to the 'Kingdom of Scotland'.

Once Malcolm was king, he agreed with Henry II of England to relinquish control of the northern counties of Cumberland, Westmorland and Northumberland. Although this temporarily improved Scotland's relationship with the English, the Scottish nobles were displeased.

THE BISHOPS AND CLERGY

The secular clergy were overseen by the bishops, who lived in major towns like St Andrews, Edinburgh, Glasgow, Elgin and Dunkeld. David added five more bishops to the four already in office. The bishops had jurisdiction over areas of the country called dioceses, and were responsible for the clergy and population of their particular diocese. They looked after the poor and helped to make people feel that by following the Christian religion they belonged to one nation.

Perhaps the greatest religious project begun at this time was at St Andrews, the site of an ancient monastery and destination for the earliest pilgrims, who came to see St Andrew's relics. The cathedral-priory was founded by the Bishop of St Andrews in about 1144, and finally completed in the thirteenth century. It stands close to the town itself and beside the sea. St Andrews became the largest cathedral complex in Scotland and the second largest in Britain after Norwich Cathedral. The ruins still indicate how impressive it once was.

Left: *Jedburgh Abbey, founded by David I*
Below: *St Andrews Cathedral, once the site of the largest cathedral complex in Scotland*

WILLIAM THE LION (1165–1214)

The next king was Malcolm IV's brother, William the Lion. His name originated in the time of the crusades, when warriors from western Europe travelled to the Holy Land in search of the sepulchre where Christ was buried. The armour which encased them from head to foot made them unrecognisable, so each knight wore an emblem to identify himself. William used the emblem of a roaring, clawing beast of blood in red on a yellow background – the Lion Rampant – which also became the emblem of Scotland. William's crest proved apt, as he spent much time waging war.

William ruled for 49 years, making him the longest-reigning monarch in Scotland up to that time. However, he will be chiefly remembered for his act of folly in 1174 when he flouted the peace that his brother had made with King Henry of England by leading his army to Northumberland to take Alnwick Castle. Underestimating the strength of his enemy, he was caught and sent to Normandy to become a prisoner in Falaise Castle. The price of release was his kingdom: he signed the Treaty of Falaise, which allowed Scotland to pass into the hands of Henry II. Henry died 15 years later, and Richard Coeur-de-Lion came to the English throne, his one ambition being to go on a crusade to the Holy Land. By obtaining 10,000 merks from William the Lion, he was able to achieve this ambition, and at the same time William was finally released from being a vassal of the English king.

ALEXANDER II (1214–49)

When William died in 1214, his son, Alexander II, succeeded him, and he made Scotland stronger than ever before. First he attended to parts of his country that were always causing trouble; in particular, he was

Above: *Alexander II*
Right: *Elgin Cathedral*
Far right: *a watercolour of Pluscarden Abbey*

determined to subdue the disturbances in the remote lands of Argyll. In 1221 he collected a strong army from Galloway and the Lothians and prepared a fleet to sail up the Clyde. Unfortunately, he had failed to take the stormy September weather and tides into account, and was forced to return to Glasgow. The following year he took his army across country to Argyll and re-established order, making sure the peace would last by transferring the titles of disloyal nobles' lands to more reliable subjects.

Later that same year, he faced a different kind of rebellion. Unwisely, Bishop Adam of Caithness had been charging the people in his diocese double the sum that was normally due for the support of his church, in spite of their repeated complaints. In the end, 300 angry people stormed their way towards his palace, prompting his servants to run to the Earl of Caithness' home nearby to ask for help. Possibly not realising the imminent danger, the Earl told the servants, 'If the bishop is afraid let him come to me at my castle.' Meanwhile, the angry crowd had seized the helpless bishop, stripped and beaten him, and then carried him to his kitchen fire and roasted him alive.

Alexander was just setting out to attack England when the news reached him. He came at full speed to Caithness and exacted a terrible penalty – no one would ever think of roasting a bishop again. He also confiscated half the lands belonging to the Earl of Caithness in punishment for his lack of assistance for Bishop Adam.

Alexander, like David I, was keen to grant land for the construction of cathedrals and abbeys. In 1223 he awarded the Bishop of Moray the seat at the magnificent Elgin Cathedral, and, in 1230, gave permission for the building of three abbeys: Pluscarden Abbey, south-west of Elgin; Beauly Abbey in Rossshire; and Ardchattan Abbey in Argyll. These communities were peopled by an order of Benedictine monks called the Valliscaulians who operated under a very strict code and initially had a very close relationship with France.

Before Alexander died he made an attempt to regain the Western Isles from King Haakon IV of Norway. Unfortunately, before he could reach them, he fell ill and died on the island of Kerrera, off Oban, on 8 July 1249.

ALEXANDER III (1249–86)

Alexander III was a boy of eight when he came to the throne, so a regent had to be appointed. The nobles could not agree who should take this responsible position, and the country suffered internal turmoil until Alexander came of age at 21.

King Haakon and the Western Isles

The first problem facing Alexander III after his coronation was the ownership of the Western Isles. The Earl of Ross had declared war upon King Haakon of Norway to try and regain possession of them, a move which had terrified local people, for strong memories of the fierce Viking raiders had persisted even into the thirteenth century.

Responding to the Earl's declaration of war, Haakon sailed from Norway in July 1263 with a fleet of over 100 vessels, each of solid oak with a golden dragon at the bow and stern. The day after his arrival in the Orkneys there was a total eclipse of the sun; astronomers confirm that this did indeed take place

on 5 August 1263. The Norwegian soldiers considered the eclipse to be a bad omen foreshadowing defeat. But Haakon continued his advance in spite of their fears until he anchored in the bay of Lamlash, south of the Isle of Arran.

Alexander, meanwhile, reinforced all the castles on the shoreline and marshalled a large army on the Ayrshire coast where he expected Haakon to land. It had always been known that terrific storms could rage around the western coasts during September. Cunningly, Alexander played a waiting game before he engaged in battle with Haakon, praying that storms would weaken the invaders' resolve.

On 1 October, the storm Alexander had been waiting for broke, sweeping ferociously through Haakon's fleet for two days and nights. The Norwegians, of course, believed that the punishment threatened by the eclipse had come, created by the magic of Scottish witches. The Scots, on the other hand, believed that the storm had been sent by St Margaret to save their country from defeat.

Although a battle did take place on land near Largs, Haakon's fleet had been so depleted by the storm that he decided not to continue his campaign. He returned by way of Orkney, landing at Kirkwall too ill to complete his journey home. A Norwegian writer concludes the tale by stating sorrowfully, 'At midnight on December 13th, Almighty God called King Haakon out of this mortal life.'

After Haakon's death, Alexander III secured a treaty with Haakon's successor, King Magnus. In the Treaty of Perth (1266), the two kings agreed that the Western Isles would become part of Scotland once again in exchange for an immediate payment to the Norwegians of 4000 merks and 100 merks a year indefinitely. (This annual payment to Norway continued to be made into the fourteenth century.) Orkney and Shetland remained under Norwegian control and, sadly, it was to be a long time before these islands also became part of Scotland.

THE STONE OF DESTINY

Alexander III was crowned King of Scotland at Scone, near Perth. Here stood Moot Hill, the sacred mound upon which the Stone of Destiny was placed for the coronation of Scottish kings – it was believed that no king could reign in Scotland unless he was crowned sitting on the *Lia Fail*, as it is known in Gaelic. When not in use, the stone was kept in Scone Abbey, within the grounds of what is now Scone Palace, the home of the Earls of

Right: the Stone of Destiny placed among the Honours of Scotland
Below: Edward I stealing the Stone of Destiny from Scone Abbey

Mansfield. The House of Scone, residence of the abbot, where the kings of Scotland lodged for their coronations, still forms the main structure of the present-day Scone Palace.

There are many legends about the Stone of Destiny. Some believe it was Jacob's pillow when he saw the angels of Bethel, others that it was brought to Scotland in the ninth century by Scota, daughter of an Egyptian Pharaoh. Some historians say that Kenneth I, 36th King of Dalriada, brought the sacred stone from Argyll.

The stone was removed from Scone Abbey by Edward I in 1296, four years after he had proclaimed John Balliol the successor to the Scottish throne. John was the last king to be enthroned on the Stone of Destiny in Scotland. Edward I took the stone to Westminster Abbey where it remained, beneath the seat of the coronation chair, for the following 700 years.

The Stone of Destiny was eventually returned to Scotland, amid great celebrations, at the end of 1996.

The succession

In the autumn of 1285 Alexander married, for the second time, in an effort to restore his succession. The deaths of both the sons he had fathered by Princess Margaret, Henry III's daughter, whom he married in 1251, had left his succession in jeopardy; Margaret herself had died in 1275. Just five months after his second wedding (to Yolande of Dreux), as he was returning to his palace at Kinghorn, his horse stumbled and the King was thrown over a cliff.

Alexander's only daughter, Margaret, had married King Eric II of Norway in 1283 as part of the reconciliation between the two countries started by the Treaty of Perth, almost twenty years earlier. In the same year, Margaret died in childbirth, leaving an infant daughter as heir to the Scottish throne. In 1286, at the time of Alexander's death, his granddaughter was still in Norway. The events which followed meant that it would take nearly half a century for Scotland to regain its own monarch and sovereignty.

AN OLD SCOTTISH TOWN

Between the days of St Columba and the reign of Alexander III, over 700 years had elapsed, and time had brought many changes to the lives of the Scottish people, not least in the nature of the towns they lived in.

Towns usually grew up around a castle, near a river where it was easily forded or bridged, or by the sea.

People felt safer living in larger groups and could defend themselves against their enemies more effectively. They could also supply each other's needs more readily, forming themselves into an efficient social group.

During Malcolm Canmore's reign, towns were created as a result of the overseas trade that Margaret, the King's wife, had encouraged. Merchants discovered towns in other European countries which were interested in trading and they brought the news home to Scotland, along with continental ideas about the way towns should operate. Towns gradually became places where raw materials were taken to be made into finished goods for trading.

By the time David began to create royal burghs, Scotland had a fiscal system. David and his successors welcomed traders who could pay the crown a tax for the right to set up a market. In return, the king gave the townspeople a charter which placed the town under royal protection. The king exacted tolls at the town gates, bridges, fords and harbours, and on goods sold in the market.

Towns were divided into royal burghs, burghs of regality and burghs of barony. Royal burghs were built on land belonging to the monarchy and the townspeople enjoyed the right to trade all over the country as well as overseas, whereas the other burghs were developed on lands belonging to abbots, bishops or barons, and were not considered as important nor allowed the same privileges.

The royal burgh

As a royal burgh town was neared, cattle or sheep would be seen grazing on the town acre of pasture. Around the town was a deep ditch, and inside that, a palisade or stockade. The only way to enter the town was through the town gates, where a gatekeeper was always on the lookout. If he was doubtful about a stranger's credentials, he would confine him in the prison – a hole in the ground – until the magistrate could be informed.

Inside the stockade was the town proper. A main street, called the high street, ran through the centre of the town with narrow closes or lanes leading from it. All the roads were of earth, not paved, and farm animals were free to roam everywhere. All kinds of refuse lay around in heaps to be cleared on to dunghills once a week. Shops, called booths, jutted out into the street so that passers-by could see what was for sale.

The largest building was the church, which had a great many uses besides religion – for example, the magistrates would meet there to conduct the business of the town. Round the church was a graveyard which, as well as for burials, was used to graze cattle, swine, sheep, goats and horses. The churchyard was sometimes even used as a rubbish tip.

When darkness fell upon the town, the inhabitants would retire to bed – they were forbidden to carry lighted torches, the only possible source of light at night, because of the risk of setting a wooden building on fire. They rose early, with the sun, to begin their day's work. In the absence of clocks they relied on the town crier

to wake them; he did so by making a loud noise on a drum or some other musical instrument.

Since early times the land had been cultivated and tilled for crops, such as oats and barley, with a plough pulled by hand, or later by horses. When the crops were ready for harvesting the whole town would come to help. The local mill, operated by water power from a stream or river, would grind the corn between two large flat stones.

Every town had its blacksmith and smithy. An apprentice would be at the blacksmith's side to learn the trade, which included fashioning horseshoes, iron cooking utensils, pots, tools, and any other iron goods that were needed.

Burgesses
The population of the town was divided into two classes: freemen and bondsmen. The freemen, or burgesses, enjoyed all the privileges that the king bestowed on a royal burgh town.

Before a man could become a burgess he had to pay a large sum of money to the king and have weapons and armour to defend the king when required. On the other hand, bondsmen, the workers, were not allowed to own a shop or trade, or to become craftsmen.

Merchants and craftsmen
The merchants, the town's traders, had their own societies, called guilds, whose members were the only ones permitted to trade. The guild looked after its members, supporting widows and helping those in business difficulties, and also dealt with matters outside the guild – the town's defence was its responsibility, as were the setting of quality standards and the fixing of prices of goods.

There were many different kinds of craftsmen, including armourers, potters, smiths, shoemakers, butchers, saddlers, masons, tailors, dyers and weavers, as well as many others. Each trade formed its own guild, and the members had their own area of the town in which to live and trade.

An apprentice to a particular craft would live in his master's shop for many years and learn from him until he was proficient. He would then be shut in a room on his own to make an appropriate article of his trade. His work was examined by the deacon of the trade. If it passed the standard, he had completed his training and was known as a journeyman from then on; if his work failed, he would have to continue his apprenticeship.

The yearly fair
The greatest activity in the town was seen on its weekly market-days and the day of the annual fair. There were other feast days and church activities during the year which brought people together and alleviated the monotony of work, but the most spectacular was the fair – always a major event, full of excitement and interest.

It attracted people from afar who came to sell articles not usually available in the town. Prices were fixed and taxes had to be paid before a craftsman could set up his stall. When the stalls were ready, a bell was rung to bring all the traders together and the fair would begin. Everyone from the town, young and old, rich and poor, took part in this tremendous occasion, either buying and selling, or providing refreshments.

Far left: *medieval town house*
Left: *the Common Seal of Edinburgh, showing the burgh's open, fortified gates*
Above: *a blacksmith's workshop*

Reforming the nation

When Alexander III died on the night of 18–19 March 1286, an immediate problem arose over who was to succeed him. His only surviving heir was his granddaughter, Margaret, the 'Maid of Norway'. Alexander had made his great lords swear to accept Margaret as Queen and they had agreed that until she came of age the country would be governed by the 'Guardians', the wisest and most important of the bishops and barons.

The Guardians sent envoys to Edward I of England, Alexander III's brother-in-law, seeking his advice. Edward, wanting to be recognised as the overlord of Scotland, secretly arranged, and was granted, a dispensation from the Pope for a marriage between his son and the young queen. No sooner had this agreement, the Treaty of Birgham, been finalised than it was tragically rendered impossible – the 'Maid of Norway' died in Orkney on her way to Scotland.

THE CLAIMANTS

Now the question was different. Who had the right to the Scottish throne? In Perth, Robert Bruce, Lord of Annandale, gathered a formidable force and was joined by the Earls of Mar and Atholl with their men.

This threat and the fear of war led the Guardians, perhaps unwisely, to seek Edward's advice in deciding which of the claimants had the strongest case for the throne. Accordingly, Edward invited the claimants and certain dignitaries of the Church of Scotland to Norham Castle on 10 May 1291. Once all had assembled, the claimants, John Hastings, John Balliol and Robert Bruce, were shocked by the King's declaration that he had come 'as the superior and lord paramount of the kingdom of Scotland'. This unethical assertion put the Scots in a vulnerable position, with the autonomy of their country at stake.

Throughout the meeting Edward had his army standing by in case of trouble. He gave the claimants three weeks to agree to his terms. The Scots were in a dilemma and the Bishop of Glasgow, who was also present at the meeting, told King Edward that he thought such manipulation was outrageous.

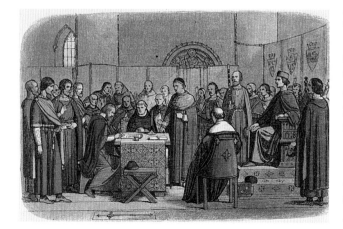

Top left: *Robert the Bruce, grandson of Robert Bruce*
Left: *Edward I being acknowledged as the supreme ruler of Scotland*
Right: *the sites and dates of Scottish battles*

ATLANTIC OCEAN

Pentland Firth

Thurso

Outer Hebrides

The Minch

Isle of Lewis

Stornoway

58°

Harris

North Uist

Inner Hebrides

Moray Firth

36

Benbecula

South Uist

Barra

Skye

Rhum

35

Inverness 31

30 SCOTLAND

33 34

32 Aberdeen

Muck Eigg

29

Coll

Fort William

Glencoe

28

Montrose

Tiree

Mull

26

Dundee

Iona

Oban 27

Perth

25

Firth of Tay

Colonsay

Jura

Firth of Lorne

23

24 22

56°

Stirling 21

19 20

18 17

Firth of Forth

Islay

Glasgow

EDINBURGH 9

8

Bute

16 15 14

11 10

7 Berwick upon Tweed

Arran

13

12

4

6 5

3

Firth of Clyde

2

Dumfries

NORTHERN IRELAND

Stranraer

1

Carlisle

Solway Firth

ENGLAND

NORTH SEA

4°

0°

BATTLES

1 Solway Moss 1542
2 Otterburn 1388
3 Homildon Hill 1402
4 Flodden 1513
5 Ancrum 1545
6 Philiphaugh 1645
7 Halidon Hill 1333

8 Dunbar 1296 and 1650
9 Prestonpans 1745
10 Pinkie 1547
11 Rullion Green 1666
12 Loudon Hill 1307
13 Drumclog 1679
14 Bothwell Bridge 1679
15 Langside 1568
16 Largs 1263
17 Falkirk 1298 and 1746

18 Kilsyth 1645
19 Sauchieburn 1488
20 Bannockburn 1314
21 Stirling Bridge 1297
22 Falkland 1298
23 Sheriffmuir 1715
24 Dupplin Moor 1332
25 Methven 1306
26 Dalrigh 1306
27 Pass of Brander 1308

28 Killiecrankie 1689
29 Inverlochy 1645
30 Glenshiel 1719
31 Culloden 1746
32 Alford 1645
33 Harlaw 1411
34 Barra Hill 1308
35 Auldearn 1645
36 Carbisdale 1650

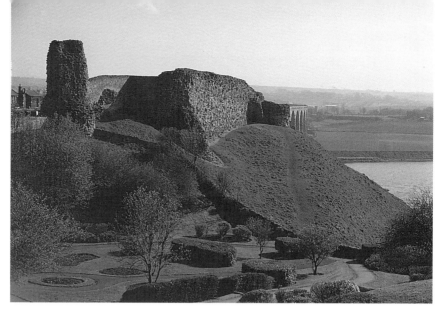

Above: *Edward I*
Right: *the ruins of
Berwick Castle*

By 6 June, the claimants had set their seals to documents acknowledging Edward I's right to govern.

Meeting at Berwick Castle

On 17 November 1292 Edward met the claimants again, this time at Berwick Castle. He rejected John Hastings outright, but Robert Bruce and John Balliol had a stronger case – they were both in line to the throne through female relatives who were sisters and great-granddaughters of David I. Edward gave the throne to John Balliol of Galloway, as John's grandmother, Margaret, was the elder sister. The new king was enthroned at Scone on 30 November, St Andrew's Day, and gave his oath of homage to Edward at Berwick on 26 December.

Berwick Station stands on the site of the original Berwick Castle, of which some ruins can still be seen. On the station there is a plaque engraved as follows:

This Station stands on the site of the Great Wall of Berwick Castle. Here on 17th November 1292 the claim of Robert Bruce for the crown of Scotland was disclaimed and the decision in favour of John Balliol was given by King Edward I of England, before the full Parliament of England and a large gathering of the nobility and populace of both England and Scotland.

EDWARD'S CONTROL OF SCOTLAND

It soon became obvious that Edward was going to use Scotland as a vassal, and that John Balliol was not strong enough to withstand him. When Edward ordered the Scots to fight for him against the French, the nobles retaliated by making a treaty with France, and this was the origin of what became known as the 'Auld Alliance' between the two countries.

Inevitably, war broke out between England and Scotland. In March 1296 Edward arrived in Scotland, seized Berwick and then routed John Balliol at Dunbar. Castles fell to Edward, including Edinburgh, and finally, on 2 July, Balliol surrendered. His crown and sceptre were removed, and his coat of arms was ripped from his tabard, earning him the nickname of 'Toom Tabard' (empty coat). He was taken as a prisoner to the Tower of London. Edward stole the Stone of Destiny and sent it to Westminster Abbey. He also took the Black Rood (crucifix) of St Margaret, said to be made from the true cross of Christ.

In the heart of Scotland, a murmur of discontent now began to gain in volume and vehemence, encouraged by the Bishop of Glasgow and many outraged loyal noblemen. Scotland needed a new leader, and found him in William Wallace.

WILLIAM WALLACE

Little is known about the background of this renowned patriot, apart from the fact that he was the younger son of a knight who lived in Paisley, and all descriptions of him stress his enormous height and strength. Certainly, he was endowed with every bit of the fighting spirit of the red-headed Scottish warriors who had withstood the Romans so long before.

Wallace gathered a huge army, consisting mainly of Highlanders and men from the north-east, to fight the English and had soon captured all the fortresses north of the Forth. He employed the same surprise tactics that the Caledonians had used so effectively to fight the Romans, completely unnerving the English forces and causing mounting alarm as the number of his attacks increased.

Further north, Sir Andrew Moray from the Moray coast, recently released from prison in England, roused his men from Banff, Moray and Aberdeen to

revolt. He used the same methods of attack as Wallace, for he too had inherited the fighting blood of his ancestors.

Both Wallace and Moray continued to fight throughout the summer of 1297.

The Battle of Stirling Bridge

At the end of August, Earl Warenne, acting on Edward's behalf, advanced towards Stirling with his army. On 11 September 1297 Wallace and Moray joined forces for the first time and waited for the English army to meet them at Stirling Bridge.

Wallace proved to be a born strategist. He waited until half the English army had crossed the bridge to the Carse of Stirling on the other side, before launching a furious attack. Over 5000 soldiers and 100 knights of the English army died in the bloody battle which ensued. Unfortunately, Moray was badly wounded and died later the same year.

In the winter of 1297, Wallace marched into the north of England and plundered widely. He also opened the Scottish ports to European merchants, encouraging commerce by writing to cities like Lübeck and Hamburg, asking for support and inviting them to trade with Scotland.

Stirling Bridge had been an outstanding victory for Wallace, but it also marked the beginning of his downfall. Most of the Scottish nobles were dissatisfied

Left: *a statue of William Wallace*
Above: *the Battle of Stirling Bridge*

with the position he had assumed as Guardian of Scotland – a knighthood for Wallace went some way towards gaining their respect. Unfortunately, his next encounter with the English was to be a disaster.

The Battle of Falkirk

On 22 July 1298 Wallace took on the English once again. He arranged his peasant army as he had before, in four schiltroms (circles of pikemen with slanted pikes). Between the schiltroms he placed the archers, and behind them, the cavalry. However, this time, Edward included a number of English bowmen in his army, carrying powerful long-range bows that were as tall as the men. The Scottish archers were mown

down by the English cavalry, and the cavalry scattered too, but the schiltroms held firm until the English bowmen came into range. The bowmen rained down arrows on the dense, packed, slow-moving schiltroms and when gaps appeared in them, Edward sent in his cavalry to finish off the Scottish troops.

William Wallace escaped, but resigned his guardianship of Scotland and became a roving thorn in the English side, continually fighting for Scottish rights. King Edward's response was to offer a large reward for his capture.

The Lake of Menteith

Inevitably, Wallace was betrayed by one of the jealous nobles - Sir John Menteith, governor of Dumbarton. Consequently, the stretch of water on Menteith's estate suffered the disgrace of being called the 'Lake of Menteith', the only loch in Scotland to be called by the English word 'lake', and thus providing a constant reminder of Menteith's treachery.

Wallace was taken to London and charged with treason at Westminster Court on 23 August 1305. His defence was, 'I never could have been a traitor to Edward, for I was never his subject.' He was condemned to be hanged, drawn and quartered, and his limbs were distributed to Newcastle-upon-Tyne, Berwick, Perth and Stirling to discourage other Scottish patriots.

ROBERT THE BRUCE (1306–29)

Between the reigns of Alexander III and Robert I there were 20 years of turmoil, war and uncertainty over who had the legal right to the throne. By 1306 the Scots were still very much dominated by the feudal system and had to submit to the dictates of their superiors in rank. Most of the noblemen's castles were

Left: *Robert the Bruce*
Right: *Bruce watches the persistent spider*

still in the hands of the English, and it was to take a strong Scottish noble to reclaim them from Edward and win back the throne.

This leader duly emerged. He was Robert the Bruce, grandson of the Robert Bruce who had made a claim to the throne many years previously at Norham Castle. He declared his right to the Scottish throne and, after a long and determined struggle, finally released Scotland from English clutches to become King of Scotland.

On 10 February 1306 Robert the Bruce met John Comyn, lord of Badenoch, to try and gain his support. Comyn, known as 'the Red', was a confidant of Edward, and both he and Bruce had strong claims to the Scottish throne, though neither of them, to their discredit, had supported Wallace. They met in the Franciscan priory at Dumfries, but unfortunately an agreement was not reached. In fact, the nobles fought and Comyn was slain.

Bruce subsequently organised his own coronation at Scone, declaring himself King of Scotland on 25 March 1306.

Although he was now king, Robert received little support from the nobles, and so Scottish lands and castles remained in English hands. Bruce knew that the only way he would be able to regain Scotland was to fight for every castle in the country and thus drive the English away.

Bruce and the spider

Bruce and a few of his men went into hiding in a cave on the small island of Rathlin, off Ireland, to escape the English after Bruce had murdered John Comyn.

A famous story tells of how, while in hiding, Bruce became entranced by watching a spider spinning its web. It made repeated attempts to fix the web to the ceiling until at last it succeeded. According to the legend, this inspired Bruce to overcome his many hardships and losses in battle, and persevere until he had won back Scotland for its people.

Bruce's campaign

Some weeks later, Bruce and a number of his men successfully established themselves on the Isle of Arran, opposite Turnberry Castle on the Ayrshire coast – Bruce's original home. After resting at their island retreat, they made plans to retake Bruce's castle.

It was decided that their allies would show a light by the castle to indicate that all was well. On the appointed night, a light was seen as planned, and Bruce and his men set sail. However, as they drew closer to the mainland, they realised the light was a fire lit by English soldiers, not a signal fire.

Bruce turned the mistake to his advantage by launching a surprise attack on the English soldiers who were stationed outside the castle, thus gaining all the food, armour and horses the rebels needed to replenish their supplies and capture the fortress.

At this time Bruce learned that three of his brothers and his wife, daughter and two sisters had been imprisoned by the English. Now, more than ever, his determination to recapture Scotland from Edward became absolute.

Edward, the 'Hammer of the Scots', decided to travel north and quash the Scots rebellion himself, but died on 7 July 1307 as he was approaching the Scottish border. His son, Edward II, took over from him, but returned south soon after. The new king immediately began to quarrel with his own subjects, which made life easier for Bruce.

Having inherited the Earldom of Carrick from his father in 1307, Bruce returned there to plan his campaign and was soon ready to wage civil war on the supporters of Comyn and Balliol. In 1308 he laid waste the Earldom of Buchan, putting down all who opposed him and slowly winning back the strongholds held by Edward II.

The freeing of Edinburgh Castle

Sir Thomas Randolph, Bruce's nephew, and son of the Earl of Moray, set out to recapture Edinburgh Castle with 30 faithful men. Among Randolph's soldiers was William Frank, who volunteered to lead an attack up a steep and rocky incline into the castle known as Wallace's Cradle, a route which he had been accustomed to use in former years when visiting his young sweetheart who worked there.

Around midnight on a stormy night in March, they started their perilous climb, with each man carrying a rope ladder. As they inched up the rock, an English sentinel shouted, 'Ah! Ah! I see you well!' and threw a stone over the wall, just missing the climbing men. They froze, hardly daring to breathe. Fortunately, the guard was only playing a joke on his colleagues. Hearing the sentinels' laughter, the climbers commenced again, more silently and cautiously than ever.

When they reached the castle, they managed to hook their ladders over the wall and began to climb. All was strangely quiet. The sentinels were nowhere to be seen. Jumping softly to the floor, they crept quickly along the inside of the wall. They edged their way into the castle, leaving two men to keep watch behind them. The attack was so sudden that the guards never had time to recover from their astonishment; the rest of the men were killed in their beds.

Randolph was delighted to have overpowered the garrison and went straight away to inform Bruce. There was much rejoicing – Edinburgh Castle was finally back in Scottish hands, and all those who had so gallantly risked their lives passed a prayer of thanks to St Margaret for their safety.

Stirling Castle

Seven years after landing at Turnberry, Bruce had regained nearly all the Scottish castles. His brother, Edward, had made a bargain with Sir Philip Mowbray, who led the English garrison at Stirling Castle, that it should be returned to the Scots if Edward II failed to defend it against Bruce by 24 June 1314.

Bruce was unhappy with the bargain made on his behalf, not having such a large army of trained knights and men as Edward, but he had to regain Stirling Castle and give Scotland back to her people. The English king, accepting Bruce's challenge, agreed to the battleground which Bruce had chosen – Bannockburn, just 3 miles (5km) from Stirling Castle.

Bruce laid the plans to receive his enemy with infinite care. Firstly, he chose his battle positions, opting for a site close to the Bannock burn, a small tidal stream, which meant the English would have to cross it to reach his army. He then prepared the land before the stream, digging holes and covering them with a thin layer of earth with the intention of tripping the enemy's horses. Then he strategically placed calthrops (spikes) on the ground to tangle and disorientate the knights on horseback.

The English are said to have had an army of 15,000 foot soldiers and 2500 knights. They must have looked magnificent in their coats of armour on their beautifully controlled horses, banners waving, as they marched behind their king toward the battlefield. It was the largest army an English king had ever led. The Scots army was much smaller: about 6000 infantry and 500 horse soldiers.

The Battle of Bannockburn

On 23 June 1314 the first of the battles to be fought at Bannockburn began. Bruce and the Scots stayed inside the wood watching the road from Falkirk. A scouting party reported 300 English knights approaching Stirling Castle, a glittering mass of banners and helmets flashing in the sun, commanded by the young Earl of Gloucester. One of the English knights, Sir Henry de Bohun, picked out Bruce riding in front of his men. Sir Henry, armed with a lance, was in full armour on a war charger, whereas Bruce was on a pony, carrying only a battleaxe. The knight charged at Bruce, hoping to gain honours by killing him and putting an end to the battle. Undaunted, Bruce made his pony swerve at just the right moment to avoid the knight, and, as he passed by at full speed, Bruce, who had risen to his full height in the saddle, swung his

axe mightily and killed his assailant with one blow. Bruce's only concern was that he had broken his axe and did not have another for the battle.

When the English knights charged the Scots, many were unseated for, just as Bruce had anticipated, the holes and spikes in the ground served to disrupt the close ranks of horsemen crossing the burn and slowed down their progress.

At the end of a day of bitter and bloody fighting, hundreds lay dead or dying. The English soldiers had been exposed to the sun all day and were parched with thirst. The army advanced with its horses through the bogs of the Carse of Stirling, and it was then decided to cross the Bannock burn before setting up camp. This took much of the night and exhausted the troops still further.

The Scots were feeling that retreat was the best option when a Scottish knight on the English side joined them under cover of darkness and urged Bruce to fight the next day, as English morale was low.

At dawn, Bruce and his men knelt in prayer calling for a blessing upon the fight that lay ahead. The English thought that they were asking for pardon.

The fighting began with a skirmish between the rival groups of archers. The English were pressed back by the Scottish schiltroms and caught between the Bannock burn and the Pelestream. There was not enough room for their cavalry to manoeuvre, and they were fighting on too narrow a front. When they tried to bring in their bowmen, Bruce brought in his own strong reserve division led by Angus Og.

Then a strange thing occurred. What looked like another Scottish army was seen coming down the hill nearby, rapidly approaching the battlefield. In fact, it was only the 'smallfolk of Scotland', a name given to the cooks and camp-followers of the Scottish army. Brandishing spades and kitchen utensils, they were determined to take part in the struggle for feedom.

The Battle of Bannockburn

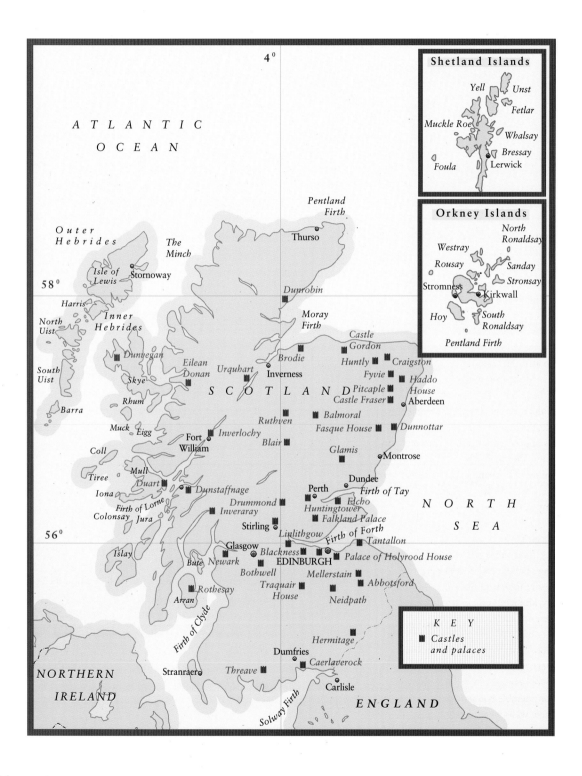

Shetland Islands

Yell Unst
Fetlar
Muckle Roe Whalsay
Bressay
Foula Lerwick

Orkney Islands

North
Ronaldsay
Westray
Rousay Sanday
Stronsay
Stromness Kirkwall
Hoy South
Ronaldsay
Pentland Firth

ATLANTIC
OCEAN

Pentland
Firth
Thurso

Outer
Hebrides The
Minch

58° Isle of
Lewis Stornoway

Harris Inner Dunrobin
Hebrides
North Moray
Uist Firth
Castle
South Dunvegan Gordon
Uist Eilean Brodie Huntly Craigston
Skye Donan Urquhart Fyvie
Barra Inverness Pitcaple Haddo
SCOTLAND Castle Fraser House
Rhum Aberdeen
Muck Eigg Ruthven Balmoral Dunnottar
Coll Fort Inverlochy Fasque House
William Blair Glamis
Tiree Mull Montrose
Duart Dundee
Iona Dunstaffnage Perth Firth of Tay
Colonsay Firth of Lorne Drummond Elcho
Jura Inveraray Huntingtower
Stirling Falkland Palace NORTH
Linlithgow Firth of Forth SEA
Islay Glasgow Tantallon
Bute Blackness Palace of Holyrood House
Newark EDINBURGH
Bothwell Mellerstain
Rothesay Traquair Abbotsford
Arran House Neidpath

Hermitage
Dumfries
Stranraer Threave Caerlaverock

NORTHERN Carlisle
IRELAND ENGLAND
Solway Firth
Firth of Clyde

4°
56°

KEY
■ Castles
and palaces

SCOTTISH CASTLES AND PALACES

The castles and palaces of Scotland are an important part of the country's heritage and a constant reminder of its turbulent history. They have also formed the background to many stories of mystery and adventure by writers of all nationalities.

Forts

Castles began as forts, strategically positioned to keep a look out for enemies. Eilean Donan in Ross-shire and Urquhart Castle by Loch Ness in Inverness-shire were located by sea lochs, and Blair Castle was uniquely situated to guard the entrance to the Scottish Highlands.

Most strongholds were designed to benefit from their particular aspect. If the castle was by the sea, for example, the living rock constituted part of its impenetrable wall. When the terrifying Viking invasions ravaged the shores of Scotland, these fortifications were vital for warning people of impending danger.

Castles

As times and needs changed, forts were enlarged by feudal lords into castles to protect their king and country, and to accommodate their families, soldiers and provisions.

Early fortresses were made of wood, but in the Middle Ages they were reconstructed in stone with extremely thick walls to withstand considerable bombardment. Slits in these walls were used by archers. Most castles had a massive drawbridge with huge doors opening on to a courtyard. When closed, these doors were fastened with iron bolts or bars. If the enemy managed to gain entry through the gates, a great iron portcullis would drop rapidly in front of the courtyard to protect the castle's interior.

Soldiers were trained in the courtyard, and, from here, stone steps led to the dungeons, deep underground. The living quarters of the resident family lay within further substantial walls; sometimes this was an inner keep, protected and guarded, as at Tantallon Castle. A winding stone staircase within the keep linked the various floors of the building and led up to the 'lookout' or 'turret' and to the balustrades.

Most castles had extensive alterations carried out, especially during the eighteenth and nineteenth centuries, whilst in the twentieth century, many owners have opened their properties to the public in a bid to offset increasing maintenance costs.

Palaces

Palaces have always been associated with royalty and this is also true of those in Scotland. Indeed, the Palace of Holyrood House, which dates originally from the days of James IV and was rebuilt by Charles II, is still used by the present royal family as their official Scottish residence.

Palaces were never regarded as being strategic buildings, but nevertheless played an important role in Scottish history.

Left: *Scottish castles and palaces*
Below: *Neidpath Castle, near Peebles*

The English mistook the 'smallfolk' for soldiers and took fright. Realising the situation, Bruce and his men fought all the harder until the enemy was fleeing in all directions.

Edward rode off to Stirling Castle, where Sir Philip Mowbray refused him admission, remembering the bargain he had made earlier with Edward Bruce.

The bloody and stormy battle of Bannockburn had brought a decisive victory over the English, the greatest the Scots had ever achieved. For the first time for many years the whole of Scotland was united, and justly proud of their king.

Scotland's independence

Bruce was soon demanding an agreement from Edward, stating that Scotland was now as free as England and he was the rightful Scottish king. Edward refused, and Bruce was forced to attack him at his weakest point, Ireland. Trouble was brewing between the English and the Irish at the time, and Bruce took advantage of this by deploying a force to support Ireland's cause. Edward found this interference most troublesome, but would still not acknowledge Bruce as King of Scotland. Bruce then tried another tactic – he attacked Northumberland, burning villages as he went. Edward raised an army and journeyed to Northumbria to fight him, but Bruce went into hiding and evaded battle, still plundering everywhere he went.

Meanwhile, the Pope had also refused to acknowledge Bruce as king because of the murder of Comyn on the altar steps of a church and because Bruce had crowned himself. In 1320, the Scottish nobles wrote a letter to the Pope asking him to persuade King Edward to leave the Scots alone:

Yet Robert himself, should he turn aside from the task that he has begun, and yield Scotland or us to the English King and people, we should cast out as the enemy of us all, as subverter of our rights and of his own, and should choose another king to defend our freedom: for so long as a hundred of us are left alive, we will yield in no least way to English dominion. We fight not for glory nor for wealth nor honours; but only and alone we fight for freedom, which no good man surrenders but with his life. (Given at the Monastery of Arbroath, in Scotland the sixth day of April in the year of Grace one thousand three hundred and twenty, and in the fifteenth year of the King named above.)

Known as the Declaration of Arbroath, this is one of the most important documents in the history of the Scottish nation. The Pope was persuaded by the appeal and encouraged the English to accept a peace treaty. In 1323 an uneasy truce was agreed. Four years later, Edward II died, probably murdered, and was succeeded by his son.

Far left: *a coin from the time of Robert the Bruce*
Left: *David II and Edward III*
Right: *the Declaration of Arbroath*

In 1328 the young King Edward III tried to engage the Scots in battle, but each time he approached the Scottish army it withdrew. Bruce then began attacking the castles of Northumberland with siege machines. Edward finally had to accept the terms demanded by Bruce and, in 1328, the Treaty of Edinburgh at last recognised Scotland's freedom and marked the end of the Wars of Independence. Scotland had been battling for liberty since 1279, and over the years the country had become impoverished, leaving its people disorganised and suffering the aftermath of conflict and uncertainty.

Reforms under Robert I

The troubles that Bruce had experienced in bringing order to his kingdom were almost entirely due to infighting between nobles, who were forever trying to gain ascendancy over each other. Many believed they had a greater right to the throne. This made Bruce's task of reforming the laws and statutes of Scotland a difficult one, but his great strength of character enabled him to overcome these discordant elements and his authority became firmly established. However, there were still significant problems with lawlessness and disorder in the Highlands and on many of the adjacent islands.

Meanwhile, burghs had grown in importance under the influence of the religious orders. Some towns had chartered privileges which equalled the powers of the nobles, and citizens elected their own municipal council. The chief magistrate was known as the provost and the others became known as baillies (city magistrates). High stone walls were built around many burghs, and the citizens were trained to defend their towns.

Not long after the peace agreement with England, Bruce contracted leprosy; he had been somewhat ill even at the time of the Treaty of Edinburgh. He returned to his home at Cardross, and died there on 7 July 1329. He was buried in Dunfermline Abbey.

Bruce had always wanted to go on a crusade to recapture the Holy Land from the Muslims, or infidels. When he died, his heart was put in a silver casket and kept by Sir James Douglas, who planned to take it to the Holy Sepulchre in Jerusalem. Sir James later joined the army of the King of Spain and, while fighting in a battle against the Saracens, his forces became hopelessly outnumbered. Throwing the casket into the midst of the battle, Sir James cried, 'Now go before, brave heart, as you always did, and I shall follow you or die.' The nobleman was killed soon after, but the casket was brought back to Scotland and buried in Melrose Abbey.

DAVID II (1329–71)

At the time of Bruce's death, his son and heir was only five years old, so once again a regent had to be found. Before dying, Bruce had obtained oil blessed by the Pope and, at the same time, received permission for it to be used to anoint his son at his coronation. The

Bishop of St Andrews officiated at the coronation which took place at Scone in 1329. It was the first time that a Scottish king had been anointed during

the crowning ceremony. The Bishop sprinkled the oil on ten areas of the young king's body: his head, breast, shoulders, armpits, elbows, and the palms of his hands. David II was then considered 'the Lord's anointed'.

Realising the vulnerability of the Scottish throne, Edward III of England again tried to conquer Scotland. He had a claimant he wished to reign there: Edward Balliol, son of John. The Scots had forgotten the lessons of warfare they had been taught by Bruce and, when they met the English in battle at Dupplin Moor, they were defeated. Edward Balliol had himself crowned, and Scotland had two kings.

Balliol was thrown out by the Scots, but he returned the next summer and the young King of Scotland was sent into safekeeping in France. Scotland was shared between Edward III of England and Edward Balliol, but David's cause was kept alive by John Randolph, Robert Steward and later, Sir Andrew Moray.

In 1337 the English sent ships to blockade Dunbar and lay siege to the castle. For five months the Countess of March, known as Black Agnes, led the defence of the castle:

> *Came I early, came I late*
> *Found I Black Agnes at the gate . . .*

Finally, in 1341, David returned home as king. In 1346 the French called on Scotland to come to their aid against England, in accordance with the terms of the Auld Alliance, and David duly marched into northern England. Unfortunately, he was severely wounded and taken prisoner by the English at the Battle of Neville's Cross.

In the meantime, Edward Balliol returned to Scotland. After nine years, David was released on a ransom of 100,000 merks to be paid at the rate of 10,000 merks a year; it was never fully paid. Edward Balliol, realising his position was futile, retired on a pension from the English king.

Though David ruled Scotland well, increasing trade and prosperity, he antagonised Parliament by entertaining the notion of a union between the Scottish and English Crowns in order to avoid having to make his ransom payments.

Having ruled for 30 years, David died unexpectedly in 1371 at the age of 46 and without a direct heir despite having been married twice.

The Black Death of 1349–50

David II's reign saw the start of the recurrent horror, the bubonic and pneumonic plague or the 'Black Death'. Originating in India, it swept across Asia and then Europe, Scotland being the last European country to suffer the epidemic. Sneezing and red rings on the skin were the first symptoms, but soon the body would be covered with the black boils or spots which gave the disease its name. Within two days most of those afflicted were dead.

The corpses could not be buried in the usual way because of the risk of contagion, so great pits were dug some distance from people's homes.

The plague returned in 1362 and 1379, and altogether a third of the population of Scotland perished.

Left: *David II*
Right: *victims of the Black Death*

THE HOUSE OF STEWART

The period following David's death was frenetic and lawless. Robert Stewart (or Steward), a grandson of Robert the Bruce, who had already been Guardian of Scotland twice, was crowned king, thus commencing the reign of the royal house of Stewart. Robert had little of his grandfather's fighting spirit and was too passive to control his family or kingdom. Once more, war broke out against England, and Scotland was assisted by France under the terms of the Auld Alliance. The English were again cleared out of Scotland.

The troubles continued under Robert III. His real name was John but he used Robert, as there had been so many ill-fated Johns. However, this superstitious re-naming does not seem to have helped. For his epitaph he chose the words: 'Here lies the worst of kings and the most wretched of men in the whole realm.' He suggested he should be buried in a rubbish-heap, but his final resting place was Paisley Abbey.

JAMES I (1406–37)

In 1406 when Robert III died, James I, his son, became king at the age of 12. His father had previously sent him to France to protect him from his uncle, the Duke of Albany, but James was captured *en route* by pirates and was handed over to Henry IV of England. He was held prisoner for 18 years, but during this time was well educated at the English court. He took part in Henry V's French campaigns and then married Lady Joan Beaufort. At 21, he was allowed to return to Scotland under the terms of the Treaty of London – a ransom for his maintenance and expenses of 60,000 merks, payable over six years.

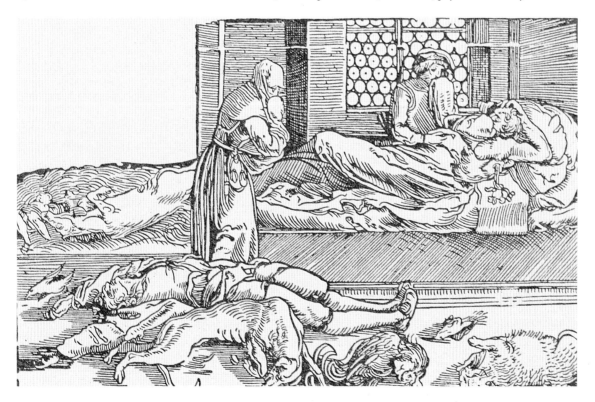

Reforms under James

When James took control of Scotland in 1424, he found the government steeped in corruption and in the hands of self-serving nobles who had allowed the country to fall into decline. No taxes were being paid. Determined to bring order to his kingdom, James dealt ruthlessly with rivals. The Duke of Albany's son, Murdoch, his sons and the Earl of Lennox were beheaded – the first state executions for 100 years.

James instigated many social reforms in the first year of his reign. When he tried to remodel Parliament on the style of the English system, the influential nobles opposed him, but James fought back by passing restrictive laws which curbed their powers and brought them to order. These laws were passed without the approval of the King's Council, thereby transgressing all the rules of law in Scotland and infuriating the nobles. Despite the ill-feeling James elicited, he did make it clear that all his subjects, high and low, were under the law's jurisdiction.

Before James' reign, Scottish students travelled to Paris to attend university rather than going to Oxford or Cambridge, since these two medieval universities were run by the Church and were training centres for appointments within the Church hierarchy. The Bishop of St Andrews, Henry Wardlaw, felt that Scotland should have its own university, and in 1411 asked the Church of Scotland to establish a university at St Andrews. Permission was granted and the university was founded in the same year.

After James had suppressed the nobles, he turned his attack on the Church, which had also fallen into disrepute, and exposed its decadent practices. The more zealous churchmen were incensed by James' action, but this did force the Church to exert greater control over its clergy.

A small group of nobles, including the Earl of Atholl, bitterly resentful of the laws James had passed, conspired to put an end to the King's rule. A plan was devised to trick the King into giving a party at Blackfriars in Perth. When all the guests had arrived, Sir Robert Graham and other dissenting nobles turned up, uninvited. It is said that the servants hastily warned the King who, fearing the worst, went straight to a secret stone on the floor of the banqueting hall. He lifted it and went down some steps to an underground room which he thought would lead him safely to the outside of the building. But only a week

Left: *memorial to the High Stewards of Scotland*
Above: *James I*
Right: *Catherine Douglas tries to save James I*

before, the exit had been blocked, supposedly because croquet balls were always running through the exit and getting lost.

At first, Sir Robert Graham thought he had also been tricked. He searched the castle with his men, but finding no one he returned to the banqueting hall. After another extensive search, they discovered the stone. They lifted it and found the King.

When James begged for mercy, he was told, 'You had no mercy on others, why should we show you any?' and forthwith a nobleman murdered him with a dagger. The murderers, though, did not have great support in the country and Queen Joan was determined to bring them to justice. Within a month they had been captured and, after two days of merciless torture, they died.

JAMES II (1437–60)

After the murder of her husband, the Queen hurried to reach the safety of Edinburgh Castle with her young son, James, who was hastily crowned at Holyrood Abbey in 1437. The new king, James II, was only six years old.

With all the work of James I unravelling, Scotland was again racked by lawlessness, plague and famine. The fifth Earl of Douglas was appointed Lieutenant General of the kingdom, with the Bishop of Glasgow as Chancellor. The Queen had custodial rights over the young king.

Known as 'the king of the fiery face' because of a birthmark, James II came of age in 1449. He immediately decided to re-establish control over the nobles and make examples of troublemakers. William, Earl of Douglas, one of the most powerful nobles in the land, was invited to dine at Stirling Castle. When James commanded him to disassociate himself from the rebels, he refused, and James murdered him with a dagger in a fit of rage.

James succeeded in bringing order to his kingdom and was able to govern in peace. In 1451, Scotland's second university was founded in Glasgow.

Unfortunately, after 11 years, James' reign ended because of an accident. He was trying to retrieve Roxburgh and Berwick Castles from the English, and had raised an army for this purpose. To accomplish his mission he had introduced the use of cannons in battle for the first time and was immensely proud of them. However, one of them blew up, killing him as he stood close by.

JAMES III (1460–88)

Once more the new heir was very young, only nine years old at his father's untimely death. Bishop Kennedy was made Guardian and he kept the country

in good order – in fact, he managed much better than James III himself when he eventually came to the throne in 1468.

James III's marriage (1469)

During the reign of Alexander III, an agreement had been made between Scotland and Norway to pay a sum of money each year to the Norwegians, but the commitment had been neglected of late. The King of Norway, who was also King of Denmark and Sweden, was demanding that the agreement be fulfilled. Something had to be done to alleviate this problem so the King's Council sent the Earl of Arran to Norway to arrange a marriage settlement.

On behalf of the Council, the Earl asked the King for his daughter Margaret's hand in marriage to James. According to the agreement, the Isles of Orkney and Shetland were to be given as security for part payment of her dowry. The King of Norway was delighted and so were all the Scots, particularly James himself, who preferred peace to war. When, in due course, the dowry failed to appear, the Orkney and Shetland Isles once again became part of Scotland.

The murder of the favourites

Unfortunately, James III became unpopular with his nobles because of a tendency to develop favourites on whom he lavished money and land to the detriment of his other subjects. Contemplating war with the English, James demanded the support of the nobles, who saw an excellent opportunity to avenge themselves on the King and his favourites.

In 1482 when the army was encamped at Lauder, in the Borders, the nobles held a meeting in the nearby church. Suddenly, there was a loud knocking on the church door, which burst open to reveal Cochrane, the King's chief favourite, lavishly dressed in a velvet coat. The nobles were infuriated. One snatched Cochrane's gold necklace and bangles, while others grabbed hold of his jacket and tied him up. At first Cochrane thought it was a joke, but then realised they were in earnest.

Several of the nobles went to the royal tent, imprisoned the King and captured the other favourites. Tent ropes and the halters of horses were tied around their necks. When he realised their intention, Cochrane begged them to use a silken rope for his neck. The nobles showed no mercy; the favourites were dragged to Lauder bridge and hanged beneath the arches.

Imprisonment

James was taken as a prisoner to Edinburgh Castle under the escort of the Earl of Atholl, but later peace was made and he was released. He soon went back to his old ways, gathering more favourites around him. The nobles could not tolerate this any longer and declared war upon James, whom they judged unfit to rule. They had kidnapped James' son, also called James, and he had agreed to lead them as long as no harm befell his father. They met at Sauchieburn, near Bannockburn. When the battle started, the King, who was not a good rider, was thrown from his horse.

The injured James was carried into the nearest building, a mill. After he had returned to his senses, the people inquired who he was, and he announced, 'I was your king this morning.' On hearing this, the miller's wife rushed out shouting, 'A priest for the King, a priest for the King!'

A man claiming to be a priest entered. Bending over the King, he asked if his wound was mortal. The King replied, 'No, but I wish to confess my sins and ask pardon.' 'This then will give you your pardon,' announced the stranger, stabbing the King in the heart. Then he made his escape before anyone could identify him.

JAMES IV (1488-1513)

After James IV's coronation in 1488, it is said that he felt so guilty about the circumstances of his father's death that he started to wear a belt with iron weights as a penance. Every year, on the anniversary of Sauchieburn, he would add another weight to the belt.

James' reign coincided with the end of the Middle Ages. Major changes were taking place in Europe, including the end of the feudal system. James was determined his realm would take its proper place in the new world. He was very much a medieval king but he reflected his times and was learned and curious, with interests including sport, hunting, the arts, and architecture.

Don Pedro de Ayala, an honest and patriotic Spanish nobleman reported in a secret cipher for his own sovereigns about James and his kingdom, saying:

He is exceptionally clever, and can speak Latin, French, German, Flemish, Italian and the barbarian Gaelic, the native tongue of nearly all his subjects. He knows the Bible well and is conversant with most subjects. He is a good historian and reads Latin and French history, committing much to memory. He does not cut his hair or his beard. He is devout and says all his prayers. He maintains

that the oath of a king should be his royal word, as was the case in bygone times. He is active and works hard, when he is not at war he hunts in the mountains. He is courageous, I have seen him undertake most dangerous things in the last wars. On such occasions he does not take the least care of himself.

Subduing the Highlands and Borders

At the beginning of James' reign the Highlands were in a state of unrest due to constant feuds between the MacKenzies and the MacDonalds. James launched at least six expeditions to the area between 1490 and 1495. He fearlessly took the Lordship of the Isles away from the MacDonalds of Islay, and, in May 1493, annexed MacDonald's lands, allowing him to remain at the royal court on an 'honourable maintenance'.

Some time later, James developed a different method of dealing with trouble, by using the strongest clans – the Campbells and the Gordons – to keep order. However, this proved unsatisfactory in the long term as the other chiefs resented the interference, and further divisions resulted.

The Borders was also an area of constant trouble. James led several raids there and, deciding that his judges were too lenient with the outlaws, he often presided in his own courts.

Education and progress

James introduced many improvements, especially in education. In 1496 Parliament passed the first Scottish Education Act, one of the earliest education acts in Europe. It became compulsory for all men of means to send their eldest sons to schools to master the arts, law and Latin, the intention being to keep the elite in positions of power. He also made it mandatory for all young men to train in the skills of warfare to safeguard the lives of the population.

In 1495, a university, along with a separate school of medicine, was established in Old Aberdeen by permission of Pope Alexander IV. Scotland now had three universities. At that time, both barbers and surgeons practised medicine. James granted the barbers and surgeons of Edinburgh the right to form a guild, or society, in 1505, and allowed them the sole right to sell whisky, a new medicine. They were also given the corpse of a hanged criminal, once a year, in order to learn more about human anatomy.

In 1507 James permitted Andrew Myllar and Walter Chapman to set up the first printing press in Scotland. Apart from books on law and Acts of Parliament, they also published two of Scotland's greatest poets, William Dunbar and Robert Henryson.

James was a keen builder and had a new palace constructed at Holyrood. Additions were made to palaces at Falkirk and Linlithgow, and the Great Hall at Stirling Castle

was completed. He also planned a new navy for the country and by 1513 he had a fleet of ships. The King's greatest joy was the *Great Michael*, the largest warship ever to have been built in Scotland.

The marriage of the Thistle and the Rose

Relations with England had already deteriorated when James invited Perkin Warbeck, the Yorkist pretender to the English throne, to Scotland. Warbeck promised to surrender Berwick to James, but when James attacked the northern border to recapture Berwick in 1496, there was no support from Warbeck, who quarrelled with the King for slaughtering his people and stealing their cattle. The siege of Berwick proved to be abortive.

However, English and Scottish relations were augmented in 1503 when James agreed to an arranged marriage with Henry VII's daughter, Margaret Tudor. James wanted to marry Margaret Drummond of Stobshall, but shortly after the politically expedient arranged marriage had been proposed to him, Margaret Drummond and her two beautiful sisters were found murdered by poisoning. James never forgot her, and had prayers said for the repose of her soul throughout his life.

Eighteen months later, James finally agreed to marry Margaret Tudor. Henry, who wanted peace with Scotland, was pleased when the marriage agreement was finally settled and James signed the Treaty of Perpetual Peace at the right horn of the altar of Glasgow Cathedral. James was 28, Margaret only 12.

The glittering ceremony to receive the young Queen surpassed anything Scotland had witnessed before. The King met her at Dalkeith on 3 August and the marriage took place in Holyrood Abbey five days later. The Queen was magnificently dressed in

Top left: *the windmill symbol of Andrew Myllar*
Left: *the marriage procession of James IV and his bride, Margaret Tudor*

white satin damask bordered with crimson velvet, with a collar of gold and pearls, a present from the King. Her long hair nearly reached the floor. The King was also dressed in white damask with gold trimmings, over a jacket slashed in crimson satin and edged with black velvet.

The Battle of Flodden

In 1513, some ten years after the sumptuous marriage feast and declaration of lasting peace between Scotland and England, James found himself at war with the English again. He had been asked by the French to honour the Auld Alliance and when Henry VIII engaged in battle with France, James felt obliged to attack the English in Northumbria.

James also had two grievances against Henry. One was that he refused to send the jewellery that his father, Henry VII, had promised his daughter Margaret as a part of her marriage dowry. The second, more pressing reason was that two Scottish ships had been seized by the English and taken into custody in London. Henry VIII had refused to return them in spite of the fact that James had returned captured English vessels during Henry VII's reign.

James amassed an army of 20,000, the most powerful army Scotland had ever put on the field, and took it into Northumbria, disrupting villages and towns wherever he went. For the battle the Scots chose an ideal position on Flodden Hill, overlooking the River Till. The English army was under the command of the Earl of Surrey, a skilful and energetic general who, realising that he had to make the Scots change position, marched his army to the north, thus cutting off their retreat. Surrey had hoped to seize Branxton Hill but the Scots took it first.

The Scots were arranged in five groups, rather like Bruce's formation at Bannockburn. The English were divided into a vanguard commanded by Admiral Howard, while at the back Surrey was in command of the larger part of the army. The Scots had cannons, but they were heavy and unwieldy, and no match for the lighter English versions manned by expert German gunners. Most of the Scottish cannon-balls missed their mark, whilst the English shot began to create great gaps in the ranks of the Scots.

James then made a fatal error. Instead of letting the English make their way up the steep slopes to face the Scots, he chose to advance. His troops were unable to present a united wall with lowered spears because the ground was too slippery. Also, the 19 ft (6m) spears of the Scots were no match for the shorter axe-like bills of the English. The central part of the Scottish army, led by James himself, had almost reached the Earl of Surrey, when James was killed.

When darkness fell, as many as 10,000 Scots of all ranks lay dead on Flodden Hill, including the King, the Archbishop of St Andrews, two bishops, three abbots, nine earls, fourteen lords and three Highland chiefs: 'The flowers o' the forest are a' wede away.' Their bodies were buried in deep pits, where a monument to the dead now stands.

St Paul's Church at Branxton, near the battlefield, has printed a booklet about the encounter. It reports:

Thus ended the last medieval battle to be fought on English soil. Never again were knights to fight in armour, their personal standards flying. Never again were arrows, swords and spears to be the decisive weapons. Small arms, still unknown at Flodden, would gradually take their place.

Flodden Wall

After James' death, the people of Edinburgh felt they would never be safe from the English unless they did something to protect themselves. They immediately started building fortifications, but the English did not attack again. When the wall around the city was completed, it was named Flodden Wall to remind everyone of the disastrous battle. Parts of it can still be seen from the Grassmarket and the Cowgate.

JAMES V (1513–42)

When James IV was killed, the heir to the throne was a baby of 17 months. James IV had made a will appointing his wife, Margaret, as Regent for James V, but only while she remained a widow.

In 1514 Margaret married the 6th Earl of Angus, and discord arose among the nobles. In 1515 the Duke of Albany arrived from France and became Guardian of the Realm, ruling well and wisely. He returned to France in 1522, and Henry VIII promptly sent troops to burn and plunder the Borders. Albany returned with French troops and drove the English out, but went back to France in 1524, and once again fighting broke out among the Scottish nobles.

Left: *James V*
Top right: *Mary of Guise, the mother of Mary, Queen of Scots*
Far right: a view of *Falkland Palace, where James V was held by his stepfather*

During the first 14 years of his life the young James V grew up being passed around from place to place while his mother, his stepfather, Archibald Douglas, Earl of Angus, then the Duke of Albany, and finally a group of nobles, ruled Scotland for him.

From 1526 until the spring of 1528, James was held in Falkland Palace by Douglas, but he finally escaped, riding at dead of night to Stirling Castle. At the age of nearly 17, James V began his rule.

James restores order

James' first act as king was to revenge himself on the Douglases for his two-year confinement. He confiscated their lands, removed their powers and decreed them outlaws. He then began to establish control over the rest of his kingdom.

Yet again the Borders, the Western Isles and the Highlands were areas of conflict. James started in the Borders which, like the Highlands, was populated by clans and ruled by chiefs, called lairds. The Armstrongs were a powerful Border clan who had burned 52 churches in Scotland and plundered much wealth from English nobles living south of the Borders. Determined to make an example of this lawless tribe, James led an army of men to conquer them, putting to death all the Armstrongs who had rebelled

against him, and thus restoring the rule of law. In 1540 James tackled the Highlands, where he executed a few of the more troublesome clan leaders. Befriending the rest of the chiefs, including those of the Western Isles, he managed to restore order.

James V also made a great contribution to Scottish society by establishing the Court of Sessions in Edinburgh in 1532, an institution which has endured as the seat of Scottish Law to the present day.

James would often roam the countryside disguised as a farmer and was called the 'poor man's king' by those who appreciated the peace he had restored to their land. However, in later years he became tyrannical, and preoccupied with increasing his own wealth.

In the interests of alliance, James married a daughter of the King of France, who sadly died six months later. A year after her death, he married Mary of Guise, another French noblewoman, who was to become the mother of Mary, Queen of Scots. Two sons were born and died in infancy before Mary's birth at Linlithgow Palace in the very same week that James V lay dying in Falkland Palace. When James heard the news of his daughter's birth, he cried out on his deathbed, 'Woe is me. My dynasty came with a lass. It will go with a lass.' At the age of six days, the baby girl was crowned Queen of Scotland.

A time of change

The sixteenth century was a time of great change in Scotland. The marriage of James IV of Scotland to Margaret Tudor, the daughter of Henry VII, had given James' heirs a claim to the crown of England, as Henry VIII lacked male heirs. By the time that James V became king, he was determined to unite the English and Scottish monarchies. These claims to the English throne coincided with a general rejection of the excesses of the Roman Church as Scotland came under the influence of Luther and the Reformation. From these new beliefs emerged the Covenanters in Scotland and the Puritans in England.

THE REGENCY OF MARY, QUEEN OF SCOTS

On James V's death, the country was once again plunged into confusion, as both France and England plotted for control. Henry VIII returned some Scottish prisoners: Archibald Douglas, Earl of Angus, together with a number of Scottish lairds seized at Solway Moss. James Hamilton, Earl of Arran, became Guardian of the Realm.

It was agreed that Mary should marry Henry's son, Edward. Then Henry began to make even greater demands, which were rejected by Mary of Guise, acting as Regent for her daughter, the future Mary, Queen of Scots. Henry sent an army north and they burned and looted Edinburgh and the abbeys in the Borders. These brutal attacks gave Mary of Guise and Cardinal Beaton an opportunity to gain control. In July 1548, when Mary, Queen of Scots was only five years old, she was betrothed to Francis, son of King Henry II of France. She was sent to live in France, accompanied by four young Scottish noblewomen, and was educated at the French court.

THE REFORMATION

When Martin Luther began to protest against the doctrines of the Roman Church and set the Reformation in motion in 1517, the monarchs of Europe were fearful of widespread religious unrest. During the reign of James V, no effort had been made to change the religion in Scotland, but by as early as 1525, books by Martin Luther had arrived in the country. Later, an Act of Parliament forbade their sale, but this did not deter men like Patrick Hamilton from following Luther's example. Serious attempts were made to crush the Protestant religion, and Hamilton and George Wishart were burned at the stake by Cardinal Beaton. Their cause was taken up by John Knox, who did more than any other man to bring about the reformation of the Church of Scotland.

In 1557 a group of Protestant lords, calling themselves the Lords of the Congregation of Jesus Christ, put their names to a Covenant aimed at establishing the Protestant religion. Finally, in 1560, Parliament

Left: *John Knox*
Right: *Mary, Queen of Scots*

abolished papal authority and established a General Assembly of the Church to head the Church as an organisation separate from the Crown.

MARY, QUEEN OF SCOTS (1542–67)

Meanwhile, Mary had been brought up in France as a Catholic. She grew into an accomplished young woman of great beauty, and in 1558 a marriage was solemnised between Mary, then only 15, and the Dauphin of France in Notre Dame. As a result, the French monarch put forth Mary's claims as the rightful sovereign of the English throne. Elizabeth I, who considered herself the sole heir to the English throne, was furious. She was jealous of Mary's beauty and feared for her own sovereignty.

Return to Scotland (1561–7)
The King of France died in 1559 in tragic circumstances, and when Mary's husband assumed the throne, she became his Queen. In June of the following year, Mary of Guise died after six years of regency in Scotland. When the King of France died, Mary, now a widow at the age of just 19 years, assumed her

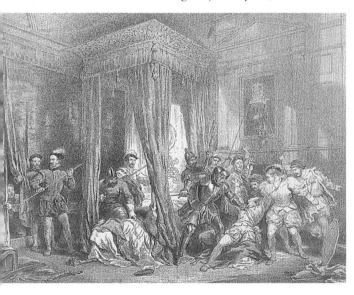

place as the Queen of Scotland, returning there on 14 August 1561.

When she landed at Leith port, by Edinburgh, five days later, the people gave her a tremendous welcome. They were enchanted by her courtesy, winning manners and radiant beauty. Unfortunately, the spell was soon to be broken, as the Scottish people began to fear the friends, opinions and Catholicism Mary had brought with her.

Marriage to Lord Darnley (1565)
A marriage was soon arranged for Mary with Henry Stewart, Lord Darnley, who was also a contender for the English throne and a Catholic. An ambitious man who wanted to reign alongside his wife, not just as her consort, he proved to be a totally unsuitable husband: ill-behaved, petulant and untrustworthy. Mary, who was six months pregnant with Darnley's child, lost patience and redirected her attentions to an Italian singer, David Rizzio, whom she made her secretary.

One night Darnley, mad with jealousy over Rizzio, arrived with a group of his friends and invaded Mary's private apartments. She was giving a supper party which included Rizzio when Darnley and his men dashed into the room. To everyone's horror, they dragged the helpless Italian into the corridor and murdered him.

Not long after this episode Mary had a temporary reconciliation with Darnley, and gave birth to a son who eventually became James VI of Scotland. Shortly after the birth, Darnley was killed in an explosion at his home. There were suspicions that he had been murdered, with evidence pointing to the culpability of James Hepburn, Lord Bothwell.

Marriage to Lord Bothwell (1567)
Lord Bothwell seems to have exerted a strong influence on Mary. She met him on her way back to Edinburgh after visiting her baby son at Stirling Castle, shortly after the death of her husband.

Left: *the murder of Rizzio*
Right: *Mary, Queen of Scots and Darnley:* A Love Duet *by Frederick William Hayes (1848–1918)*

Bothwell persuaded her that if she returned to Edinburgh her life would be in danger, and suggested she should accompany him to Dunbar Castle, where he would protect her. This she did, and they were married in May 1567 at Holyrood. Some believe Mary was forced to marry Bothwell because of a conspiracy between them over Darnley's murder.

Mary's capture

A tangled web of deceit, disloyalty and unfortunate circumstances now conspired against Mary. Her enemies were numerous. Many nobles opposed her marriage and, led by the Earl of Morton, rose in defiance against the couple, meeting them and their supporters on 15 June 1567 at Carberry Hill, near Musselburgh, with a force of 3000 men. After six hours of fighting, Bothwell was persuaded by Mary to leave the field. Surrendering herself to the insurgents, Mary was soon made aware of the treachery of her supposedly loyal subjects, and was forced to ride amidst the rebels without rest or refreshment, and with no attendant to accompany her.

On her arrival in Edinburgh, the crowds hooted and jeered. She was taken to the Provost's house and locked in a small room whilst the rioting mob outside-called for her death. Fearful of the apparent chaos, the nobles moved Mary to Holyrood under the protection of the 'blue blanket', the fighting flag of the crafts community of Edinburgh, which was used by the soldiers to shield her from the mob. Another standard displayed by the rebels illustrated Darnley's corpse beneath a tree with the proclamation, 'Judge and revenge my cause, O Lord.'

The danger was so great that Mary was then removed to a castle in the middle of Loch Leven, to the north of Edinburgh. There she was placed in the charge of her father's former mistress, Lady Margaret Douglas, formally Margaret Erskine. Several days later she was compelled to sign papers relinquishing the throne to her infant son, James VI, who was hastily crowned at Stirling.

The Earl of Moray as Regent

The Earl of Moray was made Regent for James VI. He was strongly Protestant, which allayed the fears of reformers in the country. All appeared to be going smoothly until news came of Mary's escape from Loch Leven Castle. She had fled to Hamilton Palace.

In Glasgow, the Earl of Moray at once gathered an army together, while many other nobles swore their allegiance to Mary. Battle was joined at Langside just outside Glasgow and lasted less than an hour. The Earl of Moray won a decisive victory. Mary was terrified she would fall into the hands of her enemy, and against the advice of the nobles who had supported her, she escaped to the Solway Firth and then to England and the protection, so she believed, of her cousin, Queen Elizabeth.

The execution of Mary

Mary's reign was over, but she lived for 18 years as the prisoner of Elizabeth, who thought it better to keep Mary confined under armed guard than to let her go back to Scotland, where her presence might have provoked civil war. But Mary was still an embarrassment and a threat to Elizabeth. She tried several times to escape, and finally Elizabeth accused Mary of treason and signed the warrant for her execution.

At Fotheringhay Castle, on a bitterly cold winter's day, Mary was led to her death. Scotland was too busy

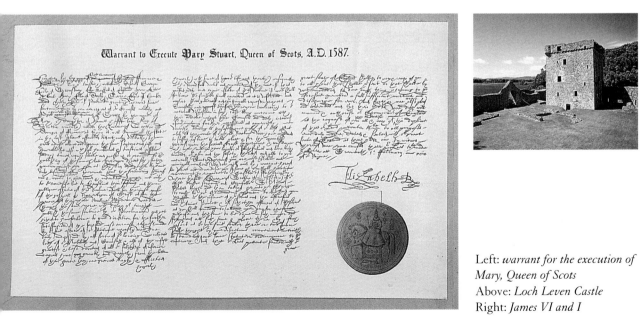

Left: *warrant for the execution of Mary, Queen of Scots*
Above: *Loch Leven Castle*
Right: *James VI and I*

with other troubles to give any thought to the execution of their former Queen, who had caused so much controversy.

JAMES VI OF SCOTLAND (1567–1625) AND I OF ENGLAND (1603–25)

The Earl of Moray did not remain Regent for very long – he was assassinated in 1570. He was followed by several other regents, all of them seeking power and position. James, son of Darnley and Mary, eventually began his rule of Scotland, as James VI, in 1585 at the age of 21. He had been baptised as a Catholic because of his mother's faith, but was brought up under the influence of a reformed Protestant Scotland in which the Catholic faith had been abolished and hearing mass was illegal. This suppression of Catholicism resulted in the imprisonment of many priests and the execution of at least one.

However, there were still divisions in the new Presbyterian Church. The people, swayed by John Knox, felt that these prevented them from following the essential teachings of Christ. Knox and the Presbyterians thought that the King should rule

Scotland for God and be an ordinary member of the Kirk; James VI thought otherwise. He believed in the divine right of kings; in other words, that they had a special relationship with God and were set by him above the people and the Church. These ideas, it

JOHN NAPIER (1550–1617)

James VI's reign saw a remarkable leap forward in the field of mathematics when John Napier, 8th Laird of Merchiston, made an outstanding contribution to the scientific world with his formulation of logarithms.

Born in Merchiston (now a suburb of Edinburgh), Napier lived in a castle that still stands today within the campus of Napier University. He was educated at St Andrews, where he matriculated at 13, before furthering his studies in Europe.

David Maxwell, in *Bygone Scotland* (1894), writes of Napier's work:

Logarithms are prepared tables of numbers, by which complex problems in trigonometry, and the tedious extraction of roots, can be performed by the simpler rules of arithmetic. [Napier] also invented the present notation of decimal fractions. Time and labour were instantly saved in many fields. In the art of navigation they enable the mariner, who may be unskilled in mathematics, to work out the most intricate calculations. In all ves-

sels on the open seas when observations could be taken, in all mathematical schools and astronomical observatories, logarithms were in daily use.

. . . the estimate by scientists of Napier's invention is, that it ranks amongst British contributions to science, second only to Newton's Principia. Kepler of Württemberg, the celebrated German astronomer (1571-1630), regarded Napier as one of the greatest men of his age . . . the only name which can be placed alongside the names of Copernicus, Tycho Brahe, Kepler and Galileo.

SEERS

Belief in second-sight (*second-sichtit* or *fey*), the ability to see into the future, has always been recognised as a gift, particularly among the Gaelic speakers in the west of Scotland.

Although not regarded as witches, people with second-sight did not always fit into their communities, and were sometimes punished for their prophecies.

The Brahan Seer

The story of Kenneth Ore, otherwise known as the Brahan Seer (*Coinneach Odhar Fiosaiche*) is told in Alexander Mackenzie's book of 1877, *The Prophecies of the Brahan Seer*. The life and personality of the Brahan Seer has been the subject of much controversy and there are many different views about the time of his birth, whether it was in the sixteenth or seventeenth century, and his prophecy on the Seaforths.

Born in Point, Isle of Lewis, and also known as the Seer of Kintoul,

the Brahan Seer's involvement with the Seaforths began when he was asked by Lady Seaforth to disclose the whereabouts of her husband. The Seer said his lordship was quite safe and well, but Lady Seaforth was not satisfied and urged him to reveal what else he could see.

Eventually, the Brahan Seer declared that the Earl of Seaforth was enjoying himself in the company of a young and beautiful woman.

It is claimed that Lady Seaforth was so incensed that she condemned the Seer to death and had him placed in a barrel of tar, rolled down hill, and then burned at the stake.

Legend maintains that as the Brahan Seer was being dragged away to his death, he drew out his precious hollow seeing-stone and placed it to his eye, saying :

I see into the far future and I read the doom of the race of my oppressor. The long descended line of the Seaforths will, ere many generations have passed, end in extinction and sorrow. I see the

chief, the last of the house, both deaf and dumb.

As the seer was led to the stake, bound with cords, Lady Seaforth was apparently heard to say he would never go to heaven. The Seer replied:

*I **will** go to heaven but you **never** shall, and this will be the sign whereby you can determine whether my condition after death is one of everlasting happiness or eternal misery. A raven and a dove, swiftly flying in opposite directions will meet, and for a second hover over my ashes, on which they will alight. If the raven be foremost, you will have spoken truly; but if the dove, then my hope is well-founded.*

Traditionally, the dove is regarded as a symbol of joy, whilst the raven is a symbol of sorrow. Of course, the dove is supposed to have landed first. A stone marking the Brahan Seer's place of death has since been erected by the lighthouse overlooking the Moray Firth, just outside Fortrosse.

seems, grew more out of political ambition than religious conviction.

Using his power to appoint bishops, James brought them back into the Kirk as a means of controlling it. He also instigated five other religious changes: baptisms could take place at home (where necessary); Christmas, Good Friday, Easter, Ascension and Whit Sunday should be observed as holy days; children of eight should be confirmed; Holy Communion could be given privately to the aged and sick; and the bread and wine of Holy Communion

should be taken while kneeling. The Church of Scotland found these demands unacceptable, but through a combination of bribery and blackmail, James forced these Five Articles of Perth, as they were known, on the General Assembly.

After the execution of Mary, Queen of Scots, James VI was determined to be crowned King of England, as well as Scotland, and worked hard to fulfill that ambition.

James married Anne of Denmark by proxy in 1589, and they eventually had seven children. Relying heavily on his Privy Council, James depended increasingly on individuals who were loyal to him. For instance, he promoted Maitland of Thrislestane (1543-95) from the ranks for good service and loyalty, followed by James Elphinstone (1553-1622) and Thomas Hamilton (1563-1637). After the Act of Annexation, they were elevated to the peerage.

Before James became King of Scotland and England, one of his chief successes was to settle the problem in the Borders by organising an Anglo-Scottish force, which was operating effectively against lawbreakers by 1605.

The Union of the Crowns (1603)

In 1603 James VI of Scotland finally achieved his life-long ambition – he became James I of England after the death of Elizabeth I and moved to London, which became his permanent home. He had governed Scotland through a Privy Council which he had trained, but instead of allowing Parliament to choose the members of the council, he continued to do so himself. After leaving Scotland he returned to his homeland only once, when he held a parliamentary session in Edinburgh in 1617.

King James I & his sonne Charles feastinge y.e Spanishe Ambassadoures.

The Union of the Crowns was the first break in the Scots' independence. The King no longer held court in Edinburgh and many nobles left Scotland to join him. Likewise, local trade drifted south to England. This caused unrest in Edinburgh, where the people had become accustomed to the presence of the Scottish Court.

Inevitably, influences from England filtered through into Scottish life as a result of this displacement of power and, by 1604, the numerous bankruptcies among tradesmen clearly showed that the King's move to London was having an adverse effect north of the border. Law and order began to break down, and vagabonds in Edinburgh gathered every night in Cowgate, Potterow, Canongate and West Port to 'pass their time in all kinds of riot and filthy lechery, to the offence and displeasure of God'.

On the other hand, the Union of the Crowns did allow an interchange of ideas between the two countries now that the warring was at an end. Scotland continued to be governed separately, with its own laws, parliamentary procedures and Church administration. Yet the Scots resented the fact that the King was ruling Scotland through his elected Privy Council without the proper united backing of the Scottish Parliament. Although each nation was acting in every respect independently, they both relied on the same decision-maker – the King.

CHARLES I (1625–49)

Charles, the second surviving son of James, succeeded his father in 1625, but did not come to Scotland for his coronation until later.

Like his father, Charles strongly believed that he was king not only in title but also by the will of God. Convinced that everyone should obey him, including the clergy, he carried this belief through into acts of

James VI and I entertains Spanish ambassadors

legislation. The nobility were particularly concerned by the Act of Revocation introduced in 1625, which seemed to endanger their rights to the numerous church properties held in their possession since 1540. The Revocation was intended to utilise some of the wealth of the former Catholic Church by distributing it more beneficially, but heavy-handed implementation aroused only suspicion and fear.

The Book of Common Prayer

This fear came to a head in 1637 when Charles imposed the *Book of Common Prayer* on Scotland, with orders that each minister should have two copies and that thereafter all churches were to follow its procedures. The Scots deeply resented these mandatory English Church services, and soon the country was in rebellious uproar as all the feelings generated by Scotland's loss of power to England were expressed.

On 23 July 1637, the first Sunday after the *Book of Common Prayer* had been received by the ministers at St Giles in Edinburgh, the Dean had just begun to read from it when an old woman named Jenny Geddes shouted from the congregation, 'Dost thou say mass at my lug?' and threw her stool at the Dean.

A great commotion immediately followed, and when the Bishop of Edinburgh mounted the pulpit to quieten the disturbance, all kinds of missiles were thrown at him. The service came to an abrupt end in a fury of disgust at the *Book of Common Prayer*, which continued in a mob demonstration outside St Giles.

The King's reaction to these disturbances was to order that all protesters should be punished.

The National Covenant (1638)

The call to rebellion was the National Covenant, a petition of protest signed by people from all over Scotland and sent to the King, in which subscribers swore to defend the Protestant religion and resist all errors and corruptions. It was drafted by Archibald Johnston of Warriston and Alexander Henderson, supported by a small group of noblemen under Lord Balmerino. When the Covenanters found that they had popular support, they demanded that a free parliament and Scottish General Assembly be held. Charles agreed to this, but did all he could to sabotage the proceedings. In November 1638, the General Assembly met in Glasgow and unanimously decided to put an end to the bishops, the Five Articles of Perth, and to the *Book of Common Prayer* – in short, to set up Presbyterianism as Scotland's religion.

The Scots decided to take an army into Newcastle to put pressure upon Charles to agree to their proposals, and a treaty was finally agreed in June 1641 by the English Parliament, who had rebelled against their king. All the proposals that had been made by the National Covenant were agreed to, plus the granting of a large sum of money to offset the cost of keeping the Scots army in Newcastle.

The Civil War

By this time, Charles was locked in a power-struggle with the English Parliament, and his attempt to arrest five of its members precipitated a civil war. Alexander Leslie brought his army of Covenanters into England to help Cromwell defeat Charles at Marston Moor. Other Covenanters remained loyal to Charles; the Marquis of Montrose, for example, who, despite his fidelity to the cause, was not given troops. Nevertheless, he put up an astonishing fight with inferior arms and considerably fewer troops than the

Left: *the National Covenant*
Right: *the execution of Charles I*

Covenanters. He won back the kingdom for the King temporarily, but his force was eventually defeated by a large faction of Covenanters who went on to butcher the defeated soldiers and camp-followers. Charles eventually surrendered to a Covenanting army in England, and was handed over to the English Parliament on condition he was not harmed.

The execution of Charles I

The English army, led by Oliver Cromwell, was now so strong that Cromwell formed an independent party against the Crown in England. The promise not to harm the King was disregarded, and he was executed at Whitehall on 30 January 1649. The Scots were outraged. In spite of their differences with Charles I over religious rights, they were indignant that Cromwell should execute their king without consulting the Scottish Parliament.

CHARLES II (1660–85)

Scotland and England were now without a king, but six days after the execution, the Earl of Argyll, who was master of Scotland, proclaimed Charles II the King. At that time, Charles was living in the Hague in Holland, and a Scottish deputation made it clear to him that they would accept him as king only if he would agree to the Covenanters' demands. Charles did not immediately agree; instead, he asked Montrose to reconquer the country. Montrose was defeated, betrayed and handed over to the Covenanters. Sentenced to death by the Scottish Parliament, he was hanged on 21 May 1650.

Later that year, Charles took an oath to accept the Covenanters' proposals and travelled to Scotland, where he was received with great rejoicing. However, the English did not want Charles as king and feared that Scotland would raise an army against them to force him onto the English throne.

CROMWELL IN SCOTLAND (1650–8)

Cromwell and General Monk fought several battles against the Scots, including one at Dunbar where the army was under the personal command of Charles II. The Scots were led by General Leslie, but were some-what hampered by the interference of zealous Covenanting ministers who had replaced many of the professional soldiers with 'clerks and ministers' sons' in order to purge the army of its 'ungodlier' elements.

However, General Leslie, whose tactics were to avoid a battle, occupied a hill position, trapping Cromwell by the sea, near the harbour at Dunbar. His plan was to stage a waiting campaign to starve Cromwell's army into submission.

Unfortunately, Leslie was thwarted by the same Covenanting ministers who had interfered with his army. They goaded the soldiers, inciting them to attack Cromwell's men: 'Go down and smite your enemies!' they shouted, drowning out the strategic commands of General Leslie to remain in position.

On 3 September 1650 the soldiers disobeyed their commander and descended to the plains. Incredulous at this sight, Cromwell exclaimed, 'The Lord hath delivered them into our hands!' The superior, more disciplined English army, commanded by General Monk, soon outmatched the unruly vigilantes.

By December, most of the fortresses and castles south of the Forth had surrendered to Cromwell, but the Scottish Parliament had moved out of danger. On 1 January 1651 Charles II was crowned King of Scotland by the Marquis of Argyll at Scone. Charles swore to the Covenanters that he would maintain and uphold the Presbyterian Kirk.

Left: *Cromwell defeating the Scots at Dunbar*
Right: *The Honours of Scotland*
Below: *Charles II*

Scotland was soon at war with England. Charles obtained enough support to attack Cromwell's army again, but was beaten. He then led his men into England, trailed by Cromwell. On 3 September 1651, a year after the Battle of Dunbar, a fight raged on the banks of the Severn, near Worcester. Three thousand Scots were slain and 10,000 taken prisoner. Many of these unfortunate soldiers were shipped off to plantations and sold into slavery. Meanwhile, Charles escaped to France, and Cromwell, represented by General Monk, gained control of Scotland.

During the years that Cromwell ruled England and Scotland, England grew strong and affluent but Scotland remained too poor to benefit from these years of peace. There was little international commerce in the country, largely because England was at war with Holland, Scotland's main partner in trade.

The Honours of Scotland

After the victory at Dunbar, General Monk tried to take possession of the 'Honours of Scotland', that is, the crown, sceptre and sword of state, but he failed to find them. The Honours had been placed in safe-keeping in the Castle of Dunnottar, on the coast of Kincardineshire. Mr Granger, a minister in the neighbourhood, fearing that the stronghold would be searched, spread a false report that the Honours had been taken abroad. Then his wife asked for the English general's permission to bring some bundles of lint out of the castle. Permission was granted and his wife carried out the lint, with the Honours wrapped inside. That night, they were hastily buried under the pulpit of her husband's church.

Today the Honours are well guarded, on display in Edinburgh Castle.

One of the most extraordinary aspects of Scottish and European society was witchcraft, a practice prevalent until the nineteenth century, but particularly powerful during the seventeenth and eighteenth centuries.

People of all cultures have a fascination with the supernatural and even today, stories about witches, ghosts and strange events continue to attract and mystify people.

Satanic influences

In the sixteenth century it was firmly believed that certain old women sold themselves to Satan, or the devil, and then used his powers against their enemies to exact revenge. These crones were believed to in secret places at certain times of the year and take part in demonic rites. There was a hardly a town or village that did not possess a witch.

Newes from Scotland,
Declaring the Damna=
ble life and death of Doctor Fian, *a*
notable Sorcerer, who was burned at
Edenbrough in Ianuary laſt.
1591.

Which Doctor *was* regeſter *to the* Diuell
that ſundry times preached at North Barrick Kirke, to a number of notorious Witches.

With the true examinations of the ſaide Doctor and Witches, as they vttered them in the preſence of the Scottiſh King.

Diſcouering how they pretended
to bewitch *and* drowne *his* Maieſtie *in the* Sea
comming from Denmarke, with ſuch
other wonderfull matters as the like
hath not been heard of at
any time.

Publiſhed according to the Scottiſh Coppie.

AT LONDON
Printed for William
Wright.

Witches were blamed for anything out of the ordinary: the death of a child, a bad thunderstorm, illness, the spread of an epidemic amongst the animals. All elderly women were suspected, but especially those who had become crotchety or bent with age, who were forced to use a walking-stick, or who were supposed to be under evil influences because they mixed herbs to cure the ailing. Whenever there was a disaster which had no obvious explanation, such as a failure of crops, these poor individuals were swooped upon by their neighbours and dragged away to the church or magistrate for judgement.

The belief in witchcraft was so strong that no one was safe. Lady Janet Douglas, who became the 16th Lady Glamis, was burned in Edinburgh as a witch in 1537 after being falsely accused by James V of Scotland. He loathed the Douglas family and relentlessly pursued a vendetta against them.

Reginald Scott wrote *The Discoveries of Witchcraft* in 1584 with the aim of preventing the further persecution of the poor, aged and simple persons who were popularly believed to be witches. The purpose of his study was 'to expose the imposters on the one hand, and the credulity on the other that supported the belief in witchcraft'. Unfortunately, this did not stop the fearsome witch-hunts.

One of the main reasons why the scourge was so prolonged was that James VI was a firm believer in witches, even suspecting that the tempest which wrecked his ship in 1590 when bringing home his bride, Anne, from Denmark, was the work of witchcraft. Following this, in May 1591, a Convention took place in Edinburgh which declared, 'anent order to be tane with sorcerers and certain practisers against his Majesty's person'. James VI felt his whole kingdom was in peril and demanded to be informed about

all cases of witchcraft. His determined fight against it fuelled people's fears and gave them greater licence to behave inhumanely.

Witch-hunts

The worst years of witch-hunting were between 1629 and 1663, with peaks of hysteria in 1630, 1649, 1650, 1661 and 1663. The order for a witch-hunt by the magistrate of the town or the minister of the church was a signal for much blood-letting, allowing the whole town or village to give vent to their superstitious fears. If someone knew something odd about an old woman, or had suspicions, they reported it to the minister or magistrate. The Church encouraged them, for this was a chance to show the dangers of the devil and keep control of the parishioners.

The investigations that followed were conducted in an atmosphere of terror, and confessions were exacted by the most hideous tortures. Most of the victims broke down, confessing to crimes of which they were innocent, to stop the cruel treatment they were receiving. Sometimes they would be dipped in the river or held under freezing water until they confessed. If, by some lucky chance, they survived, they were considered innocent. Many old women died from drowning; others were burned at the stake.

Witchfinders

Tales of witches and their powers grew to such proportions, and they were regarded with such dread and fear, that official 'witchfinders' were appointed. They had extraordinary licence to pursue their investigations, which included the practice of pricking suspects with pins until they found the 'devil's mark'.

The victims of the witchfinders had no refuge, even in their own church. Nobody dared defend the alleged witches, for then they too might be accused. In 1597 alone, twenty-three women and one man were burned in Aberdeen.

The Royal Burgh of Forfar was the only Angus Burgh to execute witches instead of burning them. Between 1661 and 1663, 42 people were suspected of witchcraft, many of whom were imprisoned in the tolbooth, their confessions heard between Sunday services. During this time, they were not permitted to sleep, had no warmth or light, and were submitted to torturous 'proddings' by witchfinder John Kincaid from Tranent. If found guilty, they were usually strung up with rope and strangled. Their bodies were taken to the

Playfield, later known as the Witches' Howe, to be burned in a tar barrel.

The last witches to die

The last witch-burning in Edinburgh was in 1726, supposedly at the top of Castlehill, close to the castle. In Forres, the last two burnings were at the beginning of the eighteenth century, the victims having first been rolled down Cluny hill in barrels. The last execution of a Scottish witch was in Dornoch in 1727. The gullibility, fear and ignorance that had been instrumental in inciting the hysterical witch-hunting had finally ended.

Top left: *North Berwick witches making cattle sick and setting fire to churches*
Far left: *the title page of* Newes from Scotland *(1591)*
Left: *Dr Fian and his companions flying widdershins around a church*
Above: *Geillis Duncan playing to King James the same tune she played to Satan*

The Restoration

After the death of Cromwell, the Scottish and English parliaments agreed that it was safer for both kingdoms to restore Charles II to his thrones. When this was made official in 1660, there was considerable excitement in Scotland. The Scots realised they were in a stronger position to hold on to their nation by having a king, in spite of the fact that he lived in London. The Earl of Lauderdale was appointed Secretary of State to keep Charles informed of affairs north of the border and carry out his orders.

An Act of Parliament was passed which deemed the King head of both Church and State, and acts in favour of the Covenanters were declared illegal. Charles re-established episcopacy in Scotland.

THE COVENANTERS

Many Scots were outraged by the King's actions and gathered to hear Presbyterian preachers. These conventicles, as they were called, were an open act of defiance against Charles and his bishops.

In November 1666, revolt broke out in Galloway, but the Covenanters were routed at Rullion Green, near Penicuick. Still, the conventicles grew larger. In 1678 a host of Highlanders was sent to quash them, but their looting and plundering only fuelled the Covenanters' resentment. They seized the hated James Sharp, Archbishop of St Andrews, and murdered him. On 1 June 1679, the Covenanters gained a victory in the Battle of Drumclog, near Loudoun Hill. The King's response was to send his troops to Bothwell Bridge, where the Covenanters were crushed by the Duke of Monmouth.

Greyfriars' graveyard

The survivors of the Battle of Bothwell Bridge were marched to Edinburgh and locked up in Greyfriars' graveyard, then a park surrounded by a high wall. The unfortunate Covenanters were left without food, shelter or bedding, in freezing cold weather. It is estimated that over 2000 were subjected to these conditions. Many died of torture and exposure. All the leaders were executed. Others gained reprieve, several hundred prisoners being sent as slaves to Barbados. This period in history has become known as the 'Killing Time'.

Left: William III *by J.Z. Kneller*
Above: *martyrs' memorial, Hamilton Parish Church*
Right: *a preacher addresses a group of Scottish Presbyterians at a conventicle*

JAMES VII OF SCOTLAND
AND II OF ENGLAND (1685–8)

After a reign of 25 years, Charles II died, with no direct heirs, and his brother James became king. Charles had prepared the way; the throne was safe and the Crown exerted great power. However, the new king was a Catholic and refused to take the Coronation Oath to defend the Protestant religion. The Scots became apprehensive, remembering his past cruelty to the Covenanters while acting for Charles.

As a result, the exiled Duke of Argyll mounted an attempt to dethrone James in Scotland whilst the Duke of Monmouth started a rising in Cheshire to achieve the same result in England. Both dukes raised strong armies, but were defeated and later executed.

James wanted freedom of worship for Catholics and tried to pass an Act of Tolerance which would have allowed the Catholics to follow their faith, but it was refused by Parliament. Finally, in 1687, James used his royal prerogative to achieve his purpose, giving complete tolerance to all his subjects, including Quakers, Covenanters and Roman Catholics. Now that Presbyterians were able to worship openly again, they did not regard the Episcopalians as a threat, but both parties were alarmed at the favoured positions being granted to Catholics.

When Mary of Modena, James' wife, gave birth to a boy on 10 June 1688, the Stuart line became secure. A number of English statesmen therefore decided to remove James VII and replace him with William of Orange, a Protestant, who had married James' eldest daughter, Mary. They officially requested that William should take over as King of England in James' place. The Scots were less certain. They wanted to be sure that William would grant them control over the Church of Scotland. The Episcopalians were equivocal too – James had treated them well.

In November 1688 William decided to accept the throne, and sailed for England from Holland with a fleet and an army prepared to support him. James

Above: *James VII and II*
Right: *William III and Mary being offered the Crown at Whitehall*

entered into battle against William, but his officers deserted him, and he was compelled to flee to France and seek the protection of Louis XIV.

WILLIAM AND MARY (1689–1702)

As soon as William and Mary were settled in London, they addressed the Scottish people, saying they would undertake to rule the country justly. A Convention of Estates was set up in Scotland on 14 March 1689 to discuss the proposals, and was clearly divided, with some still supporting James VII and II.

Although there were Williamites in Parliament and in Edinburgh, they were outnumbered in the nation at large. John Graham of Claverhouse, Viscount Dundee, accompanied by 60 horsemen, attended the Convention to represent James. He read out James' letter demanding loyalty of his subjects, but afterwards most of James' supporters deserted him.

A vote was taken in favour of accepting William and Mary as joint King and Queen of Scotland, and the coronation took place at Scone on 11 May 1689. The Convention also agreed to dethrone James for not acting according to the rightful laws of Scotland. The 'Glorious Revolution' was now complete, and had been accomplished without bloodshed. The Convention also stated that in future, if kings or queens in Scotland did not abide by the Scottish rules of law for the procedure of ruling their country, they would be dethroned. In addition, the abolition of the Committee of the Articles freed the Scottish Estates from the king's rule.

Church authority

The authority of the Church as mediator between God and the people had been accepted by everyone from the very earliest times. For centuries the Church brought balance to the established pattern of control inherent in the feudal system. The people were controlled by the Church and the aristocracy, two great influences unable to act independently of one another.

However, this state of affairs was seriously undermined by the political presence of more than one Christian Church. Disagreements about how the teaching of Christ should be delivered led to internal fighting for the absolute power and position that had once been enjoyed by the Roman Catholic Church. In 1690 the dispute between Episcopalians and Presbyterians ended when the Scottish Parliament passed an act which abolished bishops and established the Church of Scotland as Presbyterian. The Claim of Right stated that the Church would now be governed by the General Assembly, presbyteries and Kirk Sessions – and so it has remained.

'The Letters of Fire and Sword'

The struggle for church domination and the presence of a smouldering Jacobite force in Scotland set the stage for the 'The Letters of Fire and Sword'. This was a document obtained from William by those in Scotland who wanted to subdue the fierce Highlanders and their faith in James VII and the Roman Catholic Church. 'Letters of Fire and Sword' had also been issued in the past by James VI and I, who shared the ambition of pacifying the Highlanders. The document enabled those favouring the Covenanters to curb the power of the Roman Catholic Church by persecuting those who would not take the oath of allegiance to William and Mary. These included the Highlanders, who saw taking the oath as a betrayal of the Catholic Church. In the name of the declaration, people could be slain or taken prisoner and have their lands confiscated by the King.

Prominent among those who called for the declaration was the Earl of Stair, who was Sir John Dalrymple, Joint Secretary of State for Scotland. He pressurised William until he signed the declaration, giving him the powers he sought. The document made the King ultimately responsible for all the acts committed under its terms, the most abominable of which was the Massacre of Glencoe.

THE MASSACRE OF GLENCOE (1692)

After the battles of Killiecrankie and Dunkeld, fought in defence of James VII and II, the Highlanders were still restless and it was feared they would start another rebellion.

General Hugh Mackay, who had transferred his allegiance from James VII to William and Mary, was sent by Sir John Dalrymple with an army to the western Highlands to keep order. He rebuilt the fort at Inverlochy, which he called Fort William, after the new King.

The bribery

General Mackay, under the direction of Sir John Dalrymple, first offered £12,000 to be divided amongst the chiefs, to buy their loyalty to William and Mary. Some chiefs refused the money, others took it but still remained loyal to James. Then, in 1691, the government took a step that

was to culminate in the notorious events at Glencoe.

The oath

The oath of allegiance to William had already been well used. Now an order was issued stating that if the chiefs did not take the oath by 1 January 1692, they would be treated as outlaws and their lands would become the property of the King.

The chiefs were caught in a dilemma: they needed King James to release them from their solemn oath to him before they could swear loyalty to King William.

It was not until the end of December that word came from James that the clans were free to look to their own safety and pledge their allegiance to William.

By the appointed day, all the chiefs had taken the oath except one – MacIain MacDonald, chief of the clan MacDonald of Glencoe, north of Argyllshire, an old man, past 80, who had intended to take the oath but left it too late. He went to Fort William on the appointed day, but the sheriff was at Inveraray, at the other end of Argyllshire.

The road to Inverary was rough, being only a drove road for cattle, and deep in snow. MacDonald, travelling on horseback, was unable to make good progress, but eventually arrived five days after the appointed time. However, he still took the oath, which was accepted and should have saved him and his clan.

Soldiers in Glencoe

Several weeks later about 120 soldiers appeared in Glencoe. Most of them were Highlanders, some from the Campbell clan. They were commanded by Captain Robert Campbell of Glenlyon, and Major Duncanson,

who had orders 'not to trouble the government with prisoners'.

The plan was for Glenlyon and his soldiers to enter the glen, and for Major Duncanson and his men to occupy the escape routes, killing all who tried to get away.

Glenlyon and his soldiers were welcomed by their hosts, the MacDonalds, and stayed with them for about two weeks on the most hospitable terms. The MacDonalds accepted them in friendship and suspected nothing of what was to follow because the chief's daughter-in-law was Captain Glenlyon's niece.

The massacre

When the escape routes were blocked, Glenlyon gave the orders he had received from Dalrymple. At about five o'clock on the morning of 13 February 1692, the old chief was shot by one of his 'guests' as he was getting out of bed, and his wife was pushed naked into the snow to perish.

Dalrymple's plan had been to kill every MacDonald, but more than 150 escaped to the nearby mountains in

bitterly cold weather; not all of them surviving to tell the tale. Thirty-eight were slain in cold blood, including two children and two women.

This was the Massacre of Glencoe, one of the most terrible crimes in Scottish history. It turned many in the Highlands against William, and did much to exacerbate his problems there.

The government tried to use the story of the Campbells' vengeance on the MacDonalds as a screen for their devious actions, but the excuse was not really plausible – although there was animosity between the two clans, most of the Campbells involved in the massacre were Highlanders who had enlisted with the government force under General Mackay.

Top left: *order for the massacre, dated 12 February 1692, signed by Duncanson*
Far left: In the Pass of Glencoe *by Alfred de Breanski (1852–1928)*
Left: *Glenlyon as a young man*
Above: The Massacre of Glencoe *by James Hamilton*

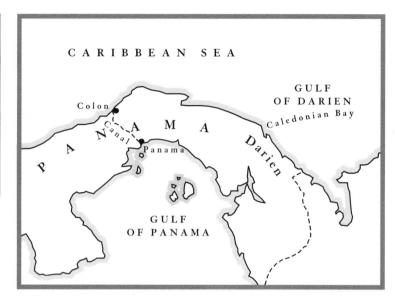

Above: *the Arms of the Company of Scotland Trading to Africa and the Indies*
Right: *the Isthmus of Panama*
Far right: *William Paterson*

Problems for the Estates

The Massacre of Glencoe shocked the Scottish people, and caused a great deal of discord within the Scottish Parliament. Many Scottish politicians resented the increasing difficulty of trying to run a country without the presence of their king or noblemen, and the fact that the massacre appeared to have been planned and ordered in London made members of the Estates fear that Scotland was again being ruled by the king's court in London. Parliament could not sit as it had been accustomed to do, and the Privy Council was unable to handle such an impossible state of affairs.

Another major problem was that Scotland was getting poorer whilst England grew richer, and many Scots felt that the main reason for England's wealth was that it possessed overseas colonies and was able to trade with them. Attempts had been made to set up Scottish colonies in New Jersey and South Carolina in the 1680s, but the more established English colonies refused to allow the Scots traders to deal with them, treating them like foreigners even though they shared the same monarch.

The Darien Scheme

William Paterson (1658-1719) was born at Skipnayre Farm in Tinwald, Dumfriesshire. After a brief spell in America, Paterson travelled to the West Indies, where he began trading. His commercial skill and seafaring knowledge soon brought him rich rewards and, having made his fortune, he returned to his native land to market his ideas about international trade.

His scheme proposed the creation of a trading route between East and West from a base on the Isthmus of Panama, the narrow neck of land between North and South America, part of which was known as Darien. Paterson canvassed the English, Dutch and Scottish people to invest in shares which would increase English and Scottish overseas trade and develop Darien, which he believed could become the centre of world trade. The plan was so well conceived that the Scottish Parliament passed an act to establish 'The Company of Scotland Trading to Africa and the Indies'. King William granted a charter.

The directors of the company were Scottish and English in equal numbers, with the investment capital coming half from England and Holland, the other half from Scotland. English investors gave their support because the new company would rival the East India Company, whose monopoly had long been resented. Over £300,000 was raised by the English and Dutch. Paterson himself also invested heavily, and took his wife and son to help set up the trading area. But the English Parliament, goaded by the East India Company and others, withdrew its consent at the last moment, forcing the English and Dutch to withdraw and leaving the Scots as sole investors.

On 12 July 1698, there was much excitement in Scotland as five ships sailed from Leith harbour. A new life beckoned for all those on board and they held high hopes of a rich return. The ships arrived at the Isthmus of Darien on 30 October 1698, but events took a tragic turn. The Spaniards attacked them, disease broke out, provisions ran short and the English colony on the Isthmus of Panama was instructed by the English government not to help the Scots – in fact, the English colonists were openly hostile. King William offered no assistance from England, instead siding with the Spaniards. The only people who befriended the emigrants were the native Indians, who helped them all they could.

Many people fell ill, including Paterson, and his wife and son both died. Eventually life became so difficult that the scheme had to be abandoned, and Paterson, greatly distressed and in poor health, managed to gain a passage on a ship bound for Hong Kong along with the surviving colonists.

In the meantime, six more ships had sailed from Leith, knowing nothing of the fate of the earlier fleet. When they arrived, the emigrants gazed in astonishment at the deserted harbour, with no means of finding out what had happened. After trying to settle where others had failed, they were attacked by the Spaniards, who fought them into an honourable capitulation. Sadly, five more ships had already sailed from Leith in total ignorance of the problems.

Only one ship returned to Scotland out of the total of sixteen that had originally sailed. Two thousand Scots lost their lives. The Darien Scheme had been a horrific disaster, quite the worst that Scotland had ever experienced. Practically the whole circulating capital of the Scottish people was involved in the project and as a result the losses completely impoverished the country.

Scots believed that the main cause was the withdrawal of support by William and the English merchants. The King had denigrated Scotland by forbidding the English to support the colonists and thus left the defenceless Scots at the mercy of the Spaniards.

When the full extent of the disaster was made known to the people of Edinburgh, they rioted. The Tolbooth was stormed and all prisoners were released. A fire broke out in Lord Crossrig's lodgings in the Cowgate and the judge was seen naked, running for his life. The fire had soon spread to the mealmarket,

the fishmarket and the Royal Exchange, and a great part of the Cowgate was destroyed:

Out of the wynds poured hundreds of terrified people, who helplessly watched the great houses, some of them 12 to 14 stories high, crash to the ground.

When King William died on 8 March 1702, few Scots mourned. Some historians believe the collapse of the Darien Scheme was instigated by English politicians to bankrupt the Scots so that union with England could be forced on them. Had the venture been a success, the sunsequent history of Scotland would certainly have been transformed. The Union of 1707 either would not have taken place or would have involved quite different terms.

A century later, the Americans engineered the Panama Canal, proving Paterson's original scheme correct in every detail and fulfilling the potential he had foreseen. In effect, he had initiated one of the best trading proposals ever devised for Scotland, and its failure was a tragic loss for the whole country.

QUEEN ANNE (1702–14)

After the deaths of William and Mary, the natural successor to the throne, Mary's sister, Anne, became queen in 1702. In 1701 the English Parliament had passed an Act of Settlement naming Sophia, the Protestant Electress of Hanover, as the heir to the throne should Anne die childless. However, there was no consultation with the Scots, who responded in 1704 by insisting they would choose their own monarch. They forced Anne to accept by refusing to vote her supplies until she did. Relations between the two countries continued to deteriorate, with the English imposing bans on some Scottish goods and the Scots hanging three English merchants for supposed piracy.

THE UNION (1707)

A war with Scotland over the succession to the throne had always been a possibility while there were two parliaments. After the disaster of the Darien Scheme, there was an even greater need for the parliaments to be unified. Since the English were Protestant, it was also imperative that they protect the throne from the Scottish Catholic Stuarts; recognition of this spurred them into action. With support from Queen Anne, they pressed ahead for the Union of the Scottish and English Parliaments, not only to support and safeguard the merged crowns, but also to uphold the English choice of Sophia as Anne's successor.

The Scots were in such a critical financial situation that many of their politicians saw no alternative but to

Left: *Queen Anne*
Right: *signatures and seals of the commissioners who negotiated the Treaty of the Union, the Scots on the left*

agree to the Union of the Parliaments. A commission was set up, with the Duke of Queensberry as Lord High Commissioner, to superintend the negotiations on behalf of Scotland:

The history of the negotiations which followed, the bribes in money and advancement offered by the English and accepted by the Scots, and the manner in which the Scottish commissioners placed their personal gain before both the honour of their nation and the wishes of those whom they were supposed to represent, makes one of the most sordid incidents in the whole history of Scotland. Not less than £20,540. 17s. 7d., was necessary to purchase their consent to the proposals; and while the Duke of Queensberry as Lord High Commissioner received the vast sum of £12,235 it cost only £11. 2s. to overcome the scruples of Lord Banff. (Extract from *Edinburgh* (1938) by Sacheverell Sitwell and Francis Bamford.)

The English statesmen were obliged to pass a separate bill meeting the demands made by the Scottish Law Lords. They were to be allowed to retain their jurisdiction over the Scottish courts of justice and to continue to practise Scottish Law independently of the English, and so it has remained to this day. The Church of Scotland also demanded that it should retain full rights of independence, and a guarantee of this was made a prerequisite to the final signing of the Treaty of the Union of the Parliaments.

The terms of the Union stated that the English national debt and tax system should be imposed on the Scots (the Scots had no national debt), and that the English choice of monarch must be upheld. This so infuriated the Scots that the English statesmen, afraid of war, offered a sum of money to help offset the losses sustained over the Darien affair. Although this gesture went some way, the initial sum was unacceptable. Before the vote on Union was taken in the Scottish Parliament, a larger sum of £398,000 (equivalent to about £33.5 million today) was suggested, and agreed.

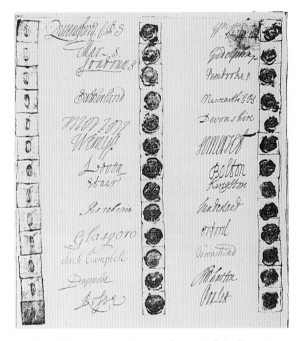

Scottish representatives in the united Parliament were to total only 61, comprising 45 members of the House of Commons and 16 peers. The commissioners finally accepted the latter when it was agreed that all their number should be raised to the English peerage, and so would not have to be elected.

When the gist of these proposals were known to Edinburgh the people were roused to a high pitch of fury. Not only were they resentful at the way in which the commissioners had signed away the birthright of their country, but they foresaw that the removal of the government from their city to London would deprive them of the chief part of their trade . . .

On 3 October 1706, in an atmosphere charged with political feeling, the people of Edinburgh lined the streets behind the troops to watch for the last time the 'Riding of the Parliament'. Between those tall houses which reach from the Palace of Holyrood to the Parliament House came all those summoned to attend on the wake of a nation . . .

When it became known, on 25 March, that the mea-sure had been passed, the people, deserted by their leaders, rose in such fury that the members of Parliament were forced to leave the house secretly and gather in a cellar in the High Street. Their presence was soon discovered, and once again they were forced to fly, finding shelter in the grounds of Moray House, occupied by the Lord High Chancellor, Lord Seafield. There in the summer-house, such of the nobility and representatives of the people as had not already appended their signatures to the act in the Union Cellar signed their names; and thus, secretly and to the accompaniment of the curses of the populace, Scotland's national independence was signed away.
(Sitwell and Bamford, *Edinburgh*)

When Lord Seafield was presented with the act for royal assent, he touched it with his sceptre, saying, 'There's an end of an auld sang.' It was rumoured that he was given a sum of £490 for his role in pro-moting the Union.

The bill was passed through the Scottish Parliament by 110 votes to 67, the figures showing there was still considerable opposition to the Union. Nevertheless, it was established in law in January 1707. The Dissolution followed in April, becoming effective in May. When the new Parliament was established, a bill was hurriedly passed ensuring that the choice of monarch would rest with the English, and giving immediate powers to marshal military forces against any dissenters. This clearly meant the Jacobites, supporters of the Stuart line.

William Paterson was asked to prepare a plan for the conversion and consolidation of the National Debt; he also helped to outline the trade and finance terms of the Treaty of the Union. He was elected to sit in the new united Parliament as a Member for the Dumfries Burghs, but never took his seat. William Pagan, a biographer of Paterson, reports that Paterson had to fight for compensation from the government over the Darien Scheme, and in 1715 received £18,000

Right: *Queen Anne receiving the Treaty of the Union*

to compensate him for his losses. He is now chiefly remembered for the terms he proposed for the foun-dation of the Bank of England in 1695.

William Paterson died in 1719. Robert Chambers, in his *Biographical Dictionary of Eminent Scotsmen* makes the comment, 'It is deeply regretted that no satisfactory memorials have been preserved of this remarkable man.'

Many differences arose between the Scottish and English politicians after the Union, largely because the Scottish Law Lords did not think that the extant laws on High Treason used in the English Law Courts should be forced on Scotland. However, an act stating: 'punishment, trial, prosecution and forfei-tures for High Treason to be passed for Scotland the same as for England', was enforced, threatening:

both the horrible disembowelling alive of the actual cul-prit, and the 'corruption of the blood' which destroyed the rights of the heirs.

Scotland was unhappy with this barbaric act and it was repealed in England in 1870, but not until 1948 north of the border. By this time the English had for-gotten that they themselves had imposed the law on the Scots in 1708.

What many English politicians seemed to forget was brought before the joint Parliament by a Scottish MP who proclaimed:

that Scotland never was or could be subject to the sover-eignty of England; that before the Union Scotland was a free, separate and independent state and since the Union, was no more a sovereignty of England than Scotland sub-sisting, both these formerly distinct sovereignties being now consolidated into the sovereignty of Great Britain, the title of Great Britain being given to the two nations at the Treaty of the Union.

These feelings were shared by many Scots and formed the initiative behind the Jacobite Uprising of 1745.

One comment relating to the Union came from Daniel Defoe in his *Tour through the Whole Island of Great Britain*, published between 1724 and 1727. Defoe worked for the English Secret Service for 20 years, during which time he was at first very much for the Union and worked wholeheartedly to bring it about. But his disgust at the behaviour of his fellow countrymen towards the Scottish nation revolted him to such an extent that he jeopardised his career with an outspoken and frank criticism of the deplorable English attitude. Defoe's *Tour* seems to have been written to assist the two countries toward a better understanding. He wrote:

Given fair play Scotland could have sent cargos to the colonies. Before the Union the embargo between the Scottish and English traders caused much ill-feeling.

Scottish languages

One of the most severe restrictions placed upon the Scottish people after the merging of the two parliaments was the imposition of the English language throughout the country.

The Scottish Gaelic language and all eight Scottish dialects were considered barbaric by the English, and their use was discouraged. This angered the Scots, and particularly the Highlanders, the majority of whom spoke no English at all.

All schools had to use the English tongue. Dr James Beattie remarked to Lord Glenbervie one day when they met in Edinburgh:

We who live in Scotland, are obliged to study English like a dead language which we can understand, but cannot speak. Our style smells of the lamp: we are slaves of the language, and are continually afraid of committing gross blunders.

Jacobite rebellions

In spite of the union of both crowns and parliaments, there was still significant support for a Stuart monarchy in Scotland which was echoed elsewhere and led to the Jacobite rebellions, causing considerable instability throughout Great Britain.

Supporters of the exiled Stuart kings came to be known as Jacobites, from 'Jacobus', Latin for James, the traditional first name of Stuart kings. The Scottish name Stewart had become Stuart after 1603, possibly as a concession to the French supporters of the Stuarts, whose language had no letter W.

BONNIE DUNDEE

The first undercurrents of Jacobite unrest surfaced almost immediately after James VII of Scotland and II of England had fled to France in 1688. In late 1689 the Duke of Gordon failed in his attempt to hold Edinburgh Castle for King James, who had by now travelled to Ireland.

John Graham of Claverhouse, Viscount Dundee, who had represented James at the Convention, left Edinburgh to gather support, and in the words of a popular old song:

Open the West Port and let us gang free
For it up withe bonnets o' Bonnie Dundee . . .

Top: *Prince Charles Edward Stuart*
Above: *Killiecrankie*
Right: *Jacobite snuff box*
Centre: *Dundee's body carried from the battle*
Far right: *Glenfinnan Monument, Loch Shiel*

He went on to raise the standard for James at Dundee. In response, King William dispatched troops under the command of General Mackay to the Highlands to deal with the rebels. Viscount Dundee managed to raise 3000 Highlanders, and they met the government forces at the Pass of Killiecrankie on 17 July 1689. As the government troops emerged from the pass, Dundee's men attacked and were victorious, though the Viscount was killed by a stray bullet.

Colonel Alexander Cannon took command, but was caught in a conflict with a Covenanting force at Dunkeld which, assisted by the Cameronians, held on to the town after heavy fighting.

THE OLD PRETENDER

James VII and II died in 1701, but his cause was taken up by his son, James Francis Edward Stuart, the Old Chevalier or Old Pretender as he came to be known. Many Jacobites were reluctant to fight Queen Anne, as she was the daughter of James VII and II, but they opposed the Union and, aware of the dissatisfaction felt by many Scots, the Old Pretender saw an opportunity to regain his kingdom.

Louis XIV of France wanted to take advantage of a weakly defended England and gave his backing to a plan to retake the throne by force, and so in 1708 the Pretender set sail from France with 6000 French troops in 30 vessels. However, bad weather weakened their resolve, and when a superior English fleet under Admiral Byng arrived to meet the invaders, the French commander took fright and, against James' wishes, the ships returned in disorder to Dunkirk.

THE 'FIFTEEN

When Anne died in 1714, the Jacobites were united in opposition to the succession of George I, the 'wee German Lairdie' from Hanover, and the following year they sought to take advantage of a general feeling of resentment towards the new king by launching another revolt. The leader of the Scottish Jacobites was the Earl of Mar, known as 'Bobbin' Johnnie', as he had been a supporter of the Union and the Hanoverians until George I refused to appoint him to a high government post, at which juncture he changed sides and became a Jacobite.

The Jacobite standard was raised at Braemar, in Aberdeenshire. Assistance from France and the south of England was anticipated, but unfortunately the many divisions among the chiefs backing James, combined with Louis XIV's recent death, conspired to erode this support. The Jacobites did, however, capture Perth, and afterwards were able to increase their forces to nearly 10,000. They met the government forces under the Duke of Argyll at Sheriffmuir on 13 November.

Mar's Highlanders routed a wing of Argyll's infantry, but the government's cavalry swept away the opposite flank of the Jacobite army. Both sides claimed a victory, but it was Mar who retreated back to Perth. Another Jacobite force under Macintosh of Borlum reached Leith and joined with an English Jacobite army, but the two groups quarrelled, despite their common aim, and the Highlanders were reluctant to fight in England.

The Old Pretender finally arrived in Scotland on 22 December, but by then his cause was already doomed, and he returned to France less than two months later. The 'Fifteen rebellion had offered a good chance of success, but ultimately it foundered for want of decisive leadership and unity between the various Jacobite factions. James VIII was never to set foot in his homeland again.

THE 'NINETEEN

A smaller rebellion took place in 1719. The Spanish were the Jacobites' allies this time, or should have been; they promised 5000 troops, and weapons for

Jacobite soldiers firing on government troops at the Battle of Glenshiel, 10 June 1719

30,000, and were planning to land both in England and Scotland. Unfortunately, the fleet carrying the troops was scattered by bad weather and only 300 men came ashore.

The Spanish soldiers were joined by Highlanders, including men from the Murrays, the Camerons, the Mackenzies and the MacGregors, but these only stayed to fight in a battle which took place at Glenshiel and then returned home. The Spaniards surrendered to the government army.

However, the Jacobites were by no means defeated. Secret meetings were arranged by the Scottish Jacobite nobility all over the country, and the government troops, known as redcoats, were forever on the look-out for rebels.

ROB ROY MACGREGOR (1671–1734)

Rob Roy was born in Glengyle, in the heart of the Trossachs, and belonged to the Protestant MacGregor clan of the Highlands. He was a powerful and agile man, skilful with the broadsword, and his muscular appearance, long arms and imposing stance gave him

a ferocious aspect – a typical Highlander of the time. It appears that he gained his nickname because he was covered by a strong growth of red hair: 'roy' is derived from the Gaelic *ruadh* (red), hence Rob Roy, meaning 'Robert the Red'.

Caught up in the turbulent political transitions from Catholicism to Protestantism, and from feudal to parliamentary rule, Rob Roy joined the Lennox Watch, a group of Highlanders who offered protection to farmers transporting cattle to the Lowlands. Assignments were obtained largely by blackmail. His offers to take cattle to market were made with an unspoken threat well understood: if Rob Roy did not get the job of protecting them, there was a good chance that the cattle would be stolen.

Under James VI a number of Acts of Proscription had been implemented in the hope of destroying the MacGregor clan. The Proscription was renewed in 1693 as a result of the Jacobite rebellion at Killiecrankie in 1689, in which Robert, his father and his eldest brother, John, had taken part. To disguise his origins, Rob Roy changed his name from MacGregor to Campbell, his mother's name.

Left: *Balquhidder Glen, the home of Rob Roy in his later years*
Above: *Rob Roy's grave at Balquhidder*

Rob Roy the cattle-dealer

Rob Roy's reputation as both fighter and cattle-drover grew, and in 1708 he became a legitimate and prosperous cattle-dealer. The clan chiefs trusted him to take their huge herds to markets in the Lowlands and even to England. Aware of Rob Roy's power, the thieves kept away. Almost 30,000 cattle crossed into the Lowlands of Scotland bound for the Scottish and English markets every year.

Between November 1711 and April 1712, Rob Roy raised £12,500 (Scots) from the Duke of Montrose and others to buy cattle for fattening and sale at Scottish and English markets. However, his partner MacDonald absconded with the letters of credit, leaving Rob Roy open to charges of theft. His debts totalled £30,000 (Scots), and legal action was duly taken against him. When he did not answer a summons to court, he was quickly deemed an outlaw.

Managing to evade arrest, Rob Roy began to support himself by stealing cattle. His family was even less fortunate, being evicted from its lands by an employee of Montrose, Grahame of Killearn.

Outlaw raids

By the age of 43, Rob Roy had become a notorious fugitive, with little to lose by becoming an outlaw proper. His first raid, at pistol-point on Grahame's stock, was in revenge for the ruin of his family. So began a life of stealing, often carried out for others who were less fortunate, as well as for his own benefit.

Unrest grew again after the death in 1714 of Queen Anne, who had been paying regular sums of money to the chiefs to ensure their loyalty to the crown. There remained much frustration among the Highlanders, especially those, like the MacGregors, who still secretly supported the Jacobite cause.

Rob Roy converted this unrest into action by gathering a large supporting force from the MacGregor clan to take part in the 1715 Jacobite uprising, led by the Earl of Mar, who had raised an army around Aberdeen. The rebellion was quashed in the Battle of Sheriffmuir. Rob Roy had decided not to fight himself, not wanting to be seen supporting the Jacobites against his kinsman, the Duke of Argyll, the commander of the government forces.

Outlaw no more

At 50, Rob Roy bought lands near Balquhidder and remained an active cattle-drover throughout the 1720s. He eventually made peace with his old enemy, the Duke of Montrose, and, through General Wade, was granted a formal pardon by the King in 1725. He died in 1734, having been converted to Catholicism, and was buried in the churchyard at Balquhidder. His three sons later played an active part in the 1745 uprising of the Jacobites under Bonnie Prince Charlie.

GENERAL WADE'S ROADS

In 1724, towards the end of George II's reign, Sir Robert Walpole, the Prime Minister, appointed General George Wade as commander-in-chief of the north, with the power to act as a government emissary in Scotland. Wade undertook a massive programme of road-building to improve communications in the Highlands, not only between the strongholds of Fort Augustus and Fort William, but in many other areas as well.

It took Wade's engineers 16 years to construct the many bridges and 260 miles of road which ensured that if there should be another Jacobite uprising, the government would be in a far better position to address the situation. The new roads also helped to disperse the ancient and formerly impenetrable order which had persevered in the Highlands.

THE 'FORTY-FIVE

The Old Pretender's first-born son was named Prince Charles Edward Stuart, and in later years came to be known as Bonnie Prince Charlie. He had one ambition: to gain the kingdom to which he was heir, an aim undoubtedly fostered by his father. Many loyal noblemen, conscious of their status as vassals of the monarch, gathered around the court of their exiled king in France.

In 1745 plans were laid to try once again to regain the Crown for James VIII and III. The prince, with the blessing of his father, set out to reclaim the kingdom, sailing secretly from France with Lord Lovat, Cameron of Locheil, the Earl of Traquair, William, Marquis of Tullibardine (elder brother of James, Duke of Atholl), and three other noblemen, followed

Right: *a pair of flintlock travelling pistols captured from an English officer at the Battle of Prestonpans*
Below: *Prince Charles Edward Stuart at the raising of the royal standard at Glenfinnan, 19 August 1745*

by a French volunteer force in another ship. The French vessel was badly damaged by British ships which were sent to intercept the invaders, and finally managed to struggle back to port. The prince, in spite of the fact that his forces were now seriously depleted, and against the advice of several of his noblemen, insisted upon continuing the quest.

Glenfinnan

Charles arrived at the Isle of Eriskay, in the Outer Hebrides, on 23 July 1745. After crossing to the mainland of Scotland, he and his party entered the sea loch, Loch Nan Uamh and finally came ashore. On 18 August they set out for Glenfinnan to join up with the other Jacobite forces, and arrived the next day to find 1200 loyal MacDonalds and Camerons waiting to welcome the prince home. The royal standard of blue, white and red silk was raised in the name of King James VIII and III by Lord Tullibardine. Under the command of the prince's noblemen, there were soon over 3000 Jacobites assembled, ready to fight for king and country.

The Jacobites marched into Perth on 4 September and were joined by Lord George Murray, brother of the Duke of Atholl. Prince Charles was fortunate, in that Sir John Cope, who had gathered a small pro-government force, marched to Inverness via Stirling and Dalwhinnie, failing to intercept the Jacobites. This left the way clear for the prince to progress to Edinburgh with very little opposition and, on 17 September, his army stormed into the capital.

Prestonpans

Cope, realising his error, transported his men by sea to Prestonpans on the east coast of Scotland, where they met the Jacobites in battle. Guided by the clever tactics of Murray, the Jacobites managed to rout the better equipped government army, who were unnerved by the fury of the Highlanders and suffered an overwhelming defeat.

Advance and retreat

After this encouraging victory, Charles decided not to forge ahead with his campaign to move further south; instead, he established himself for five weeks at Holyrood Palace in Edinburgh. Much refreshed after this, the Jacobite army left Edinburgh for Kelso, where they set up new headquarters. The Earl of Traquair offered the use of his home to the prince, while he rallied together as many Jacobite supporters of the prince's cause as he could.

In November they entered Carlisle and gained a sweeping victory. The following day they marched south to Manchester and then on to Derby, but were unable to gain as many English supporters as they had hoped. At Derby, they were awaited by two groups of government forces, one under the command of the Duke of Cumberland to the south, and another under General Wade to the north, each of the two forces bigger than the whole of Charles' army.

HARD TIMES

John MacDonald, in his book, *Travels in Various Parts of Europe, Asia and Africa*, which was published in 1790, includes an account given by the son of a Jacobite.

The narrator, born in 1741, was one of four abandoned children who set off to find their father:

I was but a child of two and half at the time, a son of a poor Highland gentleman, Grant of Grant of Keppoch, when my mother died in 1743. Two years later my father, grieve-stricken, left us in charge of a young maid, to join the Jacobite Uprising. Some time later the maid deserted us to run away with her lover.

There we were, my beautiful sister Kitty aged twelve, my two brothers, Daniel the eldest aged seven and my younger brother, Alexander, but two and half years, and myself rising five. We were quite alone in the world and would have been frightened had it not been for my sister's courage. After taking the animals to a neighbour, my sister Kitty decided to leave for Edinburgh to find our father . . . She collected all the money she could together which was fourteen pounds Scots [23 shillings odd in sterling] with this and the letter from our father in her bosom, we set out from Urquhart, in the middle of September 1745 to join our father. My sister carried the child on her back, Daniel carried the bundle and I walked or skipped alongside them.

In this manner we travelled from Inverness to Edinburgh, a distance of 150 measured miles [241km], in the space of 2 months . . . Our money being expended we were obliged to beg for bread . . . We were kindly used by some and harshly by those against the Prince, people who could not take us in would give us a bag of oatmeal . . . Our apparel looked like gentleman's children, and we had a great share of beauty . . . If we could not reach a house my sister would cover us with her plaid and cut the tops of broom with her knife to lie on and cover us over.

When we had any burn to cross my sister would carry my young brother over first, then come for me, and afterwards she went back to take my brother's hand to help him across. On one occasion my sister was whirled off her feet carrying Alexander, and nearly drowned, a farmer rescued them and brought us to his home to dry and be fed . . . When it was fine and we came to a rivulet my sister washed our second shirts and stockings.

MAC NICOL.

At last we reached Edinburgh only to find that the Jacobite army had left Edinburgh. We all sat down and cried. We were taken to the Inn, by kindly people on the boat we met as we crossed over the Forth, we were given some money that the passengers had collected for us. At the Inn, Mr. Goolem fed and housed us for some days. He said we would have to go to the workhouse. In horror my sister packed us off as fast as she could.

We roamed the streets and were often hungry . . . We were taken in one night by a kind lady whose husband had lived near us in Inverness, she recognised the Highland dress. She fed us and gave us a room in the garret and a couple of blankets, next day we left for the streets. Later in April 1746 we heard our father had been killed at Culloden. We all cried. My sister cried the most.

In the same month Kitty was knocked down by the Countess of Moray's coach, Lady Moray took us into her house on hearing our story, she set my sister into service and my brother Alexander out to nurse, my brother Daniel and I became vagrants. If we came to see my sister Kitty, she cried so much we did not go back, it upset us all so much. In time we were taken up by City Guards for begging within the city walls which was an offence. After this we lost touch with one another, although I remember I once carried a silk umbrella over my sister's head some thirty years later in London.

A woman of the MacNicol clan

Reluctantly, the Jacobites retreated to the Highlands although, had they known the terror their advance had evoked in London, they might have continued. Prince Charles strongly opposed the retreat, but was outvoted by his commanders.

As they retreated, with government armies in hot pursuit, the Jacobites grew increasingly weary. Murray's skill brought them safely to Scotland but, as they continued towards the Highlands, their supplies began to run out, and they had no option but to meet the Duke of Cumberland's army at Culloden.

THE DUKE OF CUMBERLAND

George II, eager to bring an end to the Jacobite insurrection of 57 years, had sent the Duke of Cumberland, his second son, to deal with the rebels. He had raised an army of over 8000 men, who marched from England up the east coast to Scotland, commandeering houses along the way. Camping for six weeks at Aberdeen, the soldiers created havoc among the people, who were expected to feed the army during their stay. The Aberdonians, praying secretly for a Jacobite victory, were relieved when the army departed.

The Battle of Culloden

The last battle to be fought by the Jacobite army took place on 16 April 1746 upon the bleak moor of Drummossie, at Culloden. The terrain did not suit the tactics of the Highland troops, who were exhausted and starving - the day before the battle they had eaten only one biscuit each. They fought bravely and with spirit, but were no match for the highly disciplined and better-equipped government army, twice their size and composed of well-rested and well-fed troops.

To their dismay, the Jacobites discovered they were fighting many of their own countrymen; the government force included three battalions of Lowland Scots. In fact, Culloden was a conflict between Lowlanders and Highlanders, and the last

battle ever to be fought on British soil. The Jacobites' ranks were broken by a crushing cannonade before they had even advanced through the hails of gunshot to face the steady lines of redcoats. Over 1200 Jacobites were killed on the battlefield, but only 50 government soldiers died.

Cumberland's revenge

Culloden will be remembered more for the murders committed after the battle by the 'Bloody Butcher', the Duke of Cumberland, than for the actual fighting. Cumberland, appointed to the task of pacifying the Highlands once and for all, established his headquarters at the garrison of Fort Augustus. From there he orchestrated an unrelenting regime of cruelty, debauchery and barbarism. The inhuman deeds of his command were well recorded.

Below: *targe, or shield, believed to have belonged to Prince Charles Edward Stuart* Right: *silver-hilted sword used by James Wolfe (1727-59), later to achieve fame as General Wolfe of Quebec* Far right: *government troops hunting rebels after the Battle of Culloden, after a painting by Seymour Lucas*

The following infamous act was documented by Sir Henry Seton Stewart of Allarton in the *Anti-Jacobin Review* of 1802, and confirmed by Robert Forbes in his book, *The Lyon in Mourning* (1835). It took place on Drummossie Moor, Culloden after the fighting had ceased.

The duke was inspecting the battlefield when he noticed a severely wounded young Highland soldier, who seemed to be smiling in defiance, sitting on the ground with his head propped up on his arm. The duke halted and turned to his officer (later to become the famous general who died defending Quebec). 'Wolfe,' said the duke. 'Shoot me that Highland scoundrel that dares thus look on us with such contempt and insolence.' 'My commission,' replied the gallant officer, 'is at your Royal Highness's disposal, but I never can consent to become an executioner.'

Outraged, the duke confronted his other officers, demanding that one of them draw his pistol upon the helpless Jacobite. Taking courage from their leader, Major Wolfe, they all refused. Finally, the duke called upon a private, who had no choice but to obey. The brave Highland soldier was Charles Fraser, aged 21, who had commanded the Frasers in the battle. After this callous act, Cumberland sent a contingent of soldiers to kill any surviving Jacobites.

The aftermath

The fugitive rebels were ruthlessly hunted by Cumberland's men and put to death. Many were discovered wounded and hungry, wandering up to 20 miles (32km) from the battlefield. Others were burned alive, and if prisoners were taken, they were often treated so badly that they died in custody. An officer from the duke's command boasted that he had seen as many as 72 Jacobites massacred in a single day.

One particularly disturbing report came from the garrison at Fort Augustus, regarding 19 Jacobite officers who were found hiding in the courtyard of Culloden House. They were ordered to stand against

the wall and were platooned (fusilladed). Those who survived were clubbed to death with the butt of a musket. One officer escaped with a broken nose, an eye gouged out and horrendous facial injuries. His shocking wounds stood as a damning record of Cumberland's brutality.

Highlanders who helped the Jacobites in their plight were tortured and had all their possessions stolen. Even less mercy was shown to defiant crofters – their food and property were taken and their wives brutally treated. Some 8000 cattle were taken from crofters and Jacobite landlords and brought into Fort Augustus. Many of the victims had not even played a part in the rebellion, but the savage disregard for human life continued. Over 1000 people were deported, 700 taken prisoner and 120 executed.

Starvation at Fort Augustus

Another despicable act occurred on 8 July 1746 at Fort Augustus. Cumberland forbade food to be given to the starving people in the neighbourhood. If any soldiers or their wives were caught contravening this command, they were to be flogged for the first offence and, for subsequent transgressions, the punishments

Simon, Lord Lovat *by William Hogarth*

the City of London sent £4000 to be shared between them, a huge amount in the eighteenth century. Major Wolfe recounted his complete disgust at the command at Fort Augustus:

If I stay here much longer with the regiment, I shall be perfectly corrupt, the officers are loose and profligate, and the soldiers are very devils.

SIMON, LORD LOVAT OF THE CLAN FRASER

Simon, Lord Lovat, the leader of the Fraser clan, was also one of the leaders of the prince's army. Born of Celtic lineage, he was unmatched in the strength he possessed in his youth. At the age of 16, he had already been imprisoned three times for involvement in Jacobite uprisings.

Married three times, he captivated many women with his bravery and fiery spirits. Having raised himself to the leadership of one of the most powerful clans in the Scottish Highlands, his ambition was to be awarded a dukedom. However, his support of the Jacobites was somewhat inconsistent. During the 'Fifteen he took the government side and obtained a full pardon, but in the 'Forty-five he sent his son and clan to fight for Charles whilst protesting his own loyalty to the government. Despite this capricious career, he was admired by the soldiers for his tremendous courage and resourcefulness.

were more severe. As a consequence, large numbers of innocent people died. Their livestock had been stolen, their homes ransacked by soldiers, and their produce and means of heating plundered. Such cruelty is unsurpassed in the history of the Scottish Highlands.

Government backing

Cumberland's treatment of the Jacobites was encouraged by the government in London. For example, there was much disagreement amongst the soldiers at Fort Augustus, where some of the officers had complained about 'the bleak black mountains and the dejected spirits of all their men'. Many were embittered and homesick, and so, in order to placate them,

Capture

After Culloden, Lovat was imprisoned in Fort Augustus before being taken to the Tower of London to await trial. He knew he would end up on the gallows, yet he conducted his own defence with great dignity and wit.

As he was stepping into the carriage which would carry him to his death, an old woman shouted, 'You will have your head chopped off, you ugly old Scots dog.' Without a second's hesitation he turned upon her, and, raising his hat, replied, 'I verily believe I shall, you old English bitch.'

A huge crowd gathered to see Lovat's execution, and as he went proudly to the scaffold, one of the stands for spectators collapsed, killing a number of people. With a twinkle in his eye, the old chief exclaimed, 'The more the mischief, the better the sport!' He felt the axe-blade and gave a handsome donation to the executioner. He was over 80 years old, and met death with the same mixture of cynicism and gallantry with which he had lived his life.

BONNIE PRINCE CHARLIE'S ESCAPE

The prince had escaped into hiding with the help of some of his noblemen. They had foreseen the dire outcome of Culloden and managed to reach as far as Loch Morar, 80 miles (128km) from the battlefield. They then fled to the Outer Hebrides.

There was a price of £30,000 on the prince's head whilst he remained a fugitive, but Highland loyalty was such that he was never captured in the five months he was to spend wandering throughout the Highlands and Islands.

Flora MacDonald

Bonnie Prince Charlie's escape was largely due to young Flora MacDonald. Born in South Uist in the Western Isles in 1722, Flora went to school in Sleat, where she became a firm favourite of Sir Alexander and Lady Margaret MacDonald, and would often stay at their mansion house in Mogstadt. Lady Margaret was unstinting in her efforts to help the prince, who had eventually reached the house of Ronald

Right: Bonnie Prince Charlie's brass-bound oak money box, which has a lock concealed under the hasp and iron bolts that can be lowered for securing it to a strong point

MacEachin of Corrodale, South Uist, with the help of Donald MacLeod.

Meanwhile, Flora, on her way from Skye to visit her brother in South Uist, was approached by the agents of Lady Margaret with a scheme to help the prince. The courageous girl duly met Charles in Uist and told him of the plan to disguise him as her Irish maid 'Betty Burke' so he could accompany her to Skye and elude the many government soldiers.

Whilst on South Uist, Flora was apprehended by soldiers. She demanded to see the commanding officer and was eventually ushered into his presence. He was none other than her stepfather, Hugh MacDonald. Whether or not he knew of the planned adventure has never been discovered, but the fact remains that he supplied passports for Flora, her 'maid', and a young student named Neil MacEachain with whom the prince had been residing.

Incredibly, the three managed to make their way to Benbecula in order to procure a passage on a boat to Skye. It was a hazardous journey, and the prince, clad in a dress befitting an Irish maid, nearly gave himself away twice with clumsy attempts to manipulate his long skirts. Throughout, Flora kept a very cool head for one so young, knowing that the prince's safety depended on her.

Once on Skye, the prince was met by his noblemen, who secretly escorted him to a waiting ship bound for the Isle of Raasay. In September 1746 he was finally taken to France. Despite the high reward put on the prince's head, no one had been tempted to betray his whereabouts.

Top: *Prince Charles Edward Stuart leaving Scotland for France on 20 September 1746, painting by J B MacDonald*
Left: *Charles bidding farewell to Flora MacDonald, from a painting by George W Joy*
Above: *the 'Steekit Yetts', or Bear Gates, at Traquair*

GOVERNMENT FORTS

Fort George

After the 1745 rebellion, the government ordered the construction of the massive Fort George, which lies at the entrance of the Moray Firth, 11 miles (17km) north-east of Inverness. Built to counter further uprisings, it is one of the most outstanding artillery fortifications in Europe. Today it is still an army barracks, covering 42 acres (17 hectares) and enclosed by 1 mile (2km) of ramparts.

Fort Augustus

Fort Augustus lies exactly in the centre of Glen Mor, and this natural vantage point afforded it a position of military importance. The Great Glen of Albyn, which cuts the Highlands in two from coast to coast, has formed a highway for east-west communications from the earliest times. During the Jacobite uprisings, before the construction of Fort Augustus, there was an older fort a few hundred yards away, probably erected by the Romans. Apparently, an underground passage connects the old fort with the new one.

When a trench was being dug in 1767, workmen found a blue earthenware urn containing 300 Roman coins of mixed metal dating from the time of Diocletian. As yet, there has been no concerted archaeological investigation of the area.

Fort William

Fort William was rebuilt in stone in 1698 and withstood a siege in 1745,

during the Jacobite rebellion. It was used as a base for the hunt for Bonnie Prince Charlie.

A railway station was later built on the site of the fort, but the foundations and some ruins can still be seen.

Above: *Fort George, still in use as an army barracks*

Flora, the so-called Jacobite heroine, who adamantly declared she was not a Jacobite, was captured and taken by ship to London, where she was imprisoned for nearly a year before being released under the Act of Indemnity in 1747. Her stepfather, impoverished by the costs of the episode, was also incarcerated for a short period. Flora married Allan MacDonald of Skye in November 1750, and emigrated to America with her husband and sons in 1774.

The Earl of Traquair

After the Battle of Culloden, the 5th Earl of Traquair was also imprisoned in the Tower of London for the part he played in the rebellion. The link with the Stuarts has never been forgotten, as the late Peter Maxwell Stuart, 20th Laird of Traquair, explained:

The name of Traquair is associated so vividly in the public mind not so much with the house as with its famous entrance, the 'Steekit Yetts' [stuck gates], lying at the end of a quarter-mile tree-flanked avenue. There, according to family tradition and legend, perhaps one of the most romantic in Scottish history, the gates were closed one late autumn day in 1745 by the fifth Earl after wishing his guest, Prince Charles Edward Stuart, a safe journey, with the promise that the gates would not be reopened until the Stuarts were restored to the throne.

They have remained closed ever since.

The end of the Jacobites

The prince, a disillusioned man, reached France and then drifted around Europe from one court to another, drinking heavily. He married Louisa von Stolberg in 1772, but the marriage was unhappy.

Charles left no heirs, apart from an illegitimate daughter named Caroline, and so the Jacobite cause was extinguished with his death in 1788.

The Highlanders

From the Gaelic *clann*, meaning children, comes the name of the social structure which once regulated life throughout the Scottish Highlands – the clan system. Members of a clan were like an extended family whose identity was expressed through a common name and a particular tartan. Each clan possessed its own territory, with some occupying large parts of the Scottish Highlands.

The island clans usually had an overall chief, the Lord of the Isles, who ruled his domain like a king. Clans guarded their land jealously and would often go to war with each other over territorial feuds.

There were two classes within the clan: the Saoi and the Daoi. The Saoi class were the warriors, whose duty it was to defend their tribe. This honour brought certain privileges - primarily exemption from physical toil. The Daoi class spent their lives tending the flocks or cultivating the land.

Outsiders who wished to place themselves under the protection of a powerful chief were obliged to observe a bond, or *manrent*. This meant that the outsider was bound to obey the chief and serve him 'as master, by land and sea'. In return, the chief was duty-bound to 'maintain and defend him' as he would his own kin. Chosen by the clan on merit, the chief had to demonstrate endurance, fearless leadership in battle and diplomatic ability in times of adversity. It was essential that a clan had a strong leader; the clan's survival depended on self-sufficiency and unity, and the chief had to command the respect of all his clansmen. On a chief's death, if his sons were unable to fulfil these requirements, another member of the clan would be elected to succeed him.

An English officer called Captain Burt, who visited the Highlands in the eighteenth century, described the clansman's loyalty to his chief:

The ordinary Highlander esteems it the most sublime degree of virtue to love their chief and pay him a blind obedience, although it is opposition to the government, the laws of the kingdom, or even the laws of God. He is their idol and as they profess to know no king but him . . . so will they say, they ought to do whatever he commands without enquiry.

THE LIFESTYLE OF THE CLAN

The system of smallholding within a clan was based on small lots of land rented from the chief by the clan members. This way of farming later came to be known as 'crofting', and is mainly associated with the Highlands and Islands, a 'crofter' being the holder of the smallest sub-tenancy recognised in the old Highland system of land tenure. Just below the crofters in the social order came the 'cottars', who either worked as landless farm labourers for the

Left: *a Skye islander at her spinning wheel*
Right: *Archibald McArthur, piper to the chief of Touch and Staffa*

M^cARTHUR, *PIPER*
RANALD MACDONALD Esqr. of STAFFA

I. KAY. 1810

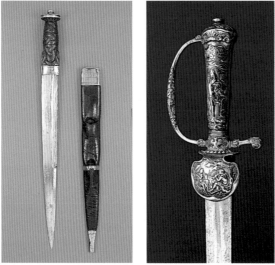

Top: Drovers striking a Bargain over Highland Cattle
by Charles James Adams (1859–1931)
Far left: *a dirk, or dagger, of about 1744*
Left: *a silver-hilted hunting sword from Drum Castle*
Above: *early eighteenth-century Highland bagpipes*

chiefs, or sub-leased strips of land ('riggs'), often part of the croft of a relative. They had no land or rights of their own, and usually led a life of insecurity and extreme poverty, moving around to find casual employment and working long hours for a pittance.

Croft houses were single-storied, built from local stone and thatched with dried heather or straw, their adjoining land being used to grow traditional Highland crops, such as oats or barley, and to graze livestock. Next to the house were drystone buildings for storing grain and straw, and sheltering animals. Typically the floor of the house itself was bare earth. The crofters slept in beds made of heather and straw. A peat fire would be set in the middle of the house to warm its inhabitants and their livestock, with an outlet in the roof for the smoke. Blackened walls resulting from the lack of a chimney may be the reason for crofters' houses becoming known as 'blackhouses'.

There are areas of peat all over the Highlands. Formed from compressed vegetation, peat can be cut and dried to be used as fuel for heating and cooking. Whole families took part in gathering and stacking peat after the men had cut it, so that it could dry out ready for use, and this practice is still followed today.

The chiefs of the larger clans employed 'tacksmen' to collect their rents, who generally leased a large part of the clan territory from the chief, then rented out some of the land, which was too large for one person to farm alone. Thus the tacksman operated both as crofter and as rent-collector for the chief. This suited those chiefs whose territory was wild and inaccessible, and hence difficult to supervise. It ensured that the chief would receive a regular rent from his tenants, providing large profits for the privileged tacksman, much to the chagrin of other, less fortunate clansmen.

Whereas the women spun the wool, the men would weave it into lengths for clothing, some in the colours of the clan. During the day the men would wrap a length of material around them, folding it over their left shoulder and securing it with a clasp; at night the same material served a second purpose, as a blanket. On their heads they wore blue shepherd's bonnets to protect them from the cold. The women draped colourful plaids around their shoulders as shawls and wore net bonnets.

Great cattle droves were organised to take the chiefs' cattle to the Lowlands of Scotland and to the English markets along drove roads, which provided the only overland routes for communication before more extensive road-building was carried out. The Highland country was rough and often boggy, so experienced cattle-drovers like Rob Roy MacGregor were employed by the chiefs to guarantee that their cattle arrived safely.

GAELIC CULTURE

The Highlanders were still influenced by the ancient Celtic culture from which they were descended, and within each clan there was always a Gaelic bard, or poet, who acted as advisor to the chief and provided a link to the clan's ancient heritage. As a representative of the people, and a kind of spiritual leader, the bard helped the clanspeople through their conflicts and troubles. In addition, talented Gaelic singers or storytellers would entertain their friends during social visits. In later centuries, musical evenings or *ceilidhs* (as they are still called) were held. The man of the house (*fear-an-taighe*), or the woman of the house (*bean-an-taighe*), would invite artists to their home.

The Gaelic language was spoken all over Scotland apart from in East Lothian, East Caithness and the Northern Isles. It is currently spoken by almost 66,000 people in the north-west Highlands, central belt, and throughout the Hebrides.

Bagpipes were also a part of the Highland culture, although their origin has never been clearly established. The most well known piper of the sixteenth century was Donald Mor MacCrimmon who devoted the whole of his life to the study of pipe music, and originated classical music for the instrument. Every chief had his own piper and the MacCrimmons played for the MacLeods of Dunvegan on Skye. Crotach MacLeod valued them so highly that he gave them land and built a college for pipers.

During battles the sound of pipes strengthened and inspired many a weary soldier. Pipes were forbidden just after the Battle of Culloden, when the government was trying to stamp out Jacobitism; even then, they continued to be played in secret.

THE IMPACT OF THE FEUDAL SYSTEM

The influences of Roman and Viking culture had already been felt in the Highlands, but the social structure persisted without radical change over the centuries, with the clan system still firmly in place. When David I, Malcolm's youngest son, introduced the Norman/English feudal system, he found it very difficult to implement across the ancient tribal structure in the Highlands. He accepted that there was a difference between nobles appointed by the king, who received lands and titles as a reward for loyalty, and Highland chieftains, who already held their territory as a vested interest for their entire people. Tribes were just beginning to form into powerful clan territories at the time, and the Highlands were so remote and the terrain so hostile that it would have been foolhardy to enforce a new system there.

Divided loyalties

The feudal system was based on land ownership and the principle that a grant of land, once given, established a noble's authority over those living there. This differed substantially from the way in which the clan system operated, where the title of chief was not gained by land right or hereditary issue, but through more democratic means.

If clan chiefs had submitted to the authority of the king, it would have led to the break up of the system, for not only would the chief have had to answer to his clan, but ultimately to the power of the king as well.

The autocratic attitude of the chiefs undermined not only the monarchy's feudal belief that they owned all the land in the kingdom, but also the notion of the divine right of kings, which supposed that they acted according to the will of God and had authority over the Church, nobles, chieftains and general populace. The conflict between the clan and feudal systems continued for many centuries, often interfering with the administration of the Church, the ruling of the country, and the rights of the people, causing divisions and upheavals throughout Scotland.

These changes filtered into Scotland over many centuries and did not have an immediate effect on the way in which chiefs managed their clans. It was not until 1493, when the chiefs were made to swear allegiance unto death to the monarchy and accept the feudal laws over the clan system, that they felt an impending danger. When they refused to take the oath, they were threatened with the loss of their territory. In return for their sworn allegiance they were promised a royal charter which would put them on a par with the nobles, entitling them to hereditary rights over their territories. The sworn allegiance from the nobles and chiefs had to be renewed each year and in the beginning most of the Highland chiefs paid only lip-service to these demands.

Over the next 300 years the Scottish kings were constantly troubled by the chiefs in the Western Isles and the western and northern Highlands, who continued to feud amongst themselves, vying for power and territorial gain. Repeated attempts were made to subordinate the clans to the rule of the king, but the fighting continued until the seventeenth century.

In the fifteenth century James I had realised that the growing power of the chiefs had to be curbed. To ensure that these formidable overlords were kept subservient to the Crown, James demanded to see their original charters. If a charter was not presented, the

A silver sword, engraved 'God Save King James the 8',
showing the enduring loyalty to the Stuart line

noble or chief had to swear his allegiance again in
order to receive another.

Dissatisfaction with the state of affairs persisted,
and, on one occasion, the feuding between the
Mackenzies and MacDonalds in the Western Isles
spread to the mainland. James IV was forced to
launch at least eight expeditions by sea and land to the
western Highlands, and, in 1493, confiscated the lordship of the Isles from the MacDonalds of Islay. He
delegated the task of keeping order to the strongest
clans in the area, the Campbells and Gordons, but this
too proved unsuccessful in the long term.

In 1608, James VI cultivated the backing of the
dominant Mackenzie and Campbell clans, determined
to bring the chiefs under his control. Setting sail for
the Isle of Mull, James, realising he would have to use
strategy and cunning, invited all the defiant chiefs to
meet him on his ship for an evening's entertainment
and a good repast. After the meal, the unsuspecting
chiefs were ambushed and were soon incarcerated in
various prisons in central Scotland, where they would
remain until ready to meet the King's demands.

A year later, James presented his commands to the
chiefs in the form of the Statutes of Iona and made
their release conditional on their agreement. The
Statutes included demands to suppress vagabonds and
beggars, to stop the bards from encouraging clan
feuds, to give their support to the reformed Church of
Scotland, and to swear allegiance yet again to the
Crown. This time the oaths had to be guaranteed,
firstly by signing each of the Statutes, and secondly by
agreeing to send their sons to the Lowlands to be educated, which essentially meant anglicising them. The
chiefs' resolve was finally breached, and the Statutes
of Iona were signed in 1609. In 1616 the chiefs had to
renew their allegiance again, and it seemed that their
loyalty to the sovereign had finally been secured.

THE DESTRUCTION OF THE CLAN

Following the death of Elizabeth I in 1603, the two
crowns of England and Scotland became one. James
VI of Scotland became James I of England and, as
joint monarch, decided to live in London. This decision marked the beginning of the end of Scotland as a
sovereign independent nation. Chiefs, noblemen,
politicians and courtiers were enticed away from
Scotland to join the court, where they were influenced
by the European ideas of class distinction and land

HIGHLAND DRESS

For 50 years Jacobitism piqued the English nation. To the English government the pro-Jacobite chiefs and their clans made up a separate entity within Scotland, and one which they needed to stamp out.

Each clan had its own colours, or tartans, a powerful visual symbol of the clan's identity. The government felt that passing an Act of Parliament forbidding anyone to wear Highland dress would help put an end to the clan system.

Such a ban was incorporated in the Act of Proscription, which was passed in 1747 and applied equally to all Highlanders, irrespective of their allegiance, except for members of Highland regiments in the British army abroad.

The act described the prohibited clothing in detail and was also used to ban the gathering of Highland people,

the playing of the bagpipes, and the carrying of arms:

No man or boy within Scotland other than such as shall be employed as officers or soldiers in the King's service, shall on any pretence whatsoever wear or put on the clothes commonly called Highland clothes, that is to say the plaid, philebeg or little kilt, trowse, shoulder-belts, or any part whatsoever of what peculiarly belongs to the Highland garb; and that no tartan or particoloured plaid or stuff shall be used for great-coats or for upper coats . . . Every such person . . . being convicted thereof by the oath of one or more witnesses . . . shall suffer imprisonment without bail during six months and no longer; and being convicted for a second offence . . . shall be liable to be transported to any of her majesty's plantations beyond the seas for seven years.

This was one of the most humiliating laws imposed on the Highlanders as a result of the 'Forty-five. Troops were always on the alert, ready to arrest anyone they suspected of sedition, and many clansmen were apprehended and imprisoned.

The act was not repealed until 35 years later, by which time the traditional usage of the Highland dress had changed. The clan identities were enshrined in the uniforms of the Highland regiments, the plaids being worn as the kilts which can still be seen today.

Above: *a chief of the Campbells of Argyll wearing truis*
Far left (from top): *Stewart dress tartan, Cameron, Graham, Macmillan Ancient and Hannay tartans*
Left: *a Drummond of Perth wearing the Grant tartan*
Right: *an early eighteenth-century brass and leather sporran*
Far right: *the Jacobite badge, a white cockade, worn by Lord George Murray*

ownership. Marriages with the daughters of English noblemen further removed the chiefs from their clans. The English had little understanding of the clan system, its history or the loyalties it demanded. Over the generations, the chiefs began to forget the clan system, regarding their Scottish land in the same way as they would their English property, and caring very little for the plight of the clansmen.

In the early eighteenth century a social revolution took place in the Scottish Highlands which broke the age-old relationship between the chief and his clan. Everyone in Scotland was forced by the government to pay allegiance directly to the monarch. As a result, the old system of shared land between the chief and his clan began to collapse, and the clansmen's utilisation of that land was no longer established by law. Castles and estates, originally assigned to the nobles and chiefs for the protection of the land and its people, were now no longer used as fortifications.

The land that had been worked by clansmen was now supervised by tacksmen, whilst the clansmen were treated as mere tenants. The chiefs had royal charters from the king stating that the lands and castles were theirs by hereditary right, whereas the clansmen's rights were not written into these charters. This left them in a vulnerable position. According to Scottish Law, the clansmen, now tenants, would have to take civil action against the landowners if they wished to establish their rights of tenure. The clansmen, who had always relied upon and trusted their chiefs to look after their interests as a family unit, did not know how to help themselves.

Nevertheless, the chiefs remained in command of their clans until the Union of the Parliaments in 1707, and many pro-Jacobite chiefs continued to exercise control over their clans until the crushing defeat of the Jacobites in the uprising of 1745.

After the Battle of Culloden in 1746, the full impact of the change began to be felt, as the enforced peace gradually divided the chiefs and their clans. The Vesting of Heritable Jurisdiction Act of 1747 formally transferred ownership of forfeited estates (mainly belonging to Jacobite supporters) to the Crown. The Annexing Act had provided for the management of such forfeited estates, and most clansmen living there, still under the influence of the clan system, sent their rent to their exiled chiefs but were also forced to pay the government. By the 1780s, Dr Samuel Johnson felt impelled to write:

There was perhaps never any change of national manners so quick, so great, and so general, as that which has operated in the Highlands by the last conquest and the subsequent laws. We came hither too late to see what we expected – a people of peculiar appearance and a system of antiquated life. The clans retain little now of their original character: their ferocity of temper is softened, their military ardour is extinguished, their dignity of independence is depressed, their contempt of government subdued, and their reverence for their chiefs abated. Of what they had before the late conquest of their country there remains only their language and their poverty. (Works, viii, p. 334, London 1787-9)

IN THE WAKE OF THE 'FORTY-FIVE

As time passed, more beneficial changes began to occur in the lives of the Highlanders. One of the most important was the introduction of the potato, which grew well in Scotland and produced a high yield. But its arrival, together with the eradication of smallpox, led to a population surge which threatened to culminate in numbers that the land could not support.

Improvements were also made in training the young for employment. They were taught spinning, sewing and other crafts, and some were sent to the Lowlands as apprentices to farmers, spinners, weavers and dyers. Generous grants were made for roads, bridges and harbours in the Highlands to improve trade and internal communications.

However, John Knox, a London-Scottish book-seller who travelled through the Highlands in 1764, was appalled by the conditions there:

My curiosity, the primary impulse, that took me to the Highlands, gave way to serious investigations . . . A tract of land that comprises a fifth part of Great Britain appeared, with some few exceptions, to be in a state of nature; a great body of people, and these the most virtuous of our island, dragging out a wretched existence, perishing through want, or forced through wild despair to abandon their country, their kindred and friends, and to embark moneyless and unknown, the indented slaves to unremitting toil and drudgery . . . at the distance of 3,000 miles [4,828km] from home.

From 1762 landlords in the Highlands introduced sheep for commercial gain, and by 1800 had begun to encroach upon the slender supply of arable land still belonging to the clansmen. Finally, some debt-ridden landowners succumbed to the temptation to remove their tenants to make space for sheep, which produced a better income. The Highlands were already over-populated and many inhabitants were forced to emi-grate to Canada, North America and Australia.

THE CLEARANCES

However, the clansmen's rights did not become an issue until they were served with eviction papers by the factors, or tacksmen, now managing the estates for the chiefs and nobles. Instructed to find other lands on the foreshore for the clansmen, the tacksmen dealt ruthlessly with any opposition and called in the law or government troops if evicted tenants refused to leave.

Despite reports in the London newspapers of the horrors of eviction, it was to be nearly a century before Gladstone ordered an investigation. Public ignorance was easily fostered; the isolation and inac-cessibility of the Highlands hid many ruthless actions.

The first wave of clearances spread steadily across Scotland from 1772 to 1820. General Stewart said of the persecution:

No one who knows anything of human nature need be told that there exists a strong propensity in the minds of those who oppress others by an undue exercise of power, to justify that proceeding to themselves by exaggerating every provocation from the objects of their hostility, including the fact that the creature dares to be different; and then they don't care for the vermin, or for its possible claim to human rights.

This first wave culminated with the notorious Sutherland Clearances, when the evicted tenants were burned out of their houses without mercy. They were savagely pushed into vacant areas along the coast and

left to their own devices to establish crofter-fisher communities on the bare shoreline.

Sir Alexander MacKenzie wrote in 1881 of the Highland Clearances:

What was generally true of the Highlands was in Sutherland carried to the greatest extreme . . . The inhabitants were literally burnt out and every contrivance and ingenious and unrelenting cruelty was eagerly adopted for extirpating the race. South country men from England were introduced and the land given over to them over the heads of the native tenantry. These strangers were made justices of the peace and armed with all sorts of authority in the country, and were thus enabled to act in the most harsh and tyrannical fashion, none making them afraid. While the oppressed natives were placed completely at their mercy.

Far left and left: *clan shields from* Vestiarium Scoticum *(1842), possibly based on a sixteenth-century manuscript*

The second continuous wave of clearances, from 1820 to 1885, was fuelled by the downturn in the demand for cattle and kelp, and the potato famine of 1846. The tacksmen served notices of eviction in Skye, the Western Isles and most parts of the Highlands, forcing tenants from their homes in ever-increasing numbers, with or without their livestock. When the crofters resisted, the authorities shamelessly burned down their homes. This occurred in Braes and Glendale in Skye, the Park and Lochs in Lewis, and all over Arran and Mull.

The Strath of Glenclavie Clearances

In the Strath of Glenclavie by Ardgay, Sutherland, where the land was divided into two estates, hitherto unknown restrictions were being imposed upon the tenants. The first eviction orders were instigated there in 1815. No longer were the remaining tenants allowed to hunt deer, kill pheasants, or fish for salmon to supplement their meagre diet, nor were they permitted to gather broken branches from the forest floor to maintain their ditches or animal enclosures, which had been a long established part of the shared system within the clans. Instead, the lands were rented out to shooting parties and sheep farmers.

Thirty years after these notorious first evictions, the tacksmen arranged a meeting with the remaining Glenclavie tenants in the church hall at Ardgay, by Bonar Bridge. The tenants, unaware of the reason for the meeting, entered the hall, were handed their eviction orders and told they would be compensated for their livestock only if they went quietly. They were given nowhere else to go.

The last of the tenants in the Strath of Glenclavie gathered in the leeway of the east window of the Croick Church awaiting their compensation. The evicted tenants scratched their names on the panes of

Left: *the east window of Croick Church, where evicted tenants scratched their names*
Above: *a memorial to the evicted tenants of Park*
Right: A Highlander *by Willem Hermanus Koekkoek (1867–1929)*

the east window, a poignant reminder of the hardships and uncertainties of the times. To the west of the church lie the ruins of a Pictish broch, a testimony to the ancient lineage of the people.

The Clearance of the Highlanders of Glenclavie was reported in *The Times* on 2 June 1845, which stated that 18 families were removed from their homes, numbering 92 people in all:

These poor Highlanders, however, apart from their naturally mild and passive natures have been so broken in spirit by many such scenes, that not a murmur, not a remonstrance escaped them in the completion of this heartless wholesale ejection.

Further reports referred to the early days of evictions:

250 persons were seated Gaelic fashion on the hillside in a semicircle facing officials, the women neatly dressed in net caps, wearing scarlet plaid shawls, the men wearing their blue bonnets and having their shepherd plaids wrapped around them, listening to the demands made of them by the factors, when the first evictions were made from the 250 persons.

Clearances in the Western Isles

On the road from Stornoway to Harris, by Loch Seaforth, stands a prominent memorial. By the gate leading to the monument is a plaque which describes an event that took place as a result of the evictions of 30 villages. The wording of the plaque is as follows:

November 1887, to the people of the Lochs who challenged the authority of the State, in order to focus people's attention on the poverty and injustice they suffered under the oppression of heartless landlords who dispossessed their forebears from over 30 villages in Park. Their inspiration was Donald MacRae, schoolmaster at Balallai, who committed his life to the Highland Land Laws Reform movements, and to the emancipation of the oppressed crofters and landless cottars over a long period.

Lady Matheson, the proprietrix of Lewis, ignored numerous pleas from landless families throughout Lochs for permission to return to some of the former villages in Park from which their forefathers had been evicted. Instead she converted the former 42,000-acre (16,800-hectare) Park Sheep Farm into a sporting deer forest in 1886.

On 22 November 1887, crofters and cottars from Lochs, having made their intentions public, marched into the Park deer forest, led by pipers carrying flags. They confronted Mrs Platt, the lessee, and her gamekeeper at Seaforth Head and continued into the forest. The authorities acted quickly, sending a detachment of the Royal Scots and some naval ships carrying marines to deal with the trespassers.

The raiders made their camp at Avridh Dhomhnoall Chairm by the shores of Loch Seaforth where they assuaged their hunger on large quantities of roasted and boiled venison.

Sheriff Fraser read the riot act at Raadh Chleit, explaining its significance in Gaelic. By this time the raiders felt that they had made their point and began to disperse. Six leaders were committed to trial in the High Court, Edinburgh. In January 1888 they were all acquitted of charges of mobbing, rioting and breaking the law of trespass.

Clearances on Skye

On Skye, the Napier Commission reported that, between 1840 and 1883, decrees of eviction against crofters involved thousands of people. At that time, there appeared to be a combined activity against the crofters by the landlords, police, sheriffs and officers of the established Church.

The *Glasgow Herald* of 9 February, 1883 reported:

To accelerate the departure of the doomed natives the heath pastures were set fire to and burnt. The act deprived the cattle of their only subsistence, heather and young grass during the spring months prior to the May term. The animals by this means were starved, lost or sold for a mere trifle (usually to the landlord's factor) . . . the houses were pulled down over the heads of the old people, the women, the children and the infirm and set on fire! The people were thus left exposed to the elements, many dying from alarm, fatigue and the cold. The barns, kilns and mills (for storing, drying and grinding corn) were burnt, except what the factor was likely to require.

It has been said that in all the years of the Clearances there seems to have been no concerted effort made by the tenants to unite against such injustice. In fact, they did try many times to resist but were forcibly suppressed. The government overpowered them by sending gun boats and police to support the landlords and the ministers of the established Church.

One man on Skye made a stand: John MacPherson, the 'Skye Martyr'. On 21 February 1882 he was addressing a meeting in Glendale aimed at establishing a Land League to protect the tenants. MacPherson was within the grounds of the Free Church and spoke with permission from the minister, the Reverend MacRae. Nevertheless, the meeting was broken up by the police, who took four men into custody, charging them with disturbing the peace. They were found guilty at Edinburgh assizes and imprisoned for two months.

An article was published in the *Isle of Skye Data Atlas* of 1993 regarding an incident concerning clansmen in the Braes who were refused the right to continue to graze their stock on Ben Lee after their leases expired, despite agreeing to pay a generous rent increase. Instead, the grazing rights were passed to a farmer who had been employed by Lord MacDonald. In 1882 MacDonald placed eviction orders upon the leaders of the Braes incident, but the clansmen demanded that the orders be ignored. Fifty police arrived from Glasgow to join the ten already on Skye, quashing the insurrection and fighting with the tenants. Five men were arrested, charged and fined at Inverness Court. The government eventually had to send troops and a gunboat to the sea loch by the Braes to quell the disturbance.

THE ROYAL COMMISSION'S REPORT (1883)

The incidents at Glendale and the Braes prompted the government to set up a Royal Commission in 1883 to enquire into the clansmen's grievances.

Commissioners were appointed, one of whom was a great lover of Skye, Sheriff Alexander Nicholson, a Gaelic scholar from Husabost. The report appalled the public when it disclosed 'a shocking state of misery, of wrong doing, and patient long suffering of the tenants without parallel in the history of our country'.

As a result of the enquiry, the Crofters' Holding Act was passed in 1886, granting the crofters security of tenure, protection from eviction (except in cases of one year's rent arrears, assignment of tenancy, bankruptcy and other specific conditions), and the right to a fair rent determined by law. However, it sadly failed to address the rights of the cottars, or smaller tenants. This was followed in 1887 by the establishment of the Crofters' Commission, which was to administer the act. Ninety years later it was agreed that the crofters, if they so desired, could buy the land on which their homes were built.

The Clearances had been taking place for over 100 years. By the time the government finally acted, thousands of clansmen had already been forced to emigrate. Some crofters alive today in the Highlands still remember tales they have heard of the evictions of their great-grandparents and other relatives who lived during the Clearances.

In a speech delivered at Inverness on 18 September 1885, Joseph Chamberlain said:

The history of the Highland clearances is a black page in the account with private ownership in land and if it were to form a precedent, if there could be any precedent for wrong doing, if the sins of the fathers ought to be visited upon the children, we should have an excuse for more drastic legislation than any which the wildest reformer has ever proposed.

Enlightenment

In the period from the Union of the Crowns to the Union of the Parliaments, the Scottish nation underwent fundamental changes which led to great hardship, privation and frustration. Many Scots suffered because of situations they could not control, or paid the price for insurrections of which they were not part. After the first union, the absence of the monarch was keenly felt – Scotland was ruled from London, a distant place in what was, in essence, a foreign country. The second union removed the parliament too, depriving the Scots of another emblem of their nation's unity.

Divided loyalties continued to confuse many people who were uncertain whether to uphold the Jacobite or the Hanoverian cause, and many a bitter and hard-fought conflict resulted from doubts over the succession. The imposition of restrictions following the 'Forty-five rebellion further alienated many Scots and dealt more blows to the embattled identity of the nation; in particular, the Highlands were all but torn apart by social and political changes which emanated largely from London.

Yet despite everything Scotland had endured, in the second half of the eighteenth century came a spiritual awakening, a 'golden age' in the fields of science, philosophy, industry, culture and medicine; an age of the mind, of art, industry and invention. It was a time when Scotland began to reassert its identity through outstanding cultural achievement and several remarkable developments which were to be of world-wide significance. This period, the Enlightenment, or Age of Reason, was part of a wider cultural explosion taking place all over Europe.

The advances and attitudes of scientists like Newton and Locke, coupled with the wonders of the incipient industrial revolution, gave rise to a growing faith in the power of reason. Indeed, it was one of the central tenets of Enlightenment thought that there was no obstacle which could not be overcome through the faculty of reason. Innovation, progress and rationality became the touchstones of European culture and, for the first time, a conflict began to emerge between Christian and scientific views of the world – the first challenge to the ancient authority of the Church as guardian of truth.

The social and political events of Scotland's past gave a unique importance and a particularly deep resonance to the Scottish Enlightenment.

GEORGE I (1714–27)

Following the death of Queen Anne in 1714, George I of Hanover came to the throne. He had little or no interest in British affairs of state, preferring to spend most of his time in Hanover. This provided the opportunity for the Scots to take full advantage of the connections that English trading agreements had

Top left: The Reverend Robert Walker skating on Duddingston Loch *by Sir Henry Raeburn (1756–1823)*
Right: Edinburgh *by Louise Rayner (1832–1924)*

opened up. These included many areas of commerce, in particular with parts of North America, where a number of merchants took the opportunity to set up new enterprises.

Tobacco, sugar, rum, hardwoods, lemons and limes were shipped to the Clyde, and linen, tools, pottery, glassware, furniture and leather goods were exported to the Americas. By 1770 Glasgow had become so successful that it was importing more than half the tobacco that came into Britain and had been transformed into a large and prosperous city.

GEORGE II (1727–60)

George II succeeded his father in 1727, becoming King of Great Britain and Ireland, and Elector of Hanover. He took a far more active part in the affairs of state than his father, and by the end of his reign the economy of Great Britain had begun to show signs of improvement, with Scotland playing a significant part in this development.

Scottish soldiers and sailors played a prominent role too in military and naval triumphs, and were part of the British force commanded by George at the Battle of Dettingen in 1743 – the last time a British monarch would lead his troops at the scene of battle.

It was under the command of the Duke of Cumberland, George's second son, that the British army was sent into Scotland for the first time, to quell the Jacobite uprising of 1745. Highland soldiers who had previously enlisted in the British army as a means of livelihood had never suspected that they would have to fight their fellow countrymen in a civil war, but nevertheless, after the 'Forty-five, many more Highlanders were lured into service and were employed in helping to establish overseas colonies. Highland regiments were noted for their courage, honesty and loyalty.

Far left: a *Highland soldier in the army of George II*
Left: *George III in 1767*

George III, grandson of George II, became King of Great Britain and Ireland and Elector of Hanover in 1760, and King of Hanover in 1815. The first of the Hanoverian line to be a true native of the British Isles, he was fiercely proud of his nationality. In his first address to Parliament he proclaimed, 'Born and educated in this country I glory in the name of Briton', and indeed he never visited Hanover. His patriotism had a profound influence on his court and ensured that his long reign unified and stabilised Britain as a whole. He ruled Scotland in an era of considerable cultural upheaval, a time when the foundations of modern life were laid.

Farmer George

George III's hobby was agriculture, and this earned him the nickname of 'Farmer George'. He even built a model farm at Windsor and moved there permanently. His interest was apt for a period when widespread changes in farming were gathering momentum across Britain. Ancient methods, such as crofting and strip-farming, were being ousted by procedures which were to form the basis of many present-day farming techniques.

By the early eighteenth century there were more than a million people living in Scotland, and most subsisted by farming. However, some were slow to adopt the new methods until the inception, in 1723, of 'The Honourable Society of Improvers' which sought to modernise Scottish agriculture. William Mackintosh of Borlum, in prison for his part in the 'Fifteen rebellion, wrote about the need for agricultural improvement, and experiments were carried out in different areas of Scotland by landlords like John Cockburn of Ormiston and Sir Archibald Grant of Monymusk, near Aberdeen. Lands began to be enclosed (that is, formed into the fields that exist today), bogs were drained, lime was used to improve the soil, grasses and clovers were introduced, new crops were grown and vegetables such as the turnip revolutionised farming.

Some parts of Scotland showed opposition to the changes, particularly in the north-east, where crofters were ruthlessly dispossessed of their holdings. Throughout the country smallholdings began to be replaced by larger lots held by single tenants on longer leases. By 1760, the pace of change was quickening, with inventions like James Meikle's threshing machine, and the plough introduced by James Small, which could be pulled by a horse rather than an ox.

However, the desolation wreaked upon the Highlands after the rebellion of 1745, already described, meant that the Highlanders did not generally feel much benefit from agricultural innovation. Even so, by the end of the eighteenth century, farming in Scotland had reached undreamt of heights in terms of the volume of food produced, with the population, approaching two million, generally becoming much fitter and healthier as a result.

ASPECTS OF THE SCOTTISH ENLIGHTENMENT

'Here I stand at what is called the Cross of Edinburgh, and can, in a few minutes, take fifty men of genius by the hand'.

So wrote an English visitor to Edinburgh in 1769. No city in the world could boast so many great men living within its walls at the time – men who were to make profound and long-lasting contributions to modern thought, and whose work would have far-reaching effects on society: its politics, economics and culture. It was the standing of these men, together with the superb classical architecture of the New Town, which earned Edinburgh the title of 'Athens of the North'.

The vacuum of power created by the displacement of national government to London, and the many terrible acts carried out to suppress Jacobitism and tame the Highlanders had denigrated the Scots' identity. The stage was set for their resilient spirit to find a new outlet; this time it did so through the pen rather than the sword. The same vitality that had driven William Wallace and Robert the Bruce to win back Scotland many years before was now channelled into intellectual activity.

As well as many advances in science and medicine, the period also saw a change in ways of thinking, with more liberal thoughts about society being expressed, based on actual experience rather than previously accepted truths. The artistic and literary worlds reflected this change, with poetry and other writing shifting the emphasis away from a reliance on ancient dogma towards the promotion of experience and reason as the best guides through life, a parallel with the movement in scientific method towards empiricism.

The 'Athens of the North', Edinburgh from Calton Hill *by a follower of David Octavius Hill*

SCOTTISH EDUCATION

Until about the middle of the eighteenth century, the Scottish way of life had been determined by two parallel power structures: the feudal system and the Church. Yet, unlike the secular authorities, the Church had a benign contribution to make to Scottish life – the gift of education.

If the Church of Scotland had not demanded financial support from the lairds and chiefs in the early seventeenth century, there would have been little or no education for the Scottish people. The Church took full responsibility for organising the schools, the teachers and even the building process itself, using funds obtained from the nobility, who erected schools on their lands.

Before the advent of organised education, children had depended solely upon their parents if they were to learn to read and write. Parish churches became aware of the need for formal education as parents

unable to teach their children sought help. As a result of pressure from the Church, several Acts of Parliament were passed with the aim of addressing this important need.

The last act, passed in the Scottish Parliament in 1696, gave equal opportunities to children to attend school by forcing landowners, or heritors, to provide a schoolhouse and employ a schoolmaster at a salary of not less than £6 a year. This important act set the course for Scottish education and provided a basis for extended learning.

It was the pioneering efforts made by the Church, and their pupils' willingness to learn, which earned Scotland its reputation for good education and played an important part in producing the creative climate in which the Scottish Enlightenment was to flourish.

Parish schools

Throughout the eighteenth century the Scottish Church maintained its management of education and supervised the enforcement of the 1696 act. From the parish schools established as a result, many children went on to university education. By the end of the eighteenth century, students were rising from the most humble beginnings to make significant contributions to their country's culture.

In 1772, the Society for the Propagation of Christian Knowledge (SPCK) introduced schools to the Scottish Highlands and soon there were 159 of these establishments, offering both ordinary lessons and technical knowledge.

In the Lowlands, John Anderson (1726–96) introduced the first radical views on education and pioneered technical colleges. He devoted two days a week to help struggling students and left an endowment for their further education. This was to form the basis of the famous Andersonian Institute in Glasgow. This eventually merged with other educational establishments to become the University of Strathclyde, where there is still an Andersonian Library.

The loss of statehood following the Act of Union brought to the forefront of writers' minds the issue of how, or indeed whether, to maintain a distinctively Scottish voice within the United Kingdom. Some writers, such as Tobias Smollett and James Boswell, wrote in a language which cannot easily be distinguished from that of English writers, such as Henry Fielding or Samuel Johnson. Others, in particular the poets Robert Fergusson and Robert Burns, sought a form of expression which could speak with the vigour and sense of national identity of Scots vernacular. A third, almost underground grouping strove to keep alive the ancient Gaelic tongue, through its mainly oral, non-literary tradition.

Allan Ramsay (1685–1758)

Ramsay was a native of Leadhills in Lanarkshire, but is now remembered as an Edinburgh figure. A poet and bookseller, he made his shop into a gathering place for men of letters and he opened Britain's first lending library in Edinburgh in 1725. As a poet he wrote humorous and satiric verses, some in Scottish dialect. As an editor, Ramsay did much to preserve the heritage of Scotland's ancient poetry. He was highly regarded by the *cognoscenti* who gathered in Edinburgh to exchange ideas in the various elegant coffee houses, convivial salons and at the meeting-place of the Select Society. Ramsay's well known poem, 'The Gentle Shepherd', describes rural life in Scotland during the early eighteenth century and won him great acclaim. His son, also named Allan, became one of Britain's finest portrait painters.

Tobias Smollett (1721–71)

Smollett, who was born at Bonhill, Dunbartonshire, began his literary career early with *The Regicide*, a play based on James I's assassination, written in 1437. He left Scotland for London thinking that the English

would appreciate Scottish history, but they did not, and he could not find a sponsor for his work. Close to starving, Smollett took a job as a surgeon's mate aboard HMS *Cumberland*. In Jamaica, he married an English planter's daughter and then returned to London, where he concentrated on writing.

Much of Smollett's literary work is based on fact. His *Tears of Scotland*, for example, focuses on the butcheries of Culloden, and clearly expresses his hatred of cruelty. He also published novels (favourably compared with those of Henry Fielding), travel writing and a journal which he founded, *The Critical Review*. His last and probably best work was *The Expedition of Humphrey Clinker*; he learnt of its success just before his death.

James Boswell (1740–95)

Born in Edinburgh, Boswell is chiefly remembered for his friendship with Dr Samuel Johnson, author of the famous *Dictionary of the English Language* and many other works. They met in London in 1763 when, having with great reluctance qualified as a lawyer, Boswell was seeking to join a guards' regiment. Thus began a lifelong friendship which was regularly to draw Boswell away from his native land.

Johnson, no great lover of Scotland, was persuaded by Boswell in 1773 to take a journey through the Highlands and Hebrides to see the richness of the country and the many interesting historical sites. Johnson returned to England an enlightened man and recorded his impressions in *Journey to the Western Islands of Scotland* in 1775. Boswell also recounted his version of their adventures in his *Journal of a Tour to the Hebrides* of 1785, which provided an illuminating picture of the life and society of the Scottish people at the time of the Enlightenment.

Johnson died in 1784, and in 1791 Boswell immortalised him by publishing a biography, a work which had taken seven difficult years to complete. Boswell then tried to enter politics in northern England, with little success and, after the death of his wife in 1789, he returned to London, where he died six years later.

Robert Fergusson (1750–74)

Fergusson was born in Edinburgh and was educated at St Andrews University, where he began writing poetry. He later returned to Edinburgh, where he worked as a clerk whilst writing in his spare time, initially in English and later in Scottish dialect. His work exhibits a racy humour and contains streetwise descriptions – elements which greatly influenced Robert Burns – and his long and witty poem, 'Auld Reekie', captures intimacies of Edinburgh folk-life.

Fergusson battled against ill health, both physical and mental, following a fall down a flight of stairs, and was confined to an institution, where he eventually died. He was buried in a pauper's grave, but fifteen years later Robert Burns erected a memorial to his 'elder brother in muse'.

Carolina Oliphant, Baroness Nairne (1766–1845)

Carolina Oliphant lived amongst Edinburgh's aristocratic society at a time when it was considered inappropriate for ladies to become poets or writers.

Baroness Nairne published some of her work under the pseudonym, 'Mrs Bogan of Bogan'. However, she became famous for her unique Jacobite lyric, 'Will Ye No' Come Back Again', which later appeared under her own name. Other famous Scottish songs of hers include 'The Auld Hoose', 'The Land o' the Leal', 'John Tod' and 'Caller Herrin'' (the refrain of which was caught from the chimes of St Giles). Her father was a staunch Jacobite of the Oliphant family of Gask, near Perth, which no doubt fuelled the Jacobite sentiments of the laments. However, these transcend their political origins and convey strong, poignant feelings which still touch many people today.

TRADITIONAL MUSIC

Traditional Scottish music is a combination of different traditions, some Gaelic, similar to Irish forms, others from Nordic sources. The ancient forms have persisted for centuries, preserved in the Scottish Gaelic oral tradition, passed on from generation to generation. Favoured instruments include the clarsach, or Celtic harp, and fiddle, as well as the bagpipes.

The origin of the pipes is not clearly established, but they first appeared in the Highlands in the sixteenth century. It is quite natural that such a renowned aspect of Scottish tradition as the pipes formed part of the inspiration and enthusiasm associated with the Scottish Enlightenment, a time when Scottish identity re-asserted itself; bagpipes are the pride of Scotland. Pipes later evoked international interest when they accompanied the expansion of the British Empire. Pipe bands were attached to military forces in Scotland and they have played an important role in the history of all the Scottish regiments.

The Scottish Enlightenment saw the blending of Italian styles with traditional Scottish musical forms, made possible by the popularity of the violin in both countries. By the late eighteenth century, opposition to this trend grew steadily as it was seen as yet another compromise of Scottish identity.

Music has always been a very important part of the lives and activities of the Highlanders, with Gaelic singers still passing songs down from one generation to another. The present revival in Gaelic is demonstrated by the popularity of The Mod, a great Gaelic musical festival, held in Scotland every year and organised by *An Comunn Gaidhealach*.

Niel Gow (1727–1807)

Gow, one of the most famous Scottish fiddlers, was born in Dunkeld in 1727, the first of a great family of fiddlers. His family intended him to be a weaver, but he preferred to play the fiddle.

ROBERT BURNS (1759–96)

Robert Burns was born at Alloway in Ayrshire, the eldest son of a poor tenant farmer. Despite the poverty and hard physical labour he had to endure throughout much of his life, he managed to become an accomplished man of letters. He first learnt the power of words and rhythm from his mother,

who would sing the 'auld' songs of Scotland softly to her children at the close of day. As he grew he developed a facility to express the native Scottish genius for song and poetry to a degree which has been unsurpassed.

He published his first collection, *Poems, Chiefly in the Scottish Dialect*, at Kilmarnock in 1786 in an edition of just 612 copies. It met with considerable success in his native Ayrshire and also in Edinburgh, where he was read with enthusiasm by the élite of Edinburgh society.

He made his way to the capital to meet Dr Dalrymple of Orangefield, a friend, who gave him an introduction to the Earl of Glencairn, hence propelling Burns into the centre of Edinburgh's literary and social scene, where he created quite a stir as the 'ploughman poet'.

A Scottish bard

With the money he received from his first book, Burns embarked on a series of tours of Scotland, taking in many

areas new to him. The tours allowed him to visit places of historical interest, such as the battlefield of Bannockburn, which provided the inspiration for his patriotic poem 'Scots, Wha Hae'.

On his travels Burns met the traditional fiddler Niel Gow, and collected hundreds of folk songs. He was still reviving old Scottish songs and ballads and setting them down for posterity right up to his death in 1796, bequeathing a priceless collection of over 300, many of which might have been lost without his work.

Burns was one of the few Scottish poets to use his native dialect in songs and poems. In addition, he wrote many letters in compelling English to his family, friends and literary acquaintances. These are now considered to be prose masterpieces.

Burns was devoted to Scotland and its history, and many of his poems and songs were dedicated to its heritage and people. 'The Cotter's Saturday Night', 'My Father was a Farmer' and 'The Farewell' depict the life of the ordinary people of Scotland, whilst 'For a' That and a' That' boldly speaks up for the common man and clearly implies the need for a more just social order:

> *What though on hamely fare we dine,*
> *Wear hoddin grey, and a' that;*
> *Gie fools their silks, and knaves their wine,*
> *A man's a man for a' that:*
> *For a' that, and a' that,*
> *Their tinsel show, and a' that;*
> *The honest man, though e'er sae poor,*
> *Is king o' men for a' that.*

Friendship, love and humour

Burns placed great value on friendship and love. Sir Walter Scott said of Burns' famous love song, 'Ae Fond Kiss', that 'it was the essence of a thousand love tales'.

Much of Burns' genius lay in his expression of feelings through words that unfolded simple, yet profoundly affecting messages. This deep interest and affection for other people led him to study his own self. He shared his sentiments in a letter to Dr John Moore, written in August 1787, in which he stated, 'To know myself had been my constant study – I weighed myself alone; I balanced myself with others.' His views are also expressed in his poem 'To a Louse':

O wad some Pow'r the giftie gie us
To see oursels as others see us.

Burns' other satirical poems, such as 'The Twa Dogs' and 'Holy Willie's Prayer', show him to have been an enlightened man: unafraid of change, and ready to challenge hypocrisy.

After his Borders and Highland tours Burns returned to farming, and in 1788 married Jean Armour. The farm was not profitable and in 1789 he became an exciseman to supplement their meagre income. During this period he wrote his masterpiece, 'Tam o' Shanter'. It is the comic tale of a citizen of Ayr who encounters a coven of witches and warlocks dancing. Captivated by the short nightdress or 'cutty sark' of one of the witches, he cries out and is then pursued; only just managing to escape over a bridge which his devilish pursuers cannot cross. His mare Meg loses her tail.

His last years and lasting fame

In the last five years of his life Burns' health began to deteriorate due, it is thought, to a rheumatic heart condition. On 21 July 1796, as Burns' life drew to an end, he said to his wife, 'I will be better known a hundred years after my death than I ever have during my lifetime.' He was right – his works have been translated into many languages, and songs such as 'Comin' thro' the Rye' are still hugely popular. Likewise, Burns' song of parting, 'Auld Lang Syne', is sung at the end of festive occasions everywhere, particularly at Hogmanay.

Top left: *Burns by an unknown artist*
Far left: *the granddaughter and great-granddaughter of Burns beside his cottage in the centenary year, 1896*
Above: The Haggis Feast
by Alexander Fraser
Below: *Walter Scott, aged 15, meeting Robert Burns, painting by C.M. Hardie*

With help from Stewart of Grandtully and the Duke of Atholl, Niel Gow began a successful performing career, playing as far afield as London. His musical compositions were soon published, some being arrangements of old tunes. Sir Henry Raeburn painted his portrait, which can be seen in the National Portrait Gallery in Edinburgh.

When Robert Burns made his tour of the Scottish Highlands, he was able to call upon Gow at Dunkeld. Burns was an accomplished violinist himself, using the instrument to help him give solid form to half-forgotten Scottish songs. He reported in his letters that they had spent:

many a pleasant hour fashioning and fiddling together, bringing to life many vivid musical renderings of the ancient Scottish songs, including 'My Heart's in the Highlands'.

This last was composed whilst Burns was with Gow and was published in his Edinburgh book of poems.

PHILOSOPHY AND HISTORY

Perhaps the most profound changes of the Enlightenment came in the areas of philosophy and history – great revisions in the way men saw themselves and the society they lived in.

Edinburgh in the eighteenth century became a melting-pot of ideas, many of them radical and challenging, and a stimulating intellectual community evolved there which was based on the principles of co-operation and innovation.

People realised that a study of their own community could be immensely informative and helpful. This reflected, as in other areas, a movement towards empiricism, or first-hand experience, and the belief that through the experience of an enquiring mind and the discipline of reason, a higher standard of living could be attained.

Francis Hutcheson (1694–1746)

George Elder Davie, in *Edinburgh: the Age of Reason*, sees Francis Hutcheson as the father of the Scottish Enlightenment. Hutcheson was a native of Ulster of Scottish descent, who studied for the Church in Glasgow and was a successful preacher in Dublin. From 1729 he held the position of Professor of Moral Philosophy in Glasgow.

Davie points out that Hutcheson's advanced ideas on reason set a pattern for the Scots and helped them to meet the new circumstances which now linked them irrevocably to the English way of life. In 'An Address to the Gentlemen of Scotland', Hutcheson discusses the 'crisis of national existence':

in which the threat or reality of assimilation to England brought home to the Scots the value of their native inheritance of institutions, legal, ecclesiastical, educational.

He regarded the Scots' past as the most important and constant factor in their recovery, reflecting their true spirit, their long history of survival and the pride they had always shown in their country. He challenged the Scots to derive strength from their national character and meet the changes imposed on them head-on.

Both the Scottish Law Courts and the Church of Scotland managed to retain their independence, as Hutcheson recommended, remaining separate from the English administration, and both these institutions were stabilising influences on Scottish society. In addition, the united Parliament did not become involved with Scottish education until the middle of the nineteenth century. Even today, education north of the border retains a certain amount of independence.

David Hume (1711–76)

David Hume is perhaps the best known of the many eminent men of learning who lived in Scotland during the Enlightenment, seeking sense, order, purpose and direction in human experience and behaviour.

Hume entered Edinburgh University to read law, but spent much of his time absorbed in Latin literature. After graduating, he studied philosophy in France for a number of years. Expounding his beliefs in *A Treatise of Human Nature*, he introduced European thought to Scotland and approached reason and culture in an innovative and intelligent way.

Hume's ideas were perhaps too different for the times in which he lived – the *Treatise* was a failure, which disappointed him and prompted him to rewrite it under the title *An Enquiry Concerning Human Understanding*. He later turned to politics and produced the acclaimed *Political Discourses*, which prepared the way for the work of Adam Smith.

The strong views, dismissing religion and attacking other established institutions, which he expressed in the thesis *Dialogues Concerning Natural Religion*, were not well received and shocked many people. He was therefore refused a professorship, instead becoming librarian to the Advocates' Library in Edinburgh, which, to his delight, turned out to be one of the best reference libraries in Europe.

Hume's agnostic theories, including that 'cause and effect had no logical relationship but was merely associated with impressions and experiences', and his opinion that 'whilst mankind worked only from a surface level, the deeper understanding would always elude him', have continued to challenge minds ever since. His death created quite a stir, since 'dying peacefully' was not the end that people expected of such an irreligious philosopher.

Thomas Reid (1710–96)

Thomas Reid's *Inquiry into the Human Mind on the Principles of Common Sense* was one of the most popular works read by students of ethics, metaphysics and logic. It was written in reaction to Hume's *A Treatise of Human Nature*. Reid was appointed Professor of

Lord Monboddo in 1784 *by John Kay (1742–1826)*

Moral Philosophy at King's College, Aberdeen, and later, Doctor of Divinity.

As the founder of the 'Common Sense' school of philosophy, which spread to France, America and Britain, Reid influenced many generations. The name of the school refers to something that is part 'good sense' and part accepted world-view upon which people must necessarily rely (hence his opposition to the radical Hume).

James Burnett, Lord Monboddo (1714–99)

Burnett was a founder member of the Select Society, a debating club formed by a group of Edinburgh intellectuals, including Hume and Adam Smith, during the Enlightenment period. An advocate at only 23 and a Lord of Session in 1767, Burnett was well known for his eccentricity – perhaps because he made no attempt to lose his Scottish accent when he become a lawyer, much to the consternation of fellow advocates.

Burnett's great work, *Of the Origin and Progress of Language*, went further in its anthropological speculation than any philosopher had thus far attempted. Dealing with the remote ancestry of mankind through language connections, it touched on the theory of evolution and traced the ancestry of man to the orangutang. Many of his contemporaries scoffed at his ideas, their ridicule no doubt fuelled by his eccentricity. He also published a highly controversial six volumes, *Ancient Metaphysics,* which dealt with the harmony of science and philosophy.

Burnett was a close friend of James Boswell's father, and also enjoyed the company of Boswell himself and his companion, Dr Johnson. Robert Burns was also welcomed to his house.

William Robertson (1721–93)

William Robertson, besides being the leading historian of his day, was also a churchman of high repute. Through his influence, a certain stability and harmony was brought to the Church's activities, which in turn exerted an effect on the Scottish people. He became the Principal of Edinburgh University in 1762 and Moderator of the General Assembly in 1763.

Robertson's works include *The History of Scotland During the Reigns of Queen Mary and James VI*, as well as volumes on the reign of the Emperor Charles V and the history of America. His elegant writing style and impeccable character earned him a position of undisputed authority and greatly enhanced the prestige of history as a discipline.

Left: David Hume *by G.B. Bosio*
Above: Adam Smith *by Jackson*

Adam Ferguson (1723–1816)

Ferguson was born in Logierait, Perthshire. After gaining a degree in Divinity, he joined the 42nd Black Watch in 1745 as chaplain and fought in the Battle of Fontenoy, where he had to be restrained from plunging into the fray, brandishing a broadsword. A fluent Gaelic speaker, he was a true man of the people.

In 1778, he was appointed Commissioner to the American Colonies and became involved in the War of Independence. Through reading travellers' reports, Ferguson made the revealing discovery that the ancient Gaelic language had a strong affiliation with Red Indian languages and with Greek, and also shared similar philosophies.

His *Essay on the History of Civil Society* (1766) had a profound and far-reaching effect, rekindling interest in ancient Greece in Scotland and elsewhere. However, not surprisingly, his speculations on the fragmentation of society and the concept of alienation were not well received by the British Government. As a result of these radical ideas, Ferguson later came to be known by some as the 'father of sociology'.

Adam Smith (1723–90)

A great friend of David Hume, Smith expounded his philosophy through lectures on *The Theory of Moral Sentiments* whilst acting as Professor of Moral Philosophy at Glasgow University. In 1764 he became tutor to the young Duke of Buccleuch and his younger brother. They travelled extensively throughout Europe, meeting many eminent philosophers. Their journeys, however, were brought to an abrupt end when both brothers contracted a severe illness, resulting in the death of the youngest.

After returning to Scotland, Smith lived with his mother in Kirkcaldy, where he wrote the hugely successful, *An Enquiry into the Nature and Causes of the Wealth of the Nations*, published in 1776. This work presents a complete theory of society and explains how each individual, merely in following his own interests, unintentionally maximises the wealth of society as a whole. Smith's notions of the 'invisible hand' controlling this interplay of individual interest and market exchange by creating a 'natural price' opened up a new and important area of study – economics.

SCOTTISH LAW

In the eighteenth century, the law gradually began to evolve from an instrument of aristocratic power into the more democratic system of modern times. Scottish law, which is mainly based on Roman law, holds a special place among the world's legal systems and has many influences, including Dutch and French aspects. Over the last century it has also been influenced in some respects by English law, although the two systems remain essentially distinct.

Sir James Balfour of Pittendreich (1520–84) is regarded as the father of Scottish law and is the author of *A System of the More Ancient Laws of Scotland*. The Lockhart family, too, made a great contribution to Scottish law between 1600 and 1782, but Alexander Lockhart (1700–82) was unable to become a judge because he had defended Jacobite prisoners in 1746 at Carlisle.

One of the major changes in the administration of the law came in 1532 during the reign of James V, when the King established a College of Justice (Court of Sessions). Before that, the law had been administered by the Church, the barons, the Highland chiefs, the monarchy and, most importantly, the Privy Council. The establishment of the Court of Sessions in Edinburgh for appeal cases was a great improvement, but the Privy Council still remained the instrument of royal authority. It was not until 1672 that Charles II's Royal Commission introduced the High Court of Justiciary, a system of courts of law in which judicial power was vested.

The Privy Council was eventually abolished after the Union in 1707, when Scottish law remained unchanged due to a specific clause in the Treaty of Union preserving it. One refinement that was made meant that anyone in Scotland could apply to the House of Lords for another hearing if their case had failed in the Scottish courts.

William Murray, Lord Mansfield (1705–93)

Murray, son of the 5th Viscount Stormont Murray, was born in Scone, near Perth, on lands that James VI had granted to his loyal subject, David Murray of Gospettie in 1605. He attended Perth Grammar before leaving for London, where he studied at Westminster School. After gaining a degree at Oxford, he was called to the English Bar in 1730. Well travelled and familiar with many figures associated with the Scottish Enlightenment, Murray was also a close friend of Alexander Pope, the distinguished English poet.

Although Murray did not practise Scottish law, he was conversant with it, and defended the city of Edinburgh against the government when it tried to deprive the city of its civic rights over the Porteous Riots. He was successful, and the Bill of Pains and Penalties imposed on the city by the government was thus invalidated.

It is easy to see how the heritage of Scone as the site for the coronation of kings might have encouraged William to have sympathies with the Jacobites, but taunts from English rivals about his historic links with the cause did not stop him from prosecuting many of those who had taken part in the 'Forty-five.

As Attorney-General, his perfect English and gift for public speaking earned him the nickname 'Silver-tongued Murray'. One of his major talents was his ability to interpret and translate the highly complex commercial law. In 1756 he became the Lord Chief Justice of England and, in 1776, was awarded the title of 1st Earl of Mansfield. He was recognised for his judgements, which were impartial and expressed in strong forthright terms, often defying contradiction.

David Dalrymple, Lord Hailes (1726–92)

Dalrymple was born near Musselburgh and was the great-grandson of the 1st Viscount Stair. He was educated at Eton and Utrecht, becoming Lord of Session in 1776. A compassionate judge, he was learned in law and history, and noted for his humour and fairness. His great interest in history led him to befriend James Boswell and his companion Dr Johnson, who greatly admired him. Hailes himself wrote many biographical outlines, including *Memorials and Letters of James I and Charles I* and *Annals of Scotland*, and the unpublished records of his extensive researches into the early documents on the Royal House of Stuart are a valuable source, revealing much of interest that was hidden within the archives.

After his retirement from the bench, he was cared for by his devoted daughter, who became hostess at his many dinner parties. His sense of fun nearly cost his daughter dearly. On his death there appeared to be no will and, in consequence, his extensive estate in Musselburgh and his town house in Edinburgh were prepared by his solicitors to be assigned to a remote relative. By some lucky chance, when his daughter was preparing to leave her home forever, her father's lost will fell to the floor from behind a window shutter; he had in fact left everything to her and she enjoyed her heritage for forty years.

Deacon Brodie (d. 1788)

Deacon William Brodie, doyen of the double life, was a greatly respected member of Edinburgh's society during the day, and the leader of a gang of burglars by night, an activity he pursued in order to finance his gambling habit.

Brodie was a town councillor of Edinburgh, as well as deacon (or head) of the Incorporation of Wrights and Masons. Part of his day job was fashioning bolts, locks and bars for the purpose of keeping burglars out; he also secretly prepared for his night activities by making skeleton keys and crowbars to let

PORTEOUS RIOTS

In 1736, Edinburgh was shaken by a great public insurrection - the Porteous Riots, when mob rule erupted and overcame the whims of the rich and powerful.

John Porteous, Captain of the Town Guard, had a reputation in Edinburgh as a profligate and a drunkard. He was detested by the poor because he sided with the affluent and influential.

Andrew Wilson, an Edinburgh merchant and a well-known smuggler, had been convicted of robbing a Customs House, and had been sentenced to death.

It was generally felt that Wilson's sentence was unfair. The crowd had some sympathy for smugglers, no doubt because some of them benefited from the illicit trade.

The Lord Provost, who feared trouble, had ordered the Welch Fusiliers to be present at the execution of Wilson's sentence, and Porteous took this to be an affront to his capabilities as captain.

During the hanging the crowd's mood was subdued, but the people broke into a great roar of anger when they saw Wilson's body swinging from the gibbet. A burly ringleader rushed forward to cut the corpse down, whereupon Captain Porteous snatched a musket from a guard and shot the man dead.

Pandemonium broke loose as the crowd's pent-up feelings exploded into a riot. They hurled stones at the guards, badly injuring several people.

Panicking, Porteous ordered his men to fire on the crowd, killing and wounding a large number. This increased the crowd's anger, and the hostile mass closed in threateningly. The town guard fired again, killing more people, but began to retreat. Under orders from Porteous they fired over the heads of the crowd as they climbed up the West Bow towards the castle.

Unfortunately, the fire fell on several citizens who were watching from windows overlooking the street, and four distinguished members of Edinburgh's high society were killed. In all 30 people were either killed or seriously wounded.

The scapegoat

Someone had to take responsibility for the atrocity, and, ironically, Captain Porteous, who had always been on the side of the rich and powerful, was now made their scapegoat. He was arrested, brought to trial for murder, and sentenced to death. The date of execution was fixed for 8 September.

George II, the reigning monarch, was away on the continent, but his regent, Queen Caroline, showed sympathy to the captain, who pleaded for mercy from his gaol. The case was duly suspended for six weeks whilst a pardon was prepared.

Hearing of the postponement of the sentence as they gathered in the Grassmarket to witness the execution, the crowd became infuriated and decided to seek vengeance. They stormed the Tolbooth in the High Street where Porteous had been

Captain Porteous lynched by the mob

imprisoned, grabbed him and marched him, screaming for mercy, to the Grassmarket, where they hanged him from a dyer's pole.

Despite a thorough investigation, it was never discovered who the ringleaders of the riots and lynching were, but many historians have supported the suggestion that such an efficient, if ruthless, affair could not have been completely spontaneous.

Some say that the feelings of the Scottish people were still running high over the Union of the Parliaments, and that the Porteous Riots allowed them to give vent to their frustration. The events of 1736 were later used by Sir Walter Scott in *The Heart of Midlothian* (1818).

Deacon Brodie in 1788 *by John Kay*

active support for the revolution in Great Britain, and Braxfield had something of a reputation for harshness towards revolutionary sympathisers.

The trial commenced on 27 August 1788. Except for the king's evidence, there was very little to incriminate Brodie until a search of his house revealed his burgling equipment and sealed his fate. After Braxfield had addressed the jury for one and a half hours, they retired and considered the verdict. Brown was released on insufficient evidence, but Brodie and Smith were found guilty and their execution was fixed for 1 October 1788.

Ironically, Brodie had recently redesigned the gibbet which was to be used at his execution. When the time came, he drew the attention of everyone, including the executioner, to his design, stating stoically that the gallows upon which he was about to die was the most efficient of its kind in existence, and, as he stood proudly beside Smith to meet his fate, he patted him on the shoulder and smiled.

The bizarre life of Deacon Brodie is said to have formed the basis for Robert Louis Stevenson's famous story of a split personality, *The Strange Case of Dr Jekyll and Mr Hyde*.

ADVANCES IN MEDICINE

The sixteenth, seventeenth and eighteenth centuries witnessed great advances in the field of medicine. Research was carried out into many aspects of anatomy, such as blood circulation, infection, the workings of muscles, digestion and the nervous system. Crucially, the importance of hygiene was beginning to be realised, and inoculation against disease was introduced during the eighteenth century. The direct link between nutrition and health was also comprehended, helping to stamp out diseases like scurvy, which occurred as a result of a poor diet.

burglars in. He had three accomplices in crime, namely Brown, Smith and Ainslie.

Brodie's downfall was the attempted burglary of His Majesty's Excise Office for Scotland in Chessrel's Court, off the Canongate, which he himself had planned. Things went disastrously wrong when Ainslie was caught and promptly turned king's evidence on his partners in crime. Brodie fled to Holland but was arrested in Amsterdam and returned to Edinburgh for trial.

The scandalous case was presided over by Lord Braxfield, nicknamed the 'Hanging Judge'. The events took place at a time when feelings were running high in Scotland in support of the new spirit of equality generated by the French Revolution. Government troops were being used to quell any

THE EDINBURGH ROYAL BOTANIC GARDEN

Present-day pharmacology has its origins in the study of plants for medicinal purposes. Man is known to have made use of plants to heal and cure from a very early period. Their use has often been associated with supernatural beliefs, such as the 'doctrine of signatures', where a plant's physical nature – its colour, shape and size – were read as clues to its use, placed there by a divine power. The walnut for example, was thought to resemble the brain, and was therefore used to treat wounds to the head, while the seeds of the pine cone were thought to ease toothache.

By the seventeenth century, herbalists such as Nicholas Culpeper were beginning to distinguish between what was merely superstition and what could be proved by observation to be effective. Medical institutions established physic gardens to provide a ready source of botanical materials for their treatments.

Physic Garden

The origins of Edinburgh's Royal Botanic Garden are to be found in the Physic Garden established in 1670 by two Scottish doctors, Andrew Balfour and Robert Sibbald. It started with a small patch of land no bigger than a tennis court at St Anne's Yard, near Holyrood. In 1676 more land was leased from the town council, east of the Nor' Loch and Trinity College, which was part of the Trinity Hospital Garden. The garden was

eventually placed under the care of James Sutherland, who received the Royal Warrant as the King's Botanist.

In 1763 these gardens were abandoned in favour of the 5 acres (2 hectares) of land called the Leith Walk Garden and all the plants were carefully transported there. Between 1820 and 1823, a new and magnificent garden was established in Inverleith Row under the direction of Robert Graham. In 1888 the Botanic Garden came under the control of the Crown.

Botanic research

With the advance of medicine and the manufacture of drugs on a more industrial scale, physic gardens have generally changed into botanic gardens. Those in Edinburgh and Kew have, however, retained their primary importance as botanical research institutions. This has been made possible by the international collections of living and preserved plants which form the core of the gardens' research into the classification and evolution of

plants and fungi. It has taken more than 300 years to build up this unique living collection.

The gardens today

The layout of the Royal Botanic Garden is superb, with many beautiful trees shading the walkways leading to different parts of the grounds, including the nine hot-houses, which exhibit many rare and exotic plants. The famous Rock Garden, with its paths and small waterfalls, also supports many uncommon specimens. The garden extends to 76.6 acres (about 31 hectares) and is the second oldest in Great Britain.

During the second half of the twentieth century a further three specialist gardens were acquired: Logan Botanic Garden near Stranraer, Younger Botanic Garden at Benmore near Dunoon, and the Dawyck Botanic Garden near Peebles.

Above: *one of the two original palmhouses*

BODY-SNATCHING

By the end of the eighteenth century, 400 of the 1,100 students at the University of Edinburgh were studying medicine. This establishment had become the most important medical school in the world.

The increased numbers of students of anatomy meant a much greater demand for human bodies for them to dissect. However, the law had not changed since the charter of 1505, which allowed only one corpse for dissection each year.

The escalating need for bodies gave rise to body-snatching, in which freshly buried corpses were dug up and sold to medical students and departments of anatomy by criminals known as 'resurrectionists'.

Burke and Hare

One enterprising pair decided to ensure they had a regular source of bodies. Rather than wait for nature to take its course, then run the risk of discovery whilst robbing the grave, they decided to short-cut the procedure by murder. Their names have entered the mythology of crime.

William Burke and William Hare came originally from Ulster to work as navvies on the Union Canal. Seeing that easier money could be had by providing corpses, they developed a way of suffocating their victims which left no trace of violence. They are believed to have murdered 16 people in this manner before they were arrested in 1827, along with Burke's mistress and Hare's wife. When they were caught there was insufficient evidence to bring them to trial unless one of them turned king's evidence. This Hare did, sending the unfortunate Burke to a public and very popular execution on the gallows on 28 January 1828.

Dr Robert Knox

After the execution a committee was set up to investigate the role of Dr Robert Knox in the affair. Knox was an eminent Edinburgh citizen

and a Fellow of the Royal College of Surgeons. He was also one of Burke and Hare's best customers for corpses.

The committee concluded that while Knox had not been directly involved in the murders, he had most probably turned a blind eye. As a consequence of the investigation, Parliament passed the Anatomy Act of 1832, which set down rules for the supply of bodies to medical schools.

Dr Knox found himself extremely unpopular in Edinburgh after the inquiry, and moved first to Glasgow and then London, where he continued a successful medical career.

Although Hare was thought to have been the mastermind behind the pair's murderous activities, his reward for betraying his partner was freedom. He fled the mob and moved to London, where he is believed to have died a pauper in the 1860s.

Top left: 'resurrectionists' going about their grisly work
Left: Burke and Hare
Above: Dr Robert Knox

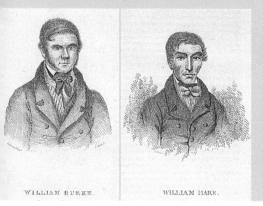

WILLIAM BURKE.   WILLIAM HARE.

In the nineteenth century, further significant progress was made when the part played by bacteria in disease was discovered. In Scotland, however, doctors were slow to adapt to changes. It was not until the reign of George I that these medical advances were practised – but they were so important that Scotland soon became the world centre of medicine.

The Monros

In 1575, a Dutch physician founded a medical school within the University of Leiden in Holland. By the eighteenth century the Dutch medical school had become world famous. A number of leading Scottish doctors studied there, including Archibald Pitcairne (1652–1713), who was made Professor of Medicine and later became one of the founders of the College of Physicians in Edinburgh, and John Monro (1670–1740), then a surgeon with King William's army, who had noticed the need for improvements in medical treatment.

Much impressed by what he had seen at the medical school in Leiden, Monro dreamt of establishing a similar school in Edinburgh. On his return to Scotland, he struggled persistently to inaugurate a medical faculty at the University of Edinburgh and was finally successful. He later became known as the 'Father of Edinburgh's Medical School'.

His son, Alexander, later known as Primus, since he was the first of three generations of Monros to be professors of anatomy in Edinburgh, helped his father to raise sufficient money by subscription to fund a site for a hospital. One was eventually found, at the head of Robertson's Close, and on 6 August 1729 the first hospital in Scotland was opened, with six beds for patients who were cared for by one matron and an assistant. John Monro's dream of a medical school and hospital had at last materialised. In 1737 a Royal Charter was granted for the building of a larger hospital, and in due course this small hospital became the Royal Infirmary of Edinburgh.

GEORGIAN ARCHITECTURE

The Scottish Enlightenment brought significant changes in architecture, and many fine buildings that resulted are preserved to this day. Georgian architecture, stressing regularity, simplicity and symmetry, revived aspects of Gothic and Greek styles, among others, to create a very formal style, often ornamented by classical devices such as pillars.

Many new towns and villages were established throughout Scotland, sometimes as a result of expansion in industries such as fishing or weaving. They often bore the hallmark of Georgian design in their uniform layout, which was usually in a grid pattern. The finest example of Georgian architecture and town-planning is Edinburgh's New Town, the largest Georgian development in Britain.

Edinburgh New Town

The transformation in Scottish cultural life was mirrored by the foundation of the New Town, built during the reign of George III, and one of the outstanding Scottish achievements of the late eighteenth and early nineteenth centuries.

The population of Edinburgh doubled in the first half of the eighteenth century, and inhabitants were crowded within the city walls, their proximity and lack of sanitation creating an environment where disease flourished. When space ran out at street level, building continued vertically, with houses of up to 13 storeys being constructed. Inside the tenements, the attics and basements were home to the poor, on the ground floor were the shops, and in between resided the lawyers, merchants, doctors and nobles.

The Edinburgh Town Council was slow to act on the problems of housing shortage and the dangers of disease, although there had been plans for an expansion of the city back in the 1680s. It was George Drummond, six times Lord Provost, who at last addressed the situation. In 1767, the council obtained

an act extending the royalty of the city to the north side. Along the steep bank on the north side of the Nor' Loch, which lay below the castle, was a straight road which ran between two field walls, called Lang Dykes. South of the walls were productive farmlands and market gardens. The New Town was planned to lie on the ridge running parallel to the castle.

The ancient Nor' Loch had to be drained. The next step was to build a bridge across the area of the Nor' Loch to the north, later to become the North Bridge. The bridge gave access to the Port of Leith, allowing the city to expand northwards.

In 1767 a competition, set up by the Town Council to find the best plan for the New Town, was won by James Craig, an unknown architect of 22. The first New Town extended as far as Queen Street and was essentially Craig's design, comprising two squares joined by the central avenue of George Street, between the single-sided terraces of Princes Street and Queen Street. To the west was Charlotte Square and, to the east, St Andrew Square.

The main streets were crossed by others arranged in a grid pattern, giving the plan its formal symmetry. The council kept the planners under strict discipline, laying down rigid rules for the width of the streets as well as for the design of houses. It had first been necessary to obtain permission from George III before the plans could be executed and he later stamped his approval on the project by naming the main streets George Street and Princes Street, after his sons.

Problems arose, however, over plans for developing Princes Street when the occupants on the north side realised that the south side was being offered in plots on the open market. They raised an action of interdiction against the Town Council, horrified by the thought of buildings blocking their view of the castle and gardens.

In the end the Scottish courts decided against them, but an appeal was carried to the House of Lords, where the judgement was reversed. At the time the case came up in the House of Lords, Lord Mansfield, son of the 5th Viscount of Scone, Perthshire, was the Lord Chief Justice of England. The appeal case came before him 'not only on the plain and open principles of justice, but from regard to the public, and from regard to that misguided Corporation' and this was the basis of his verdict in supporting the appeal.

Several more schemes extended the New Town: Playfair's plan included Leith in the neighbourhood of Calton Hill; Reid and Sibbald's laid the incline from Queen Street to the Water of Leith; Raeburn's plan was a community development around Stockbridge; and finally there was the Earl of Moray's development of Drumsheugh.

The building of the New Town was a time of great activity which gave many people employment. The combined efforts of these many gifted tradesmen and craftsmen created the fine collection of elegant and graceful Georgian town houses which still stand in Edinburgh today.

WILLIAM AND ROBERT ADAM

The history of architecture in Scotland in the eighteenth century is dominated by one family, the Adams. William Adam (1684–1748) was the son of a builder, whose business he inherited and turned into the largest construction firm in Scotland. He was Scotland's leading architect of the first half of the eighteenth century, and held important official positions which enabled him to obtain contracts for the military fortifications ordered after the 'Forty-five rebellion.

William Adam's company played an important part in the reconstruction of Hopetoun House, the magnificent Georgian house in South Queensferry, originally built in 1702 to a design by Sir William Bruce. In 1721 the owner, Sir Charles Hope, Earl of Hopetoun, decided he needed a grander home befitting his noble status. William Adam carried out the commission with the later help of two of his sons, James and Robert.

Robert Adam

William Adam had four sons, John, James, Robert and William, all of whom were builders and architects. It was Robert Adam (1728–92), however, who achieved the greatest fame, outdoing even his father.

Born in Kirkcaldy in Fife, Robert was educated in Edinburgh, where he associated with such great figures of the Scottish Enlightenment as Adam Smith and David Hume.

In 1745 Robert Adam joined the family firm, and in 1758 established

his own London practice. Stylistically, he differed from his father, favouring the use of architectural ornamentation based on classical designs which he had studied first-hand in Rome.

Adam made major advances in interior design, and his distinctive style influenced architects not only in England but in Europe as well. His fame grew quickly, and between 1760 and 1780 he was the most sought-after architect in England. However, his last great venture in London, the Adelphi development on the north the bank of the River Thames, proved to be a financial disaster.

Returning to Scotland, Robert Adam opened a practice with his three gifted sons and in 1771 designed the first purpose-built depository of national archives, Register House, at the east end of Princes Street.

Ever since the thirteenth century, a servant of the Scottish Crown had been appointed to safeguard and maintain the public records and it became imperative for a proper building to house the ever-increasing number of important documents. Register House proved to be the first of its

kind in the British Isles. The extraordinary central dome, 76ft (23m) high with a striking plasterwork ceiling, is most impressive. The formidable bronze equestrian statue of the Duke of Wellington outside the main building was sculpted by Sir John Steel and unveiled in 1852.

Adam also redesigned the famous Culzean Castle in three stages between 1777 and 1792, including the fine staircase. He died in 1792 while engaged in designing the buildings on the north side of Charlotte Square.

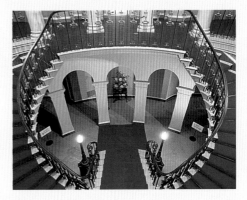

Top: *Culzean Castle, redesigned by Robert Adam between 1777 and 1792*
Above: *the castle's fine staircase*

IMPRESSIONS OF EDINBURGH

Dr Johnson thought Edinburgh 'a city too well known to admit description'. Fortunately other writers were more forthcoming. A common theme in their impressions was the contrast between the grandeur of the city and the insanitary condition of its streets and dwellings. In 1798 the Reverend Sydney Smith wrote of Edinburgh:

No smells were ever to equal Scotch smells . . . Yet the place is uncommonly beautiful, and I am in a constant balance between admiration and trepidation –

> *Taste guides the eye,*
> *where'er new beauties spread*
> *With prudence whispers,*
> *'Look before you tread'.*

Bad smells were not the only health problem. Plague had broken out on three occasions in the sixteenth century, and despite measures by the town council to convey fresh water to wells in the old town, matters were sufficiently dire by 1629 for the Privy Council to try to 'enforce some degree of decency and cleanliness'. It was singularly ineffective.

In 1636 Sir William Brereton, who travelled extensively in the British Isles and on the Continent, and was later to become a commander of the Parliamentary army, was both impressed by the 'glory and beauty of this city', and shocked by its inhabitants, whom he found to be a 'most sluttish, nasty and slothful people'.

In 1645 plague again erupted. Gradually, various measures were put in place to improve matters, such as the introduction of piped water in 1675, and an Act of Parliament to enforce street cleansing in 1686.

But there was still much that was deplorable. Daniel Defoe in *Tours through the Whole Island of Great Britain* (1724-7) commented on the appallingly cramped conditions of the dwellings. Many buildings were also unsound. In 1752 a six-storey building collapsed, provoking an anonymous writer to compose a pamphlet which attacked the state of the old town:

The narrow lanes leading to the north and south, by reason of their steepness, narrowness, and dirtiness, can only be considered as so many unavoidable nuisances. Confined by the small compass of the walls, and the narrow limits of the royalty, which scarcely extends beyond the walls, the houses stand more crowded than in any other town in Europe, and are built to a height that is almost incredible.

In contrast to the overcrowding inside the houses, many had extensive gardens; a charming feature which was to become rarer as these were sacrificed to accommodate the expanding population in ever more closely packed buildings.

However, above all else it was the foul state of the streets which seems to have made the worst impression. In his *Journal of a Tour to the Hebrides* (1785) James Boswell described how he escorted Dr Johnson through the streets one dark evening, finding himself embarrassed, as a representative of the city, by the stench which assailed them:

A zealous Scotsman would have wished Mr Johnson to be without one of his five senses upon this occasion. As we marched slowly along he grumbled in my ear, 'I smell you in the dark!'

The cause was the lack of adequate public sewers, and the citizens' habit of emptying the contents of their slop-pails (what Robert Fergusson in his satirical poem 'Auld Reekie' called 'Edina's roses') out of their windows each evening, with the cry 'Gardyloo!' to warn passers-by. Although the burgh employed people to remove the offending matter before daybreak, visitor Edward Topham, in his *Letters from Edinburgh* (1776) wrote that the smells disturbed his sleep:

I cannot help observing the intolerable stench that is produced at this season of the night on the moving of the tub of nastiness from each floor. Such a concatenation of smells I never before was sensible of; it has been sometimes so powerful as to wake me, and prevent my sleeping until it was somewhat pacified.

The situation was also satirised by Tobias Smollett in his picaresque novel *Humphrey Clinker* (1771), where a character believes the smell might actually be wholesome, for it 'took me by the nose so powerfully that I sneezed three times, and found myself wonderfully refreshed'.

93

Edinburgh citizens inspecting their newly paved streets in 1785 *by John Kay*

Despite the squalor, visitors to the 'Athens of the North' were genuinely impressed by the appearance of the city. Defoe described the High Street as the 'largest, longest and finest Street for Buildings and Number of Inhabitants, not in Britain only, but in the World'. Even Dr Johnson, according to Boswell, 'acknowledged that the breadth of the streets, and the loftiness of the buildings on each side, made a noble appearance'; while the naturalist, Thomas Pennant, wrote in his *Tour of Scotland* (1771) that Edinburgh 'possesses a boldness and grandeur of situation beyond any that I have seen'.

It was not only the buildings which aroused admiration. The Reverend Sydney Smith wrote, in his characteristically risqué manner:

I like this place extremely. It unites good libraries liberally managed, learned men without any system than that of pursuing truth; very good general society; large healthy virgins, with mild pleasing countenances, and white swelling breasts.

Another, more genteel observation of Scottish womenfolk has been left by lawyer Henry Cockburn in his description of a lady of Inverleith:

Nobody could sit down like the lady of Inverleith. She would sail like a ship from Tarshish, gorgeous in velvet or rustling in silk, and done up in all the accompaniments of fan, earrings and finger-rings, falling sleeves, scent-bottle, embroidered bag, hoop, and train – all superb, yet all in purest taste; and managing all this heavy rigging with as much ease as a full-blown swan does its plumage, she would take possession of the centre of a huge sofa, and at the same moment, without the slightest visible exertion, would cover the whole of it with her bravery, the graceful folds seeming to lay themselves over it like waves.

The house of Sir Lawrence Dundas

One of the most interesting *feus* (sites for development) in St Andrew Square, originally intended for the construction of St Andrew's Church, was quickly bought by Sir Lawrence Dundas, who had accumulated an immense fortune as Commissary-General to the army. Sir Lawrence built his house well back from St Andrew Square, and this unique departure from James Craig's master-plan was an undoubted success. Built of Ravelston stone brought from the outskirts of Edinburgh, the house was designed by Sir William Chambers, whose genius lay in his sensitive and scholarly selection of the best sources from ancient Rome.

Sir Lawrence died in 1781, and from 1788 Dundas House was used as the principal office of the Excise of Scotland. In 1828 it became the head office of the Royal Bank of Scotland. The magnificent monument to the Earl of Hopetoun by the sculptor Thomas Campbell, with an inscription by Sir Walter Scott, was planned in 1824 and erected in the forecourt of Dundas House ten years later. The royal coat of arms in the pediment dates from this time.

Above: *Dundas House, in St Andrew Square in Edinburgh*
Right: The Artist's Wife *by Allan Ramsay*

Alongside the architectural heritage bequeathed by the Scottish Enlightenment must be placed the great paintings of the age: the portraits of Allan Ramsay and Sir Henry Raeburn, and the landscapes of Alexander Nasmyth. Their paintings, and those of their fellow artists, adorned the elegant, neo-classical homes of Edinburgh's prosperous citizens, allowing them to make a living without moving to London.

Allan Ramsay (1713–84)

Allan Ramsay was the first great Scottish painter. Born in Edinburgh, he was the eldest child of the poet Allan Ramsay, and showed a prodigious talent for drawing from an early age. After an apprenticeship in London, and helped by his father's fame, he began to build a reputation as a portraitist among Edinburgh's fashionable society. A few years later he visited Italy to study Italian portraiture, and returned to Britain with a delicate, informal style.

Left: Sir John Sinclair *by Sir Henry Raeburn*
Above: Brechin Castle *by Alexander Nasmyth*

Ramsay was regarded as the equal of Sir Joshua Reynolds in portraiture, and his superior in the painting of women, and had a genius for capturing the humanity of his sitters. He painted many of the most well known characters of the Scottish Enlightenment, and associated with intellectuals such as David Hume and Adam Smith. In 1767 the patronage of the 3rd Earl of Bute won him appointment as Court Painter to George III. In 1773 he injured his arm in a fall and was unable to paint. Undaunted he threw himself into his other great passions: philosophy and literature.

Sir Henry Raeburn (1756–1823)

In contrast with Ramsay, whose fame as a portraitist was made in London as much as Edinburgh, Sir Henry Raeburn achieved his reputation almost entirely from the work he undertook in Edinburgh, where he was born, educated and spent most of his life. Apprenticed to a jeweller, he was largely self-taught. Like Ramsay he visited Italy, and though his stay was brief, he too returned with a new style: vigorous, broad brush strokes and a eye for the detail of his sitter's character. In contrast with Ramsay, his genius was best displayed in the male portrait. His society portraits are a marvellous record of most of the great figures of the Scottish Enlightenment – Robert Burns is the only notable exception – while his series of portraits of Highland chieftains created the romanticised images of Scottish noblemen which endure to this day.

Alexander Nasmyth (1758–1840)

Alexander Nasmyth is known as the father of Scottish landscape painting. He sought to place Scottish people and scenery in the poetic, allegorical world of classical harmony found in the works of Claude and Poussin. Originally trained as a portrait painter, like Ramsay and Raeburn he visited Italy, but returned to Scotland with landscape as his principal subject. He was a friend of Burns, and painted the poet's portrait, which now hangs in the Scottish National Gallery.

The workshop of the empire

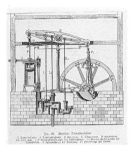

During the first decades of the nineteenth century, Scotland began to feel the effects of the social, political and economic changes which were sweeping the western world. The eruption of nationalism in Europe following the end of the Napoleonic wars was reflected in Scotland's continuing rediscovery and reinvention of itself.

Mechanisation and industrial acceleration wrought unforeseen changes on a predominantly rural economy, as small cottage industries were replaced by large-scale factory production. As Scottish coal and iron started to move along new networks of canals, roads and railways, so the population shifted from its rural homeland into the developing cities. The rural unemployed filled the swelling city slums, and poverty and deprivation were experienced on an unprecedented scale. Calls were soon made for urgent social and political reform.

Scotland was to feature significantly in the manufacturing boom of the nineteenth century. Its dockyards produced ships which transported Scottish goods across the world, its ports formed links in the expanding network of international trade and its major cities were transformed into cosmopolitan centres of commerce. Known as the 'workshop of the empire', Scotland typified the century's self-confident spirit of progress and imperial expansion. Many Scots became merchants and explorers, while others rallied against the alienating effects of mechanisation.

GEORGE IV (1820–30)

By 1811 George III's mental health had deteriorated so much that his eldest son was made Prince Regent. The Prince was the first Hanoverian monarch to show an interest in the arts, and his patronage fostered a renewed interest in painting, literature and architectural design. The great Scottish novelist and patriot, Sir Walter Scott, was determined to see this opportunity for change put to good effect north of the border.

Scott was responsible for rescuing the 'Honours of Scotland', or Scottish royal regalia, from obscurity. These comprised the crown, sceptre and sword of state which had been 'lost' since they had last been used at the time of the Union of the Crowns in 1603. After repeated requests, Scott finally obtained the Prince Regent's permission to search for them. On 4 February 1818 the Honours of Scotland were finally discovered in a great oak chest in the Crown Room of Edinburgh Castle. After this episode, Scott made persistent efforts to entice the Prince Regent to Scotland, and in 1822 the Prince, by then King George IV, finally assented, landing at Leith on 15 August. Although not a full state visit, this was the first formal appearance of the monarch in Scotland since Charles I in 1641. The King wore a kilt as a gesture to the Highlanders who only a short time before had been forbidden by law to wear tartan and Highland dress.

Left: *James Watt's revolutionary new steam engine*
Right: *early photograph of the Forth Rail Bridge, which was built by William Arrol between 1883 and 1890*

To commemorate the Scottish sailors and soldiers slain in the Napoleonic wars, it had been decided to erect a monument on Calton Hill in the form of a replica of the Parthenon. However, the 12 huge Doric pillars are the only part of the monument to have been completed when funds ran out. Some refer to the unfinished edifice as 'Edinburgh's Folly'.

While the King was still in the city, Scott persuaded him that Mons Meg, the famous fifteenth-century cannon, should be returned to its rightful home in Edinburgh Castle from the Tower of London. Royal permission was also granted to reinstate the estates and titles which had been forfeited by the Scottish noblemen during the Jacobite uprising. Scott had proved himself to be something of a distinguished ambassador for his country.

WILLIAM IV (1830–37)

The brief reign of William IV is remembered chiefly as a time of major political reform. The Parliamentary Reform Act received royal assent in June 1832. In July a Scottish bill for parliamentary reform also became law. The extension of voting rights to a larger proportion of the middle class helped to promote commerce, whilst the redistribution of parliamentary seats ensured that the expanding population of the burghs received a fairer representation in Parliament.

QUEEN VICTORIA (1837–1901)

Victoria's reign dominated the nineteenth century, and as British influence spread, the Queen came to embody the empire. She married Prince Albert of Saxe-Coburg-Gotha in 1840, and they had four sons and five daughters. Albert helped her to adapt the function of the monarchy to suit the needs of the time and in 1857 his role was officially recognised, when she made him Prince Consort.

From 1842 Victoria and Albert travelled extensively in Scotland. They were captivated by the Highlands, and their enthusiasm helped to popularise a romantic affection for the beauty and grandeur of Scotland's landscape at home and abroad. When in 1852 the opportunity arose to purchase Balmoral Estate, they made this Scottish property their summer

Left: George IV landing at Leith *by Alexander Carse*
Right: *the Crinan Canal in about 1880*

residence. With the technical advice of the Aberdeen architect, William Smith, Albert became personally involved in the planning and design of Balmoral Castle and its grounds.

IMPROVED COMMUNICATIONS

The sportsmen who brought their guns to the grouse moors of Scotland were greatly facilitated by the improvements to the roads and the introduction of railway links which were in place by the 1850s.

Scottish industry also played a central role in supporting the world-wide development of transport. The iron for which Lanarkshire became famous was, for example, exported across the Atlantic for use in the fast-developing American railway system.

Steam power propelled Scottish-built vessels all around the globe, and Scotland's dangerous coastal waters were made considerably safer by the construction of new lighthouses and harbours.

Canals

Canals were first built in England in the eighteenth century to ease the transport of heavy goods such as salt, coal and iron. By the early nineteenth century, most of the major Scottish trade routes were served by waterways. The Union Canal, for example, linked Edinburgh to Falkirk, the Forth and Clyde Canal joined Edinburgh and Glasgow, and the Crinan and Caledonian canals made the Highlands accessible.

JOHN BROWN (1826–83)

John Brown, the son of a Balmoral crofter, became Prince Albert's personal attendant, or ghillie, in 1849, and helped during grouse-shooting parties held at Balmoral Castle. The Queen found the plain-speaking servant highly amusing and, when Prince Albert died in 1861, she turned to Brown for solace, bringing him to England to act as her chief coachman.

John Brown's favoured position aroused feelings of jealousy amongst some of the Queen's courtiers, and he became the object of veiled criticism in the press, but in spite of this his undivided loyalty proved to be a great comfort to the Queen, and she began to rely upon him to provide the encouragement she needed to return to her public duties after an extended period of mourning.

Over time Brown became one of Victoria's most trusted personal servants and remained so until his death in 1883, having served the Queen for 34 years. It is said that Queen Victoria ordered that a photograph of John Brown should be buried with her, tied to her wrist.

'Brown Study', *a caricature of John Brown being baited by the British lion, from* The Tomahawk, *10 August 1867*

MOCK-ADAM-IZING – the Colossus of Roads.

Left: *caricature of John McAdam by Henry Heath, 1827*
Above: *Thomas Telford*

Roads

General Wade had partly addressed the problem of Scotland's roads in the early eighteenth century, but it was not until the involvement of engineers and innovators such as McAdam and Telford that the Scottish road network was revolutionised, setting industrial precedents which were adopted all over the world.

John McAdam (1756–1836), caricatured as the 'Colossus of Roads', was born in Ayrshire, but emigrated at the age of 14 to New York, where he made his fortune as a merchant in a family business. When he purchased an estate near his birthplace on his return to Scotland, he discovered that the roads leading to his property were almost impassable, and so set about constructing useable roads himself.

His method involved digging deep beneath the surface of the road until a layer of rock or clay was reached, which was then covered with large stones for good drainage. A layer of smaller stones was spread over the top, and a final coating of gravel left the road smooth and firm. McAdam's skill as a merchant and roadbuilder led to the development of a consultancy business which he ran with the help of his three sons.

He was also involved with the Earl of MacDonald in the tar-distilling operation of the British Tar Company at Muirkirk, and in 1827 was made Surveyor General of Roads.

Thomas Telford (1757–1834) was the son of a shepherd. His career began in the 1780s, when he worked as a stonemason during the construction of Edinburgh's New Town. Between 1788 and 1796 he established himself in London as a civil engineer and in 1801 was commissioned by the British government to improve the Scottish road system.

In 1806 Telford completed a stagecoach route between Perth and Inverness, and in 1811 his roads connected Inverness and Aberdeen. By 1819, he had constructed a route which linked the distant towns of Thurso and Wick to Inverness.

Thomas Telford spent 20 years designing roads, bridges and waterways throughout Scotland and his great engineering feats include 120 bridges and the 60-mile (96-km) Caledonian Canal, as well as many harbours and ferries. He designed the Dean Bridge in Edinburgh and was also associated with improvements to the River Clyde.

Railways and bridges

By the mid-nineteenth century, railways had begun to overtake canals and roads as a method of overland transportation. In Scotland, the idea of developing a network of railways took a long time to gather momentum but, once the benefits were appreciated, tracks were rapidly laid all over the country. Passenger and goods transport were quickly revolutionised by the railway, and some impressive station buildings displayed Scotland's new industrial self-confidence to the public. Rail transport was linked to the world's great ports. Tracks built alongside the docks enabled goods to be unloaded directly from rail wagons onto departing ships. The development of the Scottish railway network thus helped boost Scotland's overseas trade and its growing shipping industry.

Sir Robert McAlpine (1847–1935) is best known for his construction of concrete railway bridges. Some of his more famous achievements include the Mallaig extension bridge and the Glenfinnan Viaduct, which spans 21 arches and is 1,248 ft (380m) long and over 100 ft (30m) high at its highest point. The West Highland Railway, which he helped construct in 1897, is still in use and carries passengers through some of the finest country in Scotland.

In 1878, the Firth of Tay Railway Bridge of the North British Railway Company was opened. During a severe storm, the bridge collapsed into the Tay, claiming a train and many lives – an event commemorated by the Dundee handloom weaver, William McGonagall (c.1825–1902), in one of his best known 'bad' poems, 'The Tay Bridge Disaster':

Beautiful Railway Bridge of the Silv'ry Tay!
Alas! I am very sorry to say
That ninety lives have been taken away
On the last Sabbath day of 1879,
Which will be remember'd for a very long time.

PUFFERS

In the Scottish Highlands a form of transport was required to move goods between remote locations where road and rail did not exist or could not reach. The Puffer, a steam-driven coastal vessel, was developed in the 1850s and remained an integral part of Highland life until the 1960s.

Puffers travelled along Scotland's internal waterways and were designed to be compatible with the locks of the Crinan and Forth and Clyde canals. The flat bottoms of the vessels also suited them for the sandy beaches of the West Highlands and Western Isles, where they would load and unload their cargo. Their name is derived from the puffing sound, similar to that of a steam locomotive, which the early vessels made.

Examples of Puffers are preserved at the Maritime Museum at Irvine. Their work, and the lives and adventures of their crews were immortalised by the Glasgow journalist and novelist Neil Munro (1864–1930) in his Para Handy stories, which have since been adapted for television.

Retired Puffers laid up at Bowling Harbour on the River Clyde

In July 1880 an enquiry reported that the principal engineer, Thomas Bouch, had not taken account of the effects of wind pressure on the viaduct. In addition, contractors had left workmen unsupervised and substandard materials had been used in the bridge's construction. Bouch, who had subsequently been employed as chief engineer on the Forth Rail Bridge, was dismissed from his position. The new engineers appointed were Benjamin Baker and Sir John Fowler, with Scottish-born William Arrol (1839-1913) as the chief contractor. Construction began on the Forth Rail Bridge in 1883.

This impressive structure bears testimony to the remarkable achievements of Scottish engineering. The whole project took seven years to complete and cost £3 million. Stretching for one mile and 972 yards (2km) across the Firth of Forth at Queensferry, the bridge carries the railway track 157ft (48m) above the high-water level. Fifty-seven men were to lose their lives in the course of its construction, which required 6.5 million rivets and 54,000 tons (54,864 tonnes) of steel. The Forth Bridge was built to carry the main line of the London and North-Eastern Railway (LNER). In 1990 this impressive structure was specially floodlit to celebrate its centenary.

Shipbuilding

Despite the involvement of many key Scottish figures in the development of rail and steam technology, it was for its shipping industry that Scotland was best known, for it was marine engineering, centred in Clydeside, which both sustained the Scottish iron industry during the mid-nineteenth century and enabled the transportation of passengers and commodities all over the world.

For centuries, many Scottish coastal towns, such as Garmouth on the River Spey, had been well known for their small-scale shipbuilding, but it was in the late 1770s, during the American War of Independence, that the Scottish shipping industry became established. Trade with America was prohibited, and domestic alternatives had to be found to the cheap timber vessels which had previously been bought in the colonies by tobacco and sugar merchants. Scotland's dockyards

Left: *aftermath of the Tay Bridge disaster*
Above: *the Forth Rail Bridge in 1990*
Right: *the launch in 1818 of the*
SS Christian*, built by Scotts of Greenock*

soon began to meet the growing need for ships. By the mid-nineteenth century, Britain was experiencing an export boom, and the dockyards of Scotland quickly became the focus of the British shipbuilding industry.

It was in Clydeside that Scottish shipbuilding flourished. The natural advantages of Clydeside as a location were irrefutable: the docks opened directly onto the North Atlantic and the works were furnished with cheap and plentiful supplies of local iron, transported from Lanarkshire via the Monklands Canal. During the 1850s and '60s shipbuilding in Clydeside expanded in response to Britain's buoyant economy. This included the production of commercial vessels as well as ships for the Royal Navy, which was at that time the largest navy in the world.

Shipbuilding changed considerably following the invention of the separate condenser by the Scot, James Watt. Scottish expertise in steam-powered machinery was established during the 1820s in Glasgow's textile industry and, by mid-century, steam-engines were being used to generate power for sea-going vessels. From about 1834 iron and steel came into general use as an alternative to wood for hulls. Iron ships were more expensive to build, but the initial outlay was outweighed by cheaper running costs.

By 1870, ships from Clydeside accounted for two-thirds of Britain's total steam tonnage. It was the enterprise of individual shipbuilders, like Robert Napier, which helped to ensure that Scottish vessels held a large proportion of the passenger-ship market. Napier, who founded the Cunard shipping company in 1839, came from a family of pioneering steam engineers. The success of the Cunard line, which capitalised on the fast-growing traffic between Britain and North America, contributed to the rise of Clydeside as one of the world's major shipping centres.

Lighthouses

Life at sea was made considerably less perilous in the nineteenth century by the construction of lighthouses around the British coast. Many were the work of the remarkable Stevenson family.

Robert Stevenson (1772–1850) designed roads and bridges, was involved in canal-building and harbour and drainage schemes, and founded an engineering dynasty. He also built 20 lighthouses, most notably the lighthouse on Bell Rock at Arbroath, where hundreds of lives had previously been lost in wrecks. His three sons, Alan, David and Thomas, between them constructed a total of over 40 lighthouses.

Left: *James Watt in his workshop*
Above: *Alexander Graham Bell in 1892*

Alan Stevenson (1807–65) is best known for the Skerryvore Lighthouse, erected on a tiny reef, or 'skerry', near the Hebridean island of Tiree. The lighthouse took over five years to complete in harsh working conditions, the skerry being covered by the sea for long periods. Workers were marooned on the rocks by stormy weather for days at a time. This feat of great ingenuity and courage saved many lives.

SCOTTISH INVENTIVENESS

Scotland produced a remarkable number of inventors during this period who combined the new processes of mechanisation with their own ingenuity, producing a variety of inventions which were to gain them a world-wide reputation.

James Watt (1736–1819) was born in Greenock and trained as an instrument-maker. Later, he worked as a surveyor on the new canals in Scotland and then as an engineer deepening harbours and rivers. It was in 1765, whilst he was repairing an elementary Newcomen steam-engine, that he realised that by building an engine with a separate condenser, the power of steam could be harnessed in a much more efficient way. The basic improvement Watt introduced was to condense the steam before it entered the cylinder to produce movement, meaning much less fuel energy was wasted.

Watt also devised engines which used pistons to produce movement in a circle. These were used in factories to drive cotton spindles, with the result that industry no longer had to be situated near a good source of water power. These engines were also used to pump out floodwater from coal-mines. Perhaps the most striking consequence of his invention, though, was that it led directly to the locomotive steam-engine, and enabled the development of the railways.

William Murdock (1754–1839) was born in Auchinleck and trained as an engineer, working with Watt on modifying and improving the steam-engine. He went on to invent a system of gas lighting which was to illuminate the streets of Britain. Drawing on his skills as an engineer, Murdock conducted experiments with the manufacture of coal gas and, by building his own production plant, successfully lit his home by gas in 1792. In 1803 the Soho foundry in Birmingham became the first business to be commercially lit by gas; streets, homes and offices followed, and soon much of nineteenth-century Europe began to benefit from Murdock's innovation.

Charles Macintosh (1766–1843) was born and educated in Glasgow, where he studied chemistry. Among other inventions, he originated the production of chloride of lime, or bleaching powder, and in 1823 produced a waterproof material by combining india-rubber with a wool fibre. This process was used to manufacture the rainproof mackintosh worn to this day.

Alexander Graham Bell (1847–1922) was born in Edinburgh and was educated there and at London University. In 1870 he left Great Britain for Canada and established a school for the deaf and dumb in Nova Scotia, where he delivered lectures on vocal physiology. He became Professor of Vocal Physiology at Boston University in 1872.

Bell conducted a series of experiments to improve deaf students' communication through an 'apparatus for conveying sound by electricity', thus developing the techniques on which the present systems of electronic communication are based. He patented the telephone in 1876, founded the Bell Telephone Company and went on to patent the gramophone in 1887.

INDUSTRY AND SOCIAL CHANGE

The Scottish economy was still based in agriculture at the end of the eighteenth century, but farming soon began to benefit from mechanisation in the processing of grain, dairy produce and leather. The resulting fall in the need for labour led the unemployed to move from the countryside into villages, towns and cities.

Planned villages were encouraged in the Highlands to slow down the loss of population from the countryside. The resulting building work created employment opportunities for local builders, carpenters and painters. Villages and towns in the Lowlands and north-east of Scotland rapidly became more industrialised. New transport methods, financed by the capital of wealthy landowners, allowed the villages of southern Scotland in particular to thrive.

Technical advances in pig-iron smelting boosted the economy, giving Scotland a 25 per cent share of the British market by the mid-1840s. Water and steam power were soon installed in every industrial venture.

An increased demand for cotton, wool and linen led to an expanding textile market, and high wages at the beginning of the century caused by a shortage of skilled workers initially encouraged the immigration of handloom weavers from Ireland, many of whom settled in Glasgow. As machine-operated looms and factory manufacturing gradually replaced hand-crafted, home-produced goods, the effect on cottage industries was devastating. As a result, unemployed craftsmen were forced to leave their homes in search of work. These formerly independent artisans faced the prospect of unemployment and poverty, or the conditions of waged labour in the new textile industry. The seeds of industrial unrest began to grow.

Rich and poor

The changes brought by industrialisation made clear the sharp distinctions between rich and poor in nineteenth-century Scotland. Whereas merchants and adventurers lined their pockets with colonial gold, large numbers of labourers suffered unemployment and deprivation in the overcrowded city slums.

There were rich pickings for those wealthy enough to invest in lucrative trading companies, but others found their livelihoods dependent on fluctuating food prices and changing work patterns. At the same time, the numbers of the Scottish middle classes increased, due to improved living conditions and a reduction in the infant death rate, and boosted by improved education and greater technical training.

Political unrest

During the 1820s unemployment escalated throughout Scotland, as elsewhere in Britain, causing severe political and social unease. Sporadic riots and episodes

action was quickly suppressed by armed hussars and government volunteers. Fifty arrests were made under the Treason and Sedition Acts; some of those involved were acquitted, others received light sentences and 19 men were deported to Australia.

Those named as being leaders of the insurrection were not so lucky. The weavers Andrew Hardie and John Baird and their associate James Wilson, a blacksmith, were all convicted upon most unreliable evidence and were duly executed. The deaths of these 'Scottish martyrs' bear clear testimony to the heavy human cost of mechanisation and unemployment in nineteenth-century Scotland.

Urban problems

As the population of Scotland's cities grew, overcrowding, sanitation and escalating crime created a new set of problems. Urban centres such as Aberdeen, Dundee, Paisley and Glasgow recognised the need for updated systems of law and order. Private Acts of Parliament were passed which replaced the old town guards and militia with a recognised police force. Police stations were built, and local commissioners began to work closely with the Scottish legal system.

The crowded city slums made public health an issue of major concern. In 1840 Dr W.P. Alison, a specialist in public health, wrote a treatise criticising the Scottish Poor Law and its effects on the well-being of the labouring classes. Following a Royal Commission, an act was passed in 1845 which raised the number of Scottish parishes assessed by the Poor Law, and helped to guarantee medical care for the nation's destitute.

By 1867, when Scotland's Public Health Act was passed, many towns had already begun to address the hazards of unclean air and water. Glasgow was first in its construction of a town supply of water, clean and pure, taken from Loch Katrine.

of machine-breaking shook the country as both labourers and the unemployed protested against bad working conditions and high prices.

The foundations of this Scottish radical movement had been laid in the 1770s when many Scots sympathised with the calls for imperial reform voiced by their countrymen in the American colonies. This desire for change continued into the opening decades of the nineteenth century, as Europe experienced the aftermath of the French Revolution. Radical leaders among Scotland's labouring communities found, like their contemporaries in Lancashire and Yorkshire, that working-class dissatisfaction could provide the fuel for political change.

In 1820 an already volatile situation came to a head with the infiltration of the Scottish radical movement by London spies. Mass meetings were held in Paisley and Glasgow, and the government subsequently arrested 27 radicals. The workers retaliated by calling for strike action on 1 April of the same year. Sixty thousand Scots were involved, but the strike was badly organised and lasted for just one week.

Despite the attempts of Glasgow labourers to seize munitions from the Carron ironworks, and a march of radicals from Strathaven and Stirling, industrial

Education

At the beginning of the nineteenth century, educational reformers realised that a large proportion of Scotland's urban poor received little or no schooling. Rather than going to school, children were more likely to be encouraged by their parents to work in order to raise the family income by a few shillings a week. Yet by the middle of the century, Scotland, unlike England, could boast a national system of education.

After the foundation of the Educational Institute of Scotland in 1847, teaching became more professional and schools better organised. In 1872 an act was passed making schooling compulsory for all children between the ages of five and thirteen. The act also established a rating system to support underfunded schools in deprived areas. The teaching of the Gaelic language in schools was also legalised in the 1870s.

EMIGRATION, EXPLORATION AND TRADE

The Scots played an important role in the development of the British Empire, contributing significantly to overseas exploration and to the expansion of trading links around the world. Their skills as craftsmen and engineers in the design of railways, roads and ships were particularly valued in the countries in which they settled.

Scots travellers and settlers gained a reputation for good workmanship and reliability which won them many trading agreements abroad. As a result, the Scots at home benefited from the successes of their colonial countrymen. During the mid-nineteenth century, a dramatic increase in overseas trade brought wealth to the homeland, helping to ease unemployment and boost national industries.

Explorers and pioneers

Wherever they settled, the Scots had a major influence on the colonial environment and the formation of new national identities. Nova Scotia in Canada was

the first Scottish colony, founded in 1620 by Sir William Alexander, 1st Earl of Stirling. The Earl of Selkirk later founded the Canadian Red River Colony to assist the victims of the Highland Clearances.

Two Scots, John Alexander MacDonald and James Douglas, figured among Canada's most outstanding statesmen of the time, whilst the Canadian Mackenzie River takes its name from Sir Alexander Mackenzie (1764–1820), who was the first man to traverse the Northwest Passage over the Rocky Mountains to the Pacific. It was due to MacKenzie's discovery that the Canadian Pacific Railway, in 1893, was able to cross Canada from the Great Lakes to the Pacific Coast.

Australia and New Zealand remained remote and relatively undeveloped in the eighteenth century. However, by the nineteenth century, through the endeavours of inspired Scotsmen, this began to change. Lachlan Macquarie and Sir Thomas Brisbane significantly influenced the development of trade and agriculture in New South Wales by their encouragement of cattle- and sheep-farming.

In Western Australia in 1831 the Governor, James Stirling, used his position to encourage Pacific trade with Scotland. He called the capital of the colony Perth, after the Scottish town. Another Scot, John Macdouall Stuart (1815–66), is remembered for the routes he devised on his lengthy journey across the Australian continent between 1845 and 1862.

George MacLean was appointed Governor of West Africa in 1850 and he started to explore the country, opening up trade routes into the heart of previously unmapped territory. As a result, in just ten years, the level of imports into the area lying north of the Gold Coast had more than trebled.

Between 1858 and 1864 a trade route was charted from British Central Africa to the coast by David Livingstone (1813–73), who was among the greatest missionary explorers of his time. Born in Shuttle Row,

part of the cotton-mill village of Blantyre, Livingstone was working at the mill by the age of ten. After fourteen hours of work each day at the mill, he attended school and acquired a great love of learning, despite the obstacles of poverty and hard labour. He eventually qualified as a doctor, and was determined to travel and explore the world.

Livingstone's first choice, China, proved to be impossible because of the Opium Wars, so he trained to be a missionary in Africa. Once there he found it hard to settle into the missionary life and started to explore the 'Dark Continent'. He became the first European to cross and map Africa from east to west, and in 1855 was the first white man to see the Victoria Falls on the River Zambezi. During his travels he was exposed to the horrors of the slave trade, which he worked to bring to an end. His fame spread throughout the world, and his philanthropic and commercial activities in the British African colonies have contributed to the world-wide reputation of the Scots as hardy travellers and visionary explorers.

EMIGRANTS

Between the seventeenth and the twentieth centuries large numbers of Scots set sail from their native land for new homes in the Americas and the Antipodes.

Emigration in the seventeenth century was largely the effect of transportation, as Scottish Covenanters were sent to the West Indies and the American Colonies for punishment. By the eighteenth century, the Covenanters had been joined by large numbers of Jacobites who had been captured during the 'Fifteen and 'Forty-five rebellions. During the nineteenth century, the Scots were to

establish new homelands in American states such as North Carolina, where they earned a reputation for their patriotic fervour, courage and ability to withstand hardship.

Crofters who had survived the effects of the Clearances hoped to find a more rewarding life across the sea, but emigration brought its own set of problems. Those who had no relatives in the countries where they landed had to endure further privations before they settled, and many Scots died from poverty or disease. Those who survived and prospered did not

Government notice offering assistance to Scottish emigrants to Canada

forget their native land and endeavoured to keep the Gaelic language alive by passing it on to their children.

V. R.

The SECRETARY FOR SCOTLAND is enabled to offer EMIGRATION to CANADA, during the Spring of 1889, to a few selected families on the following terms:—

1. £120 will be advanced for each household, out of which will be provided travelling and all other expenses, including necessary stock and implements, and the balance will be paid over in the Colony.

2. No repayment will be demanded for four years; but during the succeeding eight years each family will be required to pay £20 17s. 8d. annually, and will then become owners of the Farms.

3. 160 acres of good land will be provided, free of charge, by the Canadian Government for each male head of a family; and the other males above 18 years of age are also entitled, if they desire it, to similar free grants.

4. No family will be selected for Emigration whose expenses, up to the time of arrival at the site of settlement, are likely to exceed £50.

5. A preference must, therefore, be given to those families which can show the possession of private resources.

The Commissioners of the Secretary for Scotland and of the Canadian Government will visit the district, for the purpose of selecting suitable families, on an early date, of which due notice will be given.

LOTHIAN,

H.M.'s Secretary for Scotland.

Andrew Carnegie, the Scottish philanthropist

Entrepreneurs

After the Act of Union in 1707, Scots had found themselves at liberty to create trading companies under the same conditions as their English contemporaries. By the nineteenth century, Scottish trading organisations had become well known for the ingenuity and enterprise of their merchants.

Lucrative export businesses, such as the jute trade of Dundee, afforded employment and assistance to many Scots. One prosperous company director, John Henderson, donated £30,000 annually to religious and charitable causes. Scottish statesmen overseas such as the Marquis of Dalhousie (1812–60), the Governor-General of India, also helped create favourable economic conditions for international commerce.

It was during the nineteenth century that Scotland also began to profit financially from the efforts of citizens who had settled abroad. One of the greatest Scottish industrialists and philanthropists was Andrew Carnegie (1835–1918). Born in Dunfermline, he was the son of a linen weaver. In 1848 his family emigrated to Pittsburgh where, at the age of thirteen, Carnegie began work in a textile mill.

With his shrewd business mind he was eventually able to invest in a wide range of America's expanding industrial activities, and particularly in railways, oil, iron and steel. Towards the end of his life Carnegie set about distributing the fortune he had accumulated to numerous good causes, creating trusts for building libraries, halls, churches, universities and parks around the world. In 1897 he returned to Scotland and bought a Highland estate, Skibo Castle, at Dornoch in Sutherland. Scotland's higher educational establishments, in particular, were to benefit greatly from his endowments.

Thomas Blake Glover (1838–1911) was born in Fraserburgh and left Scotland for the Far East as a young man. An ingenious engineer, he used his talents to develop industry and engineering in Japan and, by ordering ships from Clydeside for the Japanese Navy, helped to expand the Scottish export market.

CULTURAL ACHIEVEMENTS IN SCIENCE AND THE ARTS

Of all the small nations on this earth, possibly only the ancient Greeks surpass the Scots in their contribution to mankind. (Winston Churchill)

The nineteenth century sustained the cultural energy generated by the Enlightenment, though not perhaps on quite the same scale. Scotland's rediscovery of itself as a nation in the nineteenth century found vivid

Kelvin was a mathematical prodigy and his scientific work ranged over a broad range of specialisms. Between 1851 and 1854 he formulated the second law of thermodynamics, and he was also the mastermind behind the laying of the first telegraphic cable across the Atlantic. In addition he developed the X-ray, an innovation which assisted doctors in diagnoses and helped surgeons to perform operations with greater accuracy. He also studied and experimented with new ideas in magnetism, hydro-electric power, navigation and electric lighting.

James Clerk Maxwell (1831–79) was born in Edinburgh, and was educated there and at Cambridge, where in 1871 he became the first Professor of Experimental Physics. He studied the mysterious rings of Saturn and established that they were composed of billions of small objects held in place by the force of the planet's gravitational pull. Maxwell contributed ground-breaking work to the study of electromagnetism, which led to the discovery of radio waves. He also studied colour blindness and showed how it was caused, and in 1861 produced the first colour photograph.

By the end of the nineteenth century, Scotland was at the forefront of the world's medical advances. Many new hospitals had been built and medical faculties had opened in most Scottish universities. A number of Scotsmen made scientific discoveries and pioneered surgical techniques for which they were to become famous the world over.

Sir James Young Simpson (1811–70) was the son of a baker. From these humble origins he rose to become Professor of Midwifery at Edinburgh University in 1839. He introduced the anaesthetic use of chloroform, and thus greatly helped to reduce the pain of surgery and childbirth.

Joseph Lister, 1st Baron Lister (1827–1912), was greatly influenced by the work of Louis Pasteur. He

expression in the arts and sciences, and the achievements of the previous century bequeathed an illustrious and varied heritage to inspire emerging young writers, artists and scientists of all disciplines.

Scientists and doctors

Two of the most eminent scientists of the nineteenth century, Kelvin and Maxwell, were Scots. Both spent many years teaching in Scottish universities. William Thomson, Baron Kelvin (1824–1907) was not strictly speaking a native Scot, having been born in Belfast. However, while he was still a child his family moved to live in Glasgow, where his father had been appointed Professor of Mathematics.

introduced antiseptic surgery in the 1860s and developed important innovations in surgical techniques.

Alexander Fleming (1881–1935), should also be remembered here, although his work was undertaken in the twentieth century, for his discovery in 1928 of penicillin. Like the work of Simpson and Lister, this helped to lay the foundation of modern medicine.

Writers and poets

The two great themes of Scottish writers in the nineteenth century were history and the working of the human mind. The recent and the remote past, distant lands, the psychology of the criminal mind, creatures of legend, folklore and the supernatural, in fact everything esoteric and exotic was grist to their imaginative mills. Scottish authors excelled especially in the study of larger-than-life characters in extreme or unusual circumstances, for example: Carlyle's history of the French Revolution, Scott's Ivanhoe, Hogg's Justified

Top right: *Thomas Carlyle, the writer and historian*
Above: *Sir James Young Simpson, a pioneer of anaesthetics*
Right: *Alexander Fleming, the discoverer of penicillin*

Sinner, Stevenson's Alan Breck, Long John Silver and Jekyll and Hyde and, perhaps most famously of all, Conan Doyle's Sherlock Holmes.

Thomas Carlyle (1795–1881), born in Ecclefechan, Dumfriesshire, was educated at Edinburgh University before becoming a teacher. Dissatisfied with teaching, he turned to literary criticism, specialising in German literature and the translation of works by Goethe. His essays on Sir Walter Scott and Robert Burns were highly praised. History and philosophy also interested Carlyle, and his philosophy of appearances, *Sartor Resartus* (1834), and his account of the French Revolution (1837) are still considered classics.

James Hogg (1770–1835), nicknamed the 'Ettrick Shepherd' by *Blackwood's Magazine*, unsuccessfully invested the royalties from his first published poetry in farming. The Duke of Buccleuch, recognising the shepherd's poetic talent, gave him the use of a rent-free cottage. Hogg's poems express an energetic and typically Scottish voice, and reveal a unique perspective on life. He also wrote novels, and his study of a murderous character in *Private Memoirs and Confessions of a Justified Sinner* (1824) is a remarkable work exploring obsession and insanity.

Mary Macpherson (1821–98) was an exceptional Gaelic poet born in Skeabost, Isle of Skye. Her sensitive poems evoke sympathy for the plight of the crofters during the Clearances, as well as depicting the beauty and rustic simplicity of the Skye landscapes.

Andrew Lang (1844–1912) is famous for *The Blue Fairy Book*, and was one of the most versatile and prolific writers of his day. Born in Selkirk, Lang explored a wide range of topics, including history, religion, myths and legends, as well as contemporary affairs.

Sir Arthur Conan Doyle (1859–1930) is known all over the world for his colourful detective stories presenting the exploits and investigations of Sherlock Holmes and his assistant Dr Watson. Born in Edinburgh and educated at the city's university, Doyle qualified as a medical doctor in 1881, later became a ship's medic on a voyage to the Arctic Ocean and also served as a doctor in the Boer War. His experiences there fostered *The Great Boer War* (1900), a recollection of his time as a war correspondent. But it was his fiction that brought him the greatest acclaim. First introducing Sherlock Holmes in the novel, *A Study in Scarlet* (1887), Doyle followed this up with numerous stories featuring the shrewd pipe-smoking detective.

Robert Louis Stevenson (1850–94), one of the most popular literary figures of the nineteenth century, is known widely for his adventure novels *Treasure Island* (1883), *Kidnapped* (1886) and *The Master of Ballantrae* (1889), and for his chilling psychological study *The Strange Case of Dr Jekyll and Mr Hyde* (1886).

Stevenson was born in Edinburgh, a member of the great lighthouse-building dynasty, and read engineering and then law at university there, before deciding to devote his life to writing. He travelled widely: in Europe, America and the South Seas, where he campaigned vigorously to help the native peoples. Although unwell for most of his life with a bronchial condition, he was prodigious in his output, also composing poetry, such as the delightful *Child's Garden of Verses* (1885), and producing short stories, travel-writing and essays. He died and was buried in Samoa.

Another much respected Scot was Hugh Miller (1802–98). Born in Cromarty on the Moray Firth, Miller developed an interest in geology while working as an apprentice stonemason. In later years, as a journalist for the Church of Scotland, he became editor and then joint-owner of *The Witness*, and this allowed him the scope to express his scientific and religious convictions. A poet too, Miller published the collection *Poems Written in the Leisure Hours of a Journeyman Mason* in 1829. His findings in the fields of geology and palaeontology led to the publication of *The Old Red Sandstone* (1841), and the *Testimony of the Rocks* (1857) combined this profound knowledge of geology with a new understanding of the Creation. He is also remembered for the engaging descriptions found in *Scenes and Legends of the North of Scotland* (1835).

Composers and performers

Towards the end of the eighteenth century the folk music traditions of Scotland began to receive serious scholarly study. The published songs influenced German composer Felix Mendelssohn, who in 1829 visited Scotland, met Sir Walter Scott and began work on his Third Symphony, the 'Scottish'. His visit to Fingal's Cave on the island of Staffa provided the inspiration for the *Hebridean* overture. Mendelssohn

Left: *Sir Arthur Conan Doyle*
Below: *Robert Louis Stevenson aged about 25*
Right: Long John Silver with his parrot Captain Flint*, an illustration from* Treasure Island *by M.S.Orr*

SIR WALTER SCOTT

The great patriot Sir Walter Scott (1771–1832), the son of a Writer to the Signet, combined in his novels the optimism of the Enlightenment with the Romantic impetus of the early nineteenth century.

After graduating from Edinburgh University, Scott decided to study law

and was called to the bar in 1792. He was Sheriff-Depute of Selkirkshire from 1799 to 1832, and was Principal Clerk to the Court of Sessions from 1806 to 1830.

However, Scott's real love was literature, and he eventually came to devote most of his time to writing, emerging as the most prolific and imaginative writer of his epoch. Through his work, Scott brought Scotland to the attention of the world. His Waverley novels (1814–20), *Waverley, Ivanhoe, The Talisman, The Bride of Lammermoor* and The *Heart of Midlothian* were published alongside his ballad collection, *Minstrelsy of the Scottish Border*.

The most critical time in Scott's life came when Ballantyne, his own publishing house, went bankrupt just at the time when he was heavily involved in financial commitments towards his home, Abbotsford House. As a result, Scott was obliged to spend the rest of his life repaying debts by

putting all his efforts into writing novels and historical books. He managed to reduce his debts by two-thirds before his death.

Sir Walter Scott died at Abbotsford on 21 September 1832 and was buried with honours at Dryburgh Abbey in the Borders. A memorial was erected on Princes Street, Edinburgh shortly afterwards. His works, translated into numerous languages, continue to inspire and enthral readers around the world.

Left: Walter Scott as a young man
by Sir Henry Raeburn
Above: *Abbotsford House*

also admired the music of Scots composer John Thomson (1805–41), who was Reid Professor of Music at Edinburgh University until his early death.

Alexander Campbell Mackenzie (1847–1935) composed the famous oratorio, *The Rose of Sharon* (1884). He was born in Edinburgh into a distinguished family of musicians, his father being a celebrated violinist. Mackenzie's first composition, the Piano Quartet of 1873, and his later *Benedictus* will always retain an eminent place in Scottish musical heritage. A talented conductor, he held office as the Principal of the Royal Academy of Music in London. When Mackenzie toured Canada, he was awarded the D. Lit of McGill

University, and in 1922 he was made a Knight Commander of the Royal Victorian Order. He based many of his compositions on themes from Scottish poets, including those of Robert Burns.

A Scot who achieved household-name status with his comic songs was Harry Lauder, the stage name of Hugh MacLennan (1870–1950). Born into a working-class family in Portobello, he started work as a miner. Lauder's music-hall act presented a version of the Scotsman which became a stereotype, with his tartan image and the singing of his own words to traditional airs in such songs as 'I Love a Lassie' and 'Roamin' in the Gloamin''. He was knighted in 1919.

Painters

Scottish art had excelled during the Scottish Enlightenment, attracting international attention. This continued in the nineteenth century, when the nation's vital diversity was expressed by numerous artists in a multitude of styles.

Sir David Wilkie (1785–1841) is best known for his genre paintings, although he also painted historical subjects and portraits (including one of George IV in Highland dress). Born in Fife, he was educated at the Trustees' Academy, a school set up in Edinburgh by the Trustees of the Board of Manufacturers to promote high standards of design in Scotland's linen industry. Here he studied under David Allan, a painter of 'low' subjects such as Edinburgh's street cries. Wilkie soon developed his own style of genre painting in such works as *The Blind Fiddler*, *Village Politicians* and *Distraining for Rent*.

Like the great painters of the Enlightenment, he visited Italy to study the Old Masters. It was in some ways his undoing. He returned convinced that his real talent lay in painting grand historical subjects, but it is generally agreed that his historical paintings lack the vitality and interest of his earlier works.

One of the most interesting movements in Scottish art comprised a group of twenty-three young male painters known as the 'Glasgow Boys'. They came from all over Scotland, some even from England, producing brilliant original work bearing the influence of continental styles. The founder was William York MacGregor (1855–1923) who dynamically set the course for the young artists with his refrain, 'Flack out the subject as you would were you using an axe and try to realise it; get its bigness. Don't follow any school. There are no schools in art.'

Among the great artists of the nineteenth century, Horatio McCulloch (1805–67) stands out for his grandiose paintings, which had a particular appeal for the Victorians. McCulloch's most famous painting is *Glencoe* of 1864, now in the Glasgow Art Gallery.

Left: Mr Harry Lauder, *the music-hall star, signed postcard dated 1910*
Above: Distraining for Rent *by Sir David Wilkie*

Joseph Farquharson (1846–1935) was born in Aberdeen. He exhibited his painting *Study from Nature* at the Royal Scottish Academy in 1861 when he was only 15. His style developed under the tutelage of Peter Graham, an established landscape painter noted for his portrayal of mountains, misty glens and Highland cattle. It was Farquharson's snow and live-stock scenes that brought him fame.

Photographers

As elsewhere, the development of photography in Scotland in the nineteenth century was due to the coming together of artistic and scientific impulses. Great names in this regard are David Octavius Hill (1801–70) and Robert Adamson (1821–48), who formed a business partnership in 1844, primarily to produce photographic portraits of the ministers of the newly founded Free Church of Scotland.

Adamson and his brother John had been involved with photography almost since its beginning, and had sent an album of their work bound in tartan to the father of British photography, William Fox Talbot, in 1842. Hill was a landscape and genre painter and Secretary of the Royal Scottish Academy, and was thus able to promote photography as a respectable artistic medium rather than merely a scientific curio.

Newhaven Fishwives *by Hill and Adamson*

CHARLES RENNIE MACKINTOSH (1868–1928)

Charles Rennie Mackintosh will forever be associated with Glasgow, the city of his birth. It is where he was educated, served his apprenticeship and spent most of his working life. Many of his most important buildings and interiors are to be found in the city, and form part of the city's proud cultural heritage. Yet when he died, virtually an exile in London, his reputation was at a low ebb and his life's work misunderstood or undervalued.

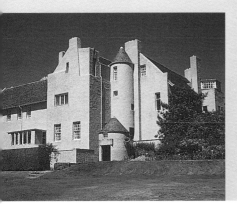

Mackintosh was the son of William McIntosh (he experimented with various spellings of his name before settling on Mackintosh) a Glasgow policeman and a keen amateur gardener. As a boy Mackintosh helped him care for his plants. From this early experience he developed a deep love and understanding of nature, which shines through his work. Trained as a professional architect, he was also a talented artist, and as a teenager attended evening classes in painting and drawing. His watercolours are among the finest by any artist in that difficult medium.

Symbolism, particularly that of flowers, plays an important part in Mackintosh's art, as does the balancing of opposites such as light and dark, straight lines and curves, and vivid colours and neutral tones. He also believed that buildings should make an emotional impact by their mass and shape. Influenced by the Scottish baronial style of architecture, he opposed the Modernist tendency to make buildings appear almost weightless by an over-extensive use of steel and glass.

Mackintosh's work is often characterised as *Art Nouveau*, although he himself rejected any attempt to categorise his art into any one style. He believed passionately that the whole was more important than the sum of its parts. He therefore strove in his architecture to create an organic whole, combining each aspect of the building into one unified work of art – from the exterior to the interior, the building materials used and the colour and texture of fabrics. Even the furniture, cutlery and light fittings were carefully considered parts of the overall design.

Outstanding examples of his work are the Glasgow School of Art, completed in 1909; Hill House in Helensburgh, completed in 1903; and the Willow Tea Rooms in Sauchiehall Street, completed in 1904, with a new tea-room added to the basement in 1917. The latter was created for Catherine Cranston, a leading figure in the Glasgow Temperance Movement, who believed tea-rooms would help combat the drunkenness of many of the city's workers.

Top left: *Charles Rennie Mackintosh*
Left: *Hill House in Helensburgh*
Above: *ladder-back chair, Hill House*

The twentieth century

The twentieth century has brought significant changes to Scotland which have continually altered the structure of its society. The considerable achievements of the nineteenth century have been eroded by the lasting effects of two world wars, with the legacy for Scottish industry too often being mass unemployment, particularly in areas which profited most from the industrial revolution, such as Clydeside. However, whilst other trades declined, the great Scottish traditions of engineering and innovation have survived, with industries like textiles and coal thriving in the earlier part of the century, and oil and gas, tourism and electronics emerging in more recent times to support the country's economy.

EDWARDIAN SCOTLAND

The long reign of Queen Victoria came to a close on 22 January 1901. The Edwardian era which followed saw the economic strength and confidence of the British Empire, to which Scots had contributed so much, reach its zenith before the nation was plunged into the catastrophe of the Great War in 1914.

Engineering Prowess

In the latter half of the nineteenth century, Scottish engineering had gained a world-wide reputation. Clydeside had become a dominant force in marine engineering, producing great sailing clippers. When sail was replaced by steam and merchant fleets required re-building, the Scots once again led the way. Associated forms of engineering including the manufacture of castings, iron and steel plates and materials for bridge building were also buoyant. This continued into the early 1900s and was largely responsible for the pre-war prosperity of the nation. Technical training in mechanical institutes and in colleges such as Herriot-Watt in Edinburgh and the Royal Technical College in Glasgow, as well as rigorous apprenticeships provided industry with a well-trained engineering elite.

Traditional Industries

The economic swing from growth to slump to growth again was experienced by several Scottish industries at this time. Coal-mining, one of the country's principal sources of income after shipping, did not escape change. Always closely related to the iron, steel and salt industries, the coal trade suffered from their fluctuations, but by 1913 the Scottish output of coal had risen to a record of 42.5 million tons.

Fishing, another of Scotland's important natural industries, by this time could claim the largest herring harvest in Europe. Agriculture remained of major importance, employing thousands of workers around the country. The Carse of Blairgowrie became known for fruit-growing, from some of the best apples in the country to soft fruits such as raspberries.

Left: *young supporter of the Scotland football team*
Right: *Princes Street from Calton Hill, Edinburgh*

The extraordinary development of Dundee's jute trade is arguably without parallel in the history of textile manufacturing. Initial technical complications were soon overcome and by the mid-nineteenth century Dundee was importing 436,985 bales of jute fibre a year. The city prospered with 40,000 employed in its jute mills by 1890, but its triumph was relatively short-lived once it had to compete with cheaper products from India and Europe. Trade declined but picked up during the Great War, due to demand from the forces, only to fall again in peace-time.

The Edwardian Cultural Scene

The economic health of the nation, and the sense of self-confidence and optimism in society heralded by the new century were reflected in a flourishing cultural scene. The International Exhibition held at Kelvingrove Park, Glasgow in 1901 to mark the opening of the Art Gallery and Museum, was an event that attracted world-wide interest.

Music Hall theatres continued to flourish in Edinburgh and Glasgow, and Scottish performers such as Sir Harry Lauder and Will Fyffe (1885-1947), famous for his song 'I Belong to Glasgow', attracted enthusiastic audiences at home and abroad.

THE GREAT WAR

The anguish and uncertainty generated by the outbreak of war in August 1914 brought people together as never before in a spirit of comradeship, and led to men volunteering all over Scotland, where one in four miners joined up in the first year.

Keep the Home Fires Burning

At home the government rationed imported goods and encouraged farmers to grow more food. Scottish miners ensured that an output of 30 million tons of coal per year was steadily maintained for industrial and domestic consumption. It was a prosperous time for heavy industries such as Clydeside shipbuilding, which in turn demanded increased output from the Scottish iron and steel industries.

The drastic changes brought about by wartime

ROYAL RESEARCH SHIP DISCOVERY

In 1899 the Dundee Shipbuilding Company was commissioned by the National Antarctic Expedition Committee to build the RRS *Discovery*, the ship which would carry Captain Robert Falcon Scott – Scott of the Antarctic – on his first attempt to reach the South Pole.

RRS *Discovery* set sail for New Zealand in March 1901. In the winter of 1901-2 it began its survey of the Antarctic region, and during its second winter there Captain Scott and two companions almost reached the Pole. The ship became trapped in the ice and rescue ships were sent to blast a way out. RRS *Discovery* returned to British shores in 1904. Scott finally reached the Pole in 1912, but he and his four companions perished on the return journey.

RRS *Discovery* continued to be used as a research ship until 1931, after which she was laid up in the East India Docks in London. Over the years she was used as a training ship, then in the late 1970s she came under the care of the Maritime Trust and on 2 April 1986, fully restored, she arrived back in Dundee where she can be seen in all her glory at Discovery Quay.

RRS Discovery *at Discovery Quay*

Sir James Matthew Barrie (1860-1937), was born in Kirriemuir, the ninth child of a weaver. After a period in journalism he turned to writing fictional sketches, sometimes described as 'Kailyard' or cabbage patch stories because of their over-sentimental depiction of rural Scottish life.

In the 1890s Barrie turned his creativity almost exclusively to writing and producing plays. *The Little Minister* appeared in 1897, *Quality Street* in 1901 and *The Admirable Crichton* in 1902. All were great successes, however Barrie's most famous and enduring creation was *Peter Pan, or The Boy Who Wouldn't Grow Up* (1904), which grew out of stories he made up for the children of friends. Its characters of Peter, Wendy, Tinkerbell,

Captain Hook and the Lost Boys have become fictional immortals in books, on stage and in films.

Detail from theatrical publicity material for Peter Pan

conditions radically affected the structure of society. Men and women came together in occupations that had hitherto been the province of men alone. Whereas before their main option had been domestic service, women now entered public transport, munitions factories and other industries to be offered skilled jobs usually denied them. Female membership of trade unions rose dramatically and four major strikes by women in this period signalled their determination to fight petty discrimination and unequal pay policies.

Red Clydeside

Due to a lack of skilled workers in the engineering industry, semi-skilled workers were employed in their place. They not only threatened the quality of goods produced but also the standing of trained engineers. The situation was exacerbated further when unskilled workers were taken on to fill vacancies. Protests, including strike action, were conspicuous during 1915-16. The military situation was so critical that the

disputes were ended by force, under the Defence of the Realm Act.

Characterised by the 'revolutionary' nature of these disputes, the area became known as 'Red Clydeside'. Glasgow was a major centre for the war effort, especially as 20,000 more people moved there to work in the munitions factories, and it was inevitable that feelings of injustice would be stirred up amongst those who were dissatisfied with working conditions, the poor standard of housing, and the excess profits being accrued by those in control. Socialist leaders such as John Maclean and William Gallacher advocated a revolutionary solution, along the lines of the Bolshevik Revolution in Russia. There was also strong support for Temperance and Pacifism.

Scotland at War

Drawing on the bravery that they had so often exhibited on their own account in past centuries, Scots played significant roles in all of the armed services.

Scottish regiments made up 22 of the 157 battalions of the British Expeditionary Force.

New industries were developed to meet the increased demand for motor vehicles, aeroplanes, and other military equipment. Similarly, more warships, merchant ships and submarines were required to replace the losses already suffered. The largest national munitions plant was established at Gretna, as it was considered to be an area safe from Zeppelin raids.

Scotland also held a strategic position in naval warfare, accounting for major bases at Invergordon, Rosyth and Scapa Flow in the Orkney Islands: the Headquarters of the British Grand Fleet. Between 31 May and 1 June 1916 it steamed into the North Sea to engage the German High Seas Fleet at Jutland.

After its surrender in 1918, the German fleet was interned at Scapa Flow, and on 21 June 1919, to the amazement of the islanders, 71 German warships were deliberately scuttled by their crews.

The Armistice Agreement with Germany was signed on 11 November 1918. The cost to Scotland of its selflessness was the loss of approximately 160,000 of its countrymen (including ten per cent -18,000- of all adult males from Glasgow). Over 300,000 were injured. The lasting effects were incalculable.

THE YEARS OF PEACE

The end of the war was welcomed by people throughout the country, but peacetime was not to herald a return to the relative security and stability of life in the pre-war era.

Left: *postcard of scuttled German battleship, Scapa Flow*
Below: The Arrival *by Bernard Meninsky, depicting Highland soldiers wearing their Balmoral caps*

New Political Parties

Politically, the war brought government activities to the consciousness of ordinary people. Due to increases in trade union membership and the establishment of a mainly working-class electorate, the Liberals' power in Scotland shifted to Labour. The Scottish Labour Party had been formed in 1888 by miners' leader James Keir Hardie (1856-1915), and was the first party of its kind in Britain. Hardie became one of Britain's first Independent Labour MPs in 1892. In the 1922 general election the Independent Labour Party won 10 out of 15 seats in Glasgow, while James Ramsay MacDonald (1866-1937) became the first British Labour Prime Minister in 1924.

In 1928 the drive for Scottish independence was given a political focus by the creation of the National Party of Scotland. This merged with the Scottish Party in 1932 to become the Scottish National Party, an uneasy coalition of left and right wing elements which achieved little electoral success until the 1940s.

Industrial Problems

After the war, and in spite of international competition, shipbuilding on the Clyde reached its peak in 1919-23 and improved its share of UK output by introducing new methods of propulsion in diesel engines. In fact, the Clyde was responsible for building 60 per cent of the entire passenger liner tonnage in the UK, including the great ocean liners *Queen Mary* and *Queen Elizabeth*. Despite such successes, the economic conditions revealed that estimates for the demand for iron and steel (the latter heavily dependent on shipbuilding) were too optimistic. During the 1920s and '30s output remained at about half the level of the war and pre-war periods.

There was also considerable unrest amongst workers in the Scottish coal industry because of a reduction in wages, an increase in hours and the pitiful working conditions which they had to endure. In 1926, British miners were supported by the Trade Union Congress (TUC), resulting in the General Strike of 4-12 May. The TUC soon gave way, however, leaving the miners in a worse plight than ever. They continued their strike for three more months but were forced back to work out of utter desperation and despair.

The emergence of gas, electricity and oil for domestic use further depressed the coal industry, but by the late 1930s a strategy of mechanisation had

---

THE BOYS' BRIGADE

Sir William Alexander Smith (1854-1914) was born in Thurso, Caithness. In 1874 he joined the Lanarkshire Rifle Volunteers, and was made a colonel in 1908. He was a keen teacher in the Sunday Schools established by the Free Church of Scotland and decided that it was imperative to offer boys a more practical way to approach their studies. In combining a military parade with his lessons, Smith thought he would increase children's interest in Christian teachings.

This inspired him to found the Boys' Brigade in 1883, 25 years before the foundation of the Boy Scouts.

The movement spread quickly all over Scotland and England, then to almost every corner of the British Empire and the USA. In Glasgow, in 1908, Smith commanded a special parade of 10,000 Boys' Brigade members before the Duke of Connaught. Today, there is an international camp held each year in a different country; district camps are also held annually.

Sir William Alexander Smith

ensured greater productivity and by undercutting the competition profits were once more attained. Even so the industry was bravely contesting a long-term and seemingly inescapable decline.

Religious Unity

Sensing a climate of change, the Church of Scotland re-initiated a plan which had originally been proposed by the General Assembly of the Church of Scotland during Edward's VII's reign (1905-10). The idea was to merge the United Free Church and the Church of Scotland, so healing a rift which had its roots in the Highland Clearances. At that time, a section of the Church had broken away to support the people who had been driven from their homes, and the resulting United Free Church spread rapidly, especially through the Highlands. An agreement for unification was finally made in 1929 with the help of Parliament, becoming a milestone in the Church's history.

Cultural Renaissance

Such a time of economic crisis tested the character of the Scottish people. Their nation's identity was once

more championed by the arts during what has become known as the 'Scottish Cultural Renaissance', led by, amongst others, the poets Edwin Muir (1887-1959) and Hugh MacDiarmid (1892-1978) and the novelists Neil Gunn (1891-1973) and James Leslie Mitchell (1901-1935), who under the pseudonym Lewis Grassic Gibbon wrote *A Scots Quair*, a trilogy of novels which deal with the effects of war and economic depression on twentieth-century Scottish society. They are regarded as amongst the first modern Scottish novels.

Continuing the momentum generated by the Glasgow Boys were the Scottish Colourists, the name given to a group of four young artists renowned for their luminous, primarily landscape painting. They looked to Europe for inspiration and were particularly influenced by artists such as Cézanne and Matisse.

Popular culture was being enjoyed by huge numbers of people in the form of radio entertainment, jazz, dance halls and cinemas (Glasgow had 114 by 1938). Football matches attracted huge crowds: in 1937 over 147,000 watched the Celtic *v.* Aberdeen Cup Final. In 1900 only one in six adults could read a newspaper compared to one in two in 1920. This rise

---

HUGH MACDIARMID

Hugh MacDiarmid was the pseudonym of Christopher Murray Grieve, generally regarded as the most important Scottish poet since Burns. He sought to write a new, vigorous Scottish poetry in a language free of what he regarded as sentimental tartanry. To this end he created his own poetic language which he called 'Lallans': a synthesis of Old Scots and various dialect words assembled from dictionaries and speech.

His masterpiece, *A Drunk Man Looks at a Thistle* (1926), is a long meditation

in which his 'drunk man' wakes up on a hillside confronted by a giant, symbolic Scottish thistle. As he rails against the debased state of contemporary Scottish culture he gradually sobers up and gains a vision of what Scotland could be.

In politics MacDiarmid was a radical, drawn to socialism as well as nationalism. He joined and was expelled at different times from both the Communist Party and the National Party of Scotland. Although the difficulty of his language has probably prevented his work from achieving a wide audience, it would

be hard to exaggerate his influence on the poets who followed him.

Hugh MacDiarmid *by Jeffrey Morgan*

PIONEERS OF TELEVISION

John Logie Baird (1888-1946) was born in Helensburgh, the son of a minister, and educated at the Glasgow Academy, after which he studied electrical engineering at Glasgow's Royal

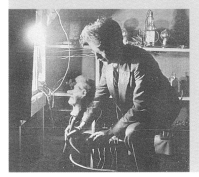

Technical College. A brilliant inventor, he made significant contributions to the science of fibre optics and radar, but it is for his work on the development of television that he is best remembered.

The theory of television had been known for some years, but it was Baird's ingenuity and perseverance which succeeded, in 1926, in creating the first workable system, based on the mechanical scanning of a disk. By 1928 he was able to demonstrate the first colour television images and the first transatlantic transmission.

In 1929 the British Broadcasting Corporation, lead by fellow Scot John

Reith (1899-1971), began experimental broadcasting using Baird's mechanical system; however, his process was eventually outdated by the Marconi-EMI electronic system, which the BBC switched to in 1937.

Baird went on to make further innovations in the technology of television, including large-screen projection, stereo sound, video disks and 3-D images. Reith, a stern and difficult man, resigned as director-general of the BBC in 1938 and entered politics. His influence on British broadcasting has been immense and long-lasting.

Left: *John Logie Baird in 1926*

in literacy was reflected in the increase in the sales of Scottish daily, Sunday and weekly newspapers.

THE SECOND WORLD WAR

Britain declared war on Germany on 3 September 1939, after Hitler's troops invaded Poland. When the news reached the people of Scotland over the radio, the nation was in shock. This was intensified by the U-boat sinking of a transatlantic liner off the Outer Isles, and the bombing of the Firth of Forth in October, 1939: the first such aerial attack of the war.

The Home Front

The war was an anxious time of furious activity. All over the country people organised themselves into what became known as the Home Front. Air raid shelters were erected and sand bags were distributed to vulnerable areas such as beaches and lighthouses. Home Guard and Civil Defence units were formed. Once more, Scotland had to adjust its daily routine drastically to play an important role in proceedings.

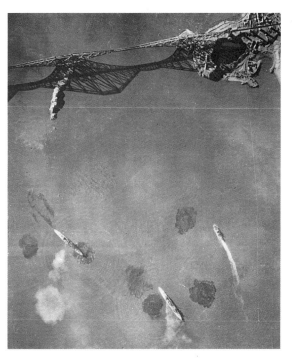

Aerial photograph taken by the Luftwaffe during its attack on the Firth of Forth, 16 October 1939

SCOTCH WHISKY

Whisky, from the Gaelic 'uisgebeatha' meaning 'the water of life', has been distilled in Scotland since at least 1494 – the date of the earliest known record of its existence there – and probably for much longer. The process of fermenting malted barley is thought to have been brought to Scotland by the Irish. Small stills sprang up all over the country, some serving only one household or family. From the seventeenth century strict licensing laws and taxation led to the setting up of illicit stills in secret hiding places, especially in the remoter parts of the Highlands.

The Scotch whisky industry did not really begin to thrive until the mid-nineteenth century when distillery companies using grain as its raw material, merged with traditional malted barley distilleries to create blended whisky.

Today blended whisky is one of Scotland's major exports, and whisky, both blended and malt, is a major boost to Scottish tourism. Scotch Whisky Centres are open to the public across Scotland, with guided tours of distilleries and tastings of the product.

WHISKY GALORE

In 1941 the merchant ship SS *Politician* foundered off the tiny Hebridean island of Eriskay, mercifully with no loss of life. Amongst the cargo abandoned aboard the sinking ship were 20,000 cases of whisky, which to the islanders, suffering under war-time spirit rationing, was like manna from heaven. Their salvage of part of this precious cargo and the authority's subsequent search for its hiding places, formed the basis of the novel *Whisky Galore* (1947) written by Sir Compton Mackenzie (1883-1972). For his story he changed the ship's name to the SS *Cabinet Minister* and renamed and divided the island

into the Protestant and Catholic communities of Great and Little Todday.

In 1948 Eriskay's near-neighbour, the island of Barra, was used as the location for the classic Ealing film comedy based on the novel and directed by Scottish director Alexander Mackendrick. Bottles from the wreck of the SS *Politician* are still occasionally recovered by divers, and are highly prized as souvenirs.

Top: *a selection of malt whiskies*
Above: *scene from* Whisky Galore
Right: *whisky distilleries*

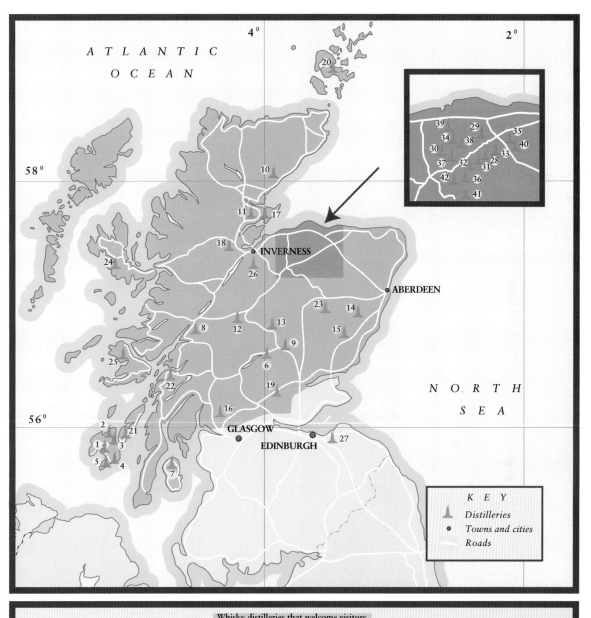

ATLANTIC

OCEAN

58°

56°

58°

56°

4°

2°

INVERNESS

ABERDEEN

GLASGOW

EDINBURGH

NORTH

SEA

39
34
29
30
38
35
37
32
40
42
28
33
31
36
41

KEY

Distilleries
Towns and cities
Roads

Whisky distilleries that welcome visitors

Islay Malt	Highland Malt			Lowland Malt		
1 Bowmore	6 Aberfeldy	13 Edradour	20 Highland Park	27 Glenkinchie	31 Glenallachie	38 Macallan
2 Bunnahabhain	7 Arran, Isle of	14 Fettercairn	21 Jura, Isle of		32 Glenfarclas	39 Miltonduff-
3 Caol Ila	8 Ben Nevis	15 Glencadam	22 Oban	Speyside Malt	33 Glenfiddich	Glenlivet
4 Lagavulin	9 Blair Athol	16 Glengoyne	23 Royal Lochnagar	28 Aberlour-	34 Glen Grant	40 Strathisla
5 Laphraoig	10 Clynelish	17 Glenmorangie	24 Talisker	Glenlivet	35 Glen Keith	41 Toumintoul-
	11 Dalmore	18 Glen Ord	25 Tobermory	29 Auchroisk	36 Glenlivet, The	Glenlivet
	12 Dalwhinnie	19 Glenturret	26 Tomatin	30 Cardhu	37 Knockando	42 Tormore, The

Women again replaced men in schools, factories, light industry, transport and the administration of local councils. Many took up crucial positions, including radio operators and drivers on the front line or elsewhere. The Scottish Women's Land Army also made a vital contribution.

The Coalition Government sanctioned several pertinent reports addressing Scotland's social problems. In 1943 a Scot, John Boyd Orr (1880-1971), compiled a study for the Scottish Health Department which led to major advances in medical treatment and a heightened concern for the living and working conditions of Scottish families. Another Scot, Thomas Johnston (1881-1965), played a key role in the development of Scotland and was one of the few Scots to receive high office in the British Government at that time. He was declared Secretary of State for Scotland in 1941 and immediately began to tackle the economic and social regeneration of the country. In 1943, as Chairman of the Hydro-Electric Board of Scotland, he was authorised to provide electricity to northern Scotland from water-power. As a result, 720 new enterprises emerged between 1942 and 1945 employing over 90,000 people: a dynamic contribution to Scotland's economy and society.

Scotland's War Effort

A purposeful national unity was evident as the Scots toiled hard towards a conclusion of the terrible conflict. As the war progressed, Glasgow became a vital port for the Merchant Navy, carrying out the dangerous task of bringing supplies in convoys from North America across the U-boat infested Atlantic Ocean. New factories were built and equipped, and by 1943 five ships a week were being launched on the Clyde. Numerous airfields and bases were constructed along the east coast of Scotland providing strategic positions for reconnaissance and training. On Loch Ryan a major sea-plane base was established. Scotland also offered camping space for the allied forces from Poland, Norway, America and France, whilst in the Orkney Islands and in the Lowlands large prisoner of war camps were built.

The Cost of Conflict

Although Scotland escaped the heavy bombing inflicted on English cities, there was a devastating 'blitz' on Clydebank between 13-14 March 1941. Civilian lives lost amounted to 1,200, while many industrial plants were completely destroyed. Only eight houses out of a

Walter Rankin, Local Defence Volunteer,
by Sir William Oliphant Hutchinson, August 1940

total of 12,000 in the area escaped damage. Rebuilding began almost immediately.

One of the major factors which helped win the war was the development of radar. By 1940, thanks to the work of Brechin-born physicist Sir Robert Watson-Watt (1892-1973) it was recognised that radio waves could detect the presence of an object within a certain range, such as the movements of incoming aircraft, thus establishing a vital early warning system.

In Europe, North Africa and the Far East Scottish men and women played significant roles throughout the war. It has been estimated that Scotland supplied 450,000 men for the armed forces and 30,000 men for the Merchant Navy, whilst 70,000 women were enlisted in their own services. Scots killed in combat during the Second World War numbered 34,000 whilst 6,000 civilians died during air raids.

The war against Germany ended on 8 May 1945 and against Japan on 15 August. The sound of celebrations resounded throughout the country, but for those who had lived through two world wars, it was clear that life must change yet again.

POST-WAR RECONSTRUCTION

The two world wars undermined the social order of the nineteenth century, leaving the government with the task of combining new welfare initiatives, such as public housing and health care, with rapid economic growth. The Clyde Valley Plan, begun in 1946, developed new towns, such as East Kilbride and Cumbernauld, to rehouse slum-dwellers. By extending welfare and intervening more in trade and industry, the government through the Secretary of State for Scotland hoped to devise a strategy which would offer the people a greater sense of freedom and opportunity.

Nationalisation and Automation

The Labour government's nationalisation of the coal trade in 1947 rejuvenated an ailing industry. Under the National Coal Board, working conditions improved significantly. The government also introduced a series of Acts to support farmers with price controls. Westminster was attempting to revitalise the Scottish economy. The railways were nationalised in 1948, merging the two remaining giants in Scotland, the LNER and the LMS.

This period witnessed the beginnings of a significant and lasting shift away from heavy manufacturing to service industries and light engineering: producing less goods and more services. The electronic revolution took root in the 1950s and updated many production methods. The jute and steel industries were automated, the coal trade received power-loading machinery, and tanker building on the Clyde benefited from the new technology.

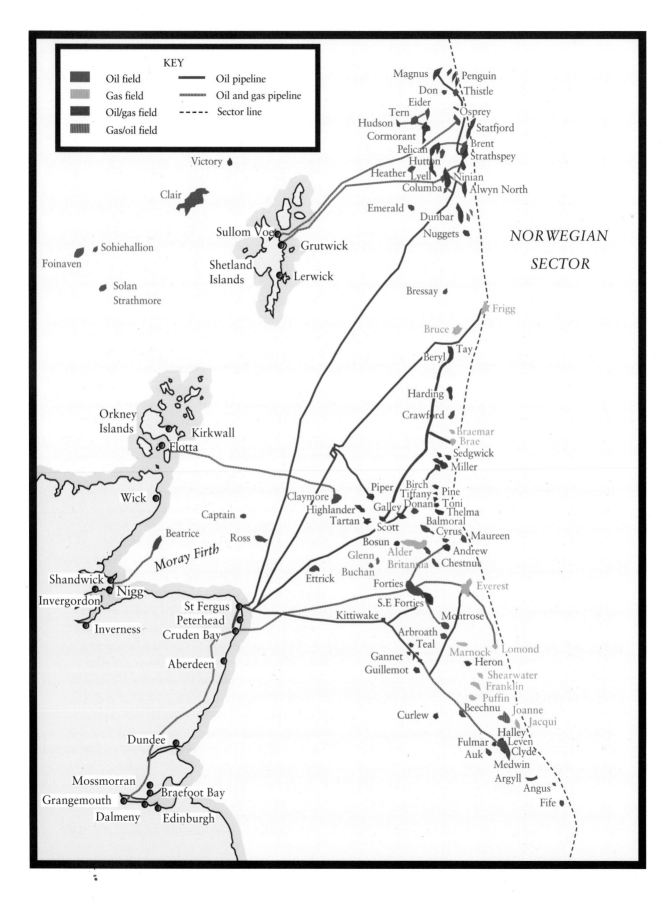

KEY

Oil field		Oil pipeline	
Gas field		Oil and gas pipeline	
Oil/gas field		Sector line	
Gas/oil field			

Victory

Clair

Sohiehallion

Foinaven

Solan
Strathmore

Sullom Voe
Grutwick

Shetland
Islands

Lerwick

NORWEGIAN

SECTOR

Magnus
Penguin
Don
Thistle
Eider
Osprey
Tern
Statfjord
Hudson
Cormorant
Brent
Pelican
Strathspey
Hutton
Heather
Lyell
Ninian
Columba
Alwyn North
Emerald
Dunbar
Nuggets

Bressay

Frigg

Bruce

Tay
Beryl

Harding
Crawford

Braemar
Brae
Sedgwick
Miller

Orkney
Islands

Kirkwall

Flotta

Wick

Captain

Beatrice

Ross

Moray Firth

Shandwick

Nigg

Invergordon

Inverness

St Fergus
Peterhead
Cruden Bay

Aberdeen

Claymore
Highlander
Tartan
Scott

Piper
Galley
Donan

Birch
Tiffany
Pine
Toni
Thelma
Balmoral
Cyrus
Maureen
Andrew
Chestnut

Bosun
Glenn
Alder
Britannia
Ettrick
Buchan
Forties

Everest

S.E Forties
Kittiwake
Montrose
Arbroath
Teal
Marnock
Lomond
Gannet
Heron
Guillemot
Shearwater
Franklin
Puffin
Curlew
Beechnut
Joanne
Jacqui
Halley
Leven
Fulmar
Clyde
Auk
Medwin
Argyll
Angus
Fife

Dundee

Mossmorran

Grangemouth
Braefoot Bay

Dalmeny
Edinburgh

Decline of Traditional Industries

Despite the benefits of new technology Scotland was entering the start of a major decline of traditional industries. By the 1960s there had been a collapse in shipbuilding which brought the industry to near disaster. The situation was reflected in the demise of many other industries, with new technologies and modernisation proving too competitive for companies such as the famous Carron Iron Works, which closed in 1982 after over 220 years in continous production.

Scottish coal, in spite of several pit closures and competition from cheaper fuels, increased its output through new markets and electricity generation. In the long term, however, its future could not be guaranteed, and the exhaustion of raw indigenous materials and the decline of heavy industries which used coal hastened its decline. By the 1980s the industry was employing only 2,000 men.

Educational Improvements

In 1945 a Scottish statute was passed to raise the school leaving age from 14 to 15. Equal opportunities through improving educational standards allowed both sexes to enter universities to train for professional positions, social services and industrial leadership. New universities were inaugurated in Strathclyde, Edinburgh (Heriot-Watt) and Dundee, and a new campus was constructed in Stirling. In 1951 the University of Edinburgh established the School of Scottish Studies, the first centre to offer study and research into a wide range of Scottish activities.

North Sea Exploration

As far back as 1930 it was suspected that oil and gas were present around Scotland's coast, but it took significant advances in technology before the first well was capped in 1967. By 1975 the first pipe line from

Left: *North Sea oil and gas fields*
Right: *Stirling University campus*

the Forties Field was run into Cruden bay, near Peterhead. By the 1980s North Sea oil and gas were contributing £6 billion each year in revenues to the Exchequer. In 1996 a new Shetland field, Foinaven, was opened up, the first in the Atlantic Ocean.

The effect upon the economies of ports such as Aberdeen and Dundee has been enormous, but the Scottish economy has been boosted generally by the demand for equipment, transportation and provisioning. Overall an estimated 300,000 people have found employment through the industry. The industry has had its disasters too, notably the fire on the oil platform, Piper Alpha, in 1988, when 166 lives were lost. While the dangers from pollution were shown by the wreck of the *Braer* off the Shetland Islands in 1993.

The Political Dimension

The 1997 General Election saw the Labour Party elected to power after 18 years of Conservative government, with a manifesto commitment to hold a referendum on the election of a Scottish Parliament. The election also saw the Labour Party retain its dominant position in Scotland, winning 57 out of the 72 seats, while the Liberal Democrat Party and the Scottish National Party consolidated their positions without making the decisive breakthrough they had hoped for. The Conservative Party suffered one of its heaviest defeats and was left with no seats at all in

ST KILDA

St Kilda is the name given to a group of islands in the Outer Hebrides now owned by the National Trust for Scotland, the largest of which is Hirta. Before their evacuation in 1930, there had been a largely self-supporting community here for over 2,000 years. The Kildans fished in small boats and trapped sea birds, such as puffin, fulmar and gannet, which live in vast numbers on the sheer cliffs of the islands. The birds were cured for food and also provided medicine, oil for lighting, feathers for mattresses and skin for shoes. Nothing was wasted.

When smallpox hit the island in the early nineteenth century the population dwindled to four adults and twelve children. But even at its height the island supported only 260 people. Accidents and disease kept their numbers down. The childbirth rate was low too, and 77 babies died in the years between 1830 and 1891 from a mysterious form of tetanus known as Kildan lockjaw. In 1930 an era ended when the 36 remaining inhabitants agreed to leave Hirta and start new lives on the mainland, where many saw trees and horses for the first time in their lives.

The islands were sold by MacLeod of MacLeod to the Marquis of Bute, who

St Kildans face the modern world

left them to the National Trust for Scotland in his will. In 1986 UNESCO designated St Kilda a World Heritage site, and declared the islands a 'testimony to the powerful work of nature and the tenacity but ultimate fragility of human settlement.'

Scotland, leaving the Liberal Democrats and the SNP disputing each other's claims to be the official opposition on Scottish affairs at Westminster.

On 11 September 1997 the electorate in Scotland was asked to vote in the second referendum on devolution in less than 20 years. Under the terms of the 1979 Referendum there were insufficient votes in favour of a Scottish Assembly to allow it to go ahead. In 1997 over 74% of the votes cast agreed that there should be a Scottish Parliamement, while over 63% agreed it should have tax-varying powers. Elections for the first Scottish Parliament in nearly 300 years will be held in 1999. Although the decision on a devolved parliament in Scotland has now been made, questions of who governs Scotland and demands for independence are unlikely to go away.

Tourism

The tourist industry is vital for the trade it generates for Scotland. It has a direct effect on the economy as so many businesses produce commodities and services aimed at visitors. In the past 50 years Scottish tourism has expanded enormously and is now one of the nation's leading industries. The tourist trade employs 177,000 people in Scotland, with an annual income from tourists of £2.4 billion.

Conservation

The world-wide interest in conservation is reflected in the recognition by the public and the government of the importance of Scotland's unique architectural and natural heritage. Two organisations, Historic Scotland and the National Trust for Scotland, act as trustees of some of the country's finest historic buildings, ancient monuments and areas of outstanding natural beauty and scientific interest.

Historic Scotland is a government agency responsible for protecting Scotland's built heritage: the ancient monuments and historic buildings of which it has such a glorious, if endangered abundance. It has over 300 monuments in its care ranging from Pictish carved stones to castles, from gasworks to pubs.

The National Trust for Scotland was formed in 1931 to act as guardian of the country's magnificent array of architectural, scenic and historic treasures, and to encourage public enjoyment of them. It is an

❦ The National Trust for Scotland

independent charity and Scotland's largest voluntary conservation body. Today it is the fourth largest landowner in Scotland. In addition it has over 100 properties in its care, including , gardens, castles, mansions and smaller buildings of architectural or historic interest.

ASPECTS OF CONTEMPORARY SCOTTISH CULTURE

Scotland today has a cultural scene to rival any major European country. The Edinburgh International Festival of Music and Drama with its vibrant Fringe festival, has been held annually since 1947 and is the largest festival of its kind in the world. In 1990 Glasgow was made European City of Culture, helping to bring its exuberant culture to the world's attention.

Literature

A rich body of Scottish poetry emerged in the immediate wake of Hugh MacDiarmid's colossal achievement, from poets writing in English and Scots, such as Sydney Goodsir Smith, Norman MacCaig, Iain Crichton Smith, Edwin Morgan, George Mackay Brown and Robert Garioch. The work of the poet Sorley Maclean (1911-1996), known as Somhairle MacGill-Eain in Gaelic, has helped to establish Gaelic as a language capable of modern as well as traditional expression. In the 1960s and 70s major poets such as Douglas Dunn and Liz Lochhead emerged and continue to delight. In recent years a younger generation of poets such as Robert Crawford, Carol Anne Duffy, Kathleen Jamie, Jackie Kay and Don Patterson have established reputations which seem certain to deepen.

Novels and shorter fiction from Scottish writers such as Booker prize winning James Kelman, Alasdair Gray, Iain Banks and Irvine Welsh have achieved a wide readership. Indeed the film

BAXTERS OF SPEYSIDE

The Baxter family came to Fochabers in Moray in the 1740s. In 1868 George and Margaret Baxter ran the village grocery shop there. George Baxter recognised that there was a potential market for home-made goods, and the business grew into a company which could supply a much larger population.

George extended the family business by encouraging his wife to provide recipes used for Baxter's soups, jams and other food products. In the next generation William Baxter, known as 'WAB', and his wife Ethel, kept true to George and Margaret's original intention of producing quality foods, and through their commercial vision, and that of their sons Gordon and Ian, the turnover of the business rose from £40,000 in 1947 to £40 million in 1996. The company has successfully entered the overseas market in 30 countries and increased its staff from 11 to over 600. A fourth generation of Baxters now runs the family business.

The cellar shop, Fochabers

Trainspotting, directed by Danny Boyle and based on Welsh's novel of Edinburgh's drug culture, has attracted a cult following akin to that of a rock band.

Music

Scottish music makers in every musical form from classical and rock to jazz and folk, continue to attract appreciative international audiences. The Royal Scottish National Orchestra is recognised for its versaility and innovative programme planning, and for its commissioning of new works, while folk-rock bands such as Runrig have successfully combined rock music with traditional Gaelic music and song.

Sport

The enjoyment of sport has a major role in the life of contemporary Scotland. Golf of course Scotland gave to the world, which still regards it as the home of the

Above: Poets' Pub *by Alexander Moffat*
Below: *dancing at Glasgow's Highland Games*

Stories of fabulous beasts inhabiting lochs and firths are common in Celtic folklore. The earliest reference to a strange creature in Loch Ness dates from AD 565 when St Columba is supposed to have pacified a 'water horse' which was terrorising the locals. Surprisingly, given the good views of the loch afforded by the surrounding glen, little else was reported until the 1930s, when the press got hold of stories of strange sightings and exploited them to their full.

The recorded sightings seem to agree upon a large aquatic animal, with a multi-humped back, a long neck and small head. So far the banks of scientific equipment directed at the loch have failed to provide most people with convincing proof. What is evident, however, is that Nessie has given many people hours of mostly

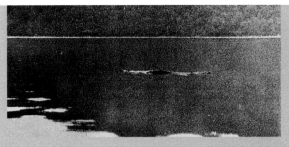

Loch Ness's 'monster' … spotted in 1958

harmless fun. If there is anything lurking there, Loch Ness is certainly big, dark and deep enough to hide it for a good many years yet.

game. It is thought to have originated in the fifteenth century, and its name to be derived from the Old Scots word 'gowff', meaning to stroke or strike.

Football continues to be a great crowd puller, and the most popular team sport played and watched in Scotland as in the rest of the world. The great rival Glasgow clubs, Celtic and Rangers, known as 'the old firm', are among the perennial top teams in the Scottish Football League, and attract fanatical devotion from their fans, drawn in the main from the city's Catholic and Protestant communities respectively. The national soccer and rugby teams also attract fervent support, with many of their fans adorned in patriotic colours and symbols.

Highland Games are held each summer all over Scotland, and are based on traditional tests of strength and skills, such as tossing the caber, throwing the hammer and stone, running, jumping, dancing and piping. The first organised games were held in the 1820s and have been exported around the world to wherever there are local communities of Scottish descent, such as Canada, the USA and New Zealand.

Winter sports such as curling and skiing are popular, the latter bringing thousands of people to the slopes. The Highlands also attract thousands of climbers. For many climbers the sport of 'Munro bagging' is an obsession. The Munros are mountains named after Sir Hugh Munro (1856-1919), who in 1891 drew up a table of 238 peaks over 3000 ft. in height. The Scottish Mountaineering Club has recently announced plans to add eight more mountains. Climbers who had 'bagged' the lot now must add another eight climbs if they are to complete the table.

Scotland's future

Scotland today stands on the brink of a new millennium. A thousand years from now will the concept of 'Scotland' as a place with its own identity still have meaning or will it have become, like Caledonia or Dalriada, an historical location only? Without a time-machine the answer must remain a matter of opinion; and yet, by whatever name it is known, by whatever method its affairs are governed, its economy managed, its culture expressed, it is dificult to imagine that it will not still have sufficient differences to mark it out as distinctive within these isles, this continent, this planet. At the very least its geography and the geology which underpins it will ensure that it will remain a place apart as long as there are still people to appreciate its unique beauty and grandeur.

Select bibliography

Burton, John Hill, *History of Scotland* (1852)
Bygone Scotland (printed for the author by T & A Constable,1924)
Carnegie, Andrew, *My Own Story* (Houghton Mifflin,1920)
Charnley, Bob, *A Voyage to St Kilda* (Maclean Press,1993)
Charnley, Bob, *Last Greetings from St Kilda* (Stenlake & McCourt,1989)
Chitnis, Anand C, *The Scottish Enlightenment* (Groom Helm,1976)
Collins Encyclopaedia of Scotland, ed. J Keay and J Keay (HarperCollins,1994)
Cruden, Stuart, *An Introduction to the Medieval Abbeys and Priories of Scotland* (HMSO,1960)
Defoe, Daniel, *Tour Through the Whole Island of Great Britain* (1724–7)
Dewar Gibb, Andrew, *The Scottish Empire* (Alexander Maclehose,1937)
Donnachie, I, and Hewitt, G, *A Companion to Scottish History* (Batsford, 1989)
Edinburgh in the Age of Reason (Edinburgh University Press,1967)
Edwards, Samuel, *Alexander MacKenzie* (printed by Alvin Redman,1965)
Fisher, Andrew, *A Traveller's History of Scotland* (Windrush Press,1990)
Geddie, John, *The Fringes of Edinburgh* (W & R Chambers)
History of Dundee (Winter, Duncan & Co., Dundee,1878)
Grant, James, *Cassell's Old and New Edinburgh: Its History, its People, and its Places* vols I-III (Cassell, Peter, Galpin & Co.,1882)
Hutcheson Campbell, Roy, *Carron Company* (Oliver & Boyd,1961)
Hutton, Ronald, *Pagan Religions of the Ancient British Isles* (Blackwell,1993)
Johnson's Journey to the Western Islands of Scotland and Boswell's Journal of a Tour to the Hebrides with Samuel Johnson, LL.D., ed. R W Chapman (OUP,1924)
Lindsay, Ian G, *Georgian Edinburgh* (Oliver & Boyd,1865)
Lynch, Michael, *Scotland: A New History* (Pimlico,1995)
MacDonald, John, *Travels in Various Parts of Europe, Asia and Africa* (J Forbes,1790)
McEwan, John, *Who Owns Scotland?* (EUSPB,1972)

Macgregor, Forbes, *Famous Scots* (Gordon Wright Publishing,1984)
MacKenzie, Alexander, *The Highland Clearances* (Mercat Press,1883)
MacKenzie, Alexander, *The Prophecies of the Brahan Seer* (Eneas MacKay, 1924)
Maclean, Fitzroy, *Scotland: A Concise History* (Thames & Hudson,1993)
MacPherson, G W, *John MacPherson, the Skye Martyr* (Skye Graphics,1982)
Martin, Martin, *A Voyage to St Kilda 1697* (James Thin,1986)
Masson, Rosaline, *Edinburgh*, (A & C Black,1931)
Maxwell, Sir Herbert, *Edinburgh: A Historical Study* (Williams & Norgate,1916)
Nicolson, Alexander, *History of Skye* (McLean Press,1930)
Piggott, Roger, *Cairnpaple* (HMSO,1951)
Prebble, John, *Culloden* (1961)
Prebble, John, *Glencoe* (1966)
Prebble, John, *The Highland Clearances* (1962)
Prebble, John, *The Lion in the North* (1971)
Quine, David A., *St Kilda Revisited* (Dowland Press, 1983)
Reid, J M, *Scotland, Past and Present* (OUP, 1959)
Ritchie, Anna, *Picts* (HMSO,1989)
Ritchie, Anna, *Scotland BC* (HMSO,1988)
Ritchie, Anna, and Breeze, David J, *Invaders of Scotland* (HMSO,1991)
Ritchie, J N G, *Brochs of Scotland* (Shire Publications,1988)
Robertson, William, *History of Scotland* (c.1770)
Scott, Reginald, *Discoveries of Witchcraft* (1584)
Scotland: A Concise Cultural History, ed. Scott (Mainstream Publishing,1993)
Scotland, A New Study, ed. Clapperton (David & Charles,1983)
Scottish Pageants, vols I–III, ed. Mure MacKenzie (Oliver & Boyd,1946–50)
Sitwell, Sacheverell, and Bamford, F, *Edinburgh* (Faber and Faber,1938)
Steel, Tom, *The Life and Death of St Kilda*, (1975)
Tappan, E M, *In Feudal Times*, revised edn (George G Harrap, 1939)
Thompson, Francis, *The Crofting Years* (Luath Press, 1984)
Wilson, Andrew P, *Milestones in the Royal Mile* (John McQueen & Son,1947)

Picture acknowledgements

The publisher is grateful to the following people and organisations for permission to reproduce copyright images in their possession (numbers refer to pages in this book): Abbotsford Collection 131 bottom and 166; The Ancient Art & Architecture Collection Ltd 23, 26, 66 and 68, and J Beecham 48 right, and Cheryl Hague 14 right, and Ronald Sheridan 16, 18 both, 20, 21, 33, 46 top, 56 right, 60, 79 left, 82 left, 84 left and 90, and John P Stevens 35 and 37, and Charles Tait 13 and 15 top, and Brian Wilson 69 and 124 right; Argyll, the Isles, Loch Lomond, Stirling & Trossachs Tourist Board 98 both; Baxters of Speyside Ltd 185; Burns Monument Trust 130 both and 131 top; Carnegie Birthplace Trust 161; Crown Copyright: Reproduced by Permission of Historic Scotland 14 left, 15 bottom, 19, 24, 39, 40 right, 43 right, 72 right, 79 right and 107; Crown Copyright: Keeper of the Records for Scotland 57, 76, 90 and 160; Dundee Heritage Trust/Spanphoto 172; Graham Ellis 153; Express Syndication 187; Fine Art Photographs 27, 71, 86 bottom, 110 top, 119, 123, 126 and 147 right; Pluscarden Abbey 41; Glasgow Museums: 87 top, 155; Dennis Hardley cover (see below for details); Jim Henderson AMPA cover (see below for details); Imperial War Museum, London 174 bottom and 177 bottom; Chief Superintendent Cooper, Leith Police, D. Division and Edinburgh Council 150; Mary Evans Picture Library 22 bottom, 28 top, 31, 32 both, 34 left, 36, 40 top, 42, 43 left, 45, 46 bottom, 48 left, 51, 56 left, 58, 59, 61, 62, 70, 72 left, 75, 77, 78, 80 both, 81 both, 83, 84 right, 89, 93, 94 bottom right, 97, 100, 103, 104, 108, 109, 114 Stewart, Cameron and Graham tartans, 120, 128, 133, 134 both, 137, 140 (four), 145, 148, 151 both, 152 both, 154 both, 156 both, 158, 159, 162, 163 bottom left and right, 164, 165 both, 167 left, 173, 174 top and 177 top, and Jeffrey Morgan 176; Private Scottish Collection 50; National Gallery of Scotland 122, 138, 146 right, 147 left and 167 right; National Library of Scotland 64 top and 86 top; National Library of Scotland/Roxburghe Estates 34 right; The National Trust for Scotland 28 bottom, 73, 94 top and bottom left, 99 top, 102 both, 105, 110 bottom left and right, 113, 114 bottom right both, 124 left, 143 bottom,163 top, 169 three, 184 and cover (see below for details); John Neil, Boys' Brigade Glasgow Battalion 175; Antonia Reeve 146 left; Royal Commission on the Ancient and Historical Monuments of Scotland 10, 82 right and 149; Scotsman Publications Ltd 170; the Scottish National Portrait Gallery 49 right, 53, 63, 64 bottom, 67 both, 87 bottom, 129, 168, 180 and 186 top; Mrs Maxwell Stuart 106 bottom right; Tony Stone Images/ Marcus Brooke bottom 186; UGC UK Ltd 178 bottom. Malt whisky selection 178 (left to right) Aberlour: Campbell Distillers; Blair Athol: United Distillers; The Edradour: Campbell Distillers; Glenfiddich: William Grant & Sons; Glenmorangie: the Glenmorangie Distillery Company; The Glenturret: Matthew Gloag & Son; Knockando: Justerini & Brooks; Loch Ranza: Isle of Arran Distillers; Talisker: United Distillers; and Cardhu: United Distillers. All other illustrations are either copyright Jarrold Publishing or out of copyright.

Cover images (clockwise from the top left): posthumous portrait of Mary, Queen of Scots at Falkland Palace, Fife (The National Trust for Scotland); Fyvie Castle, Aberdeenshire (Jim Henderson AMPA); swords of the Marquis of Tullibardine, Prince Charles Edward Stuart and the Earl of Cromarty, from the Swords and Sorrows Exhibition (The National Trust for Scotland); and Loch Etive and Ben Cruachan, Connel, Argyll and Bute (Dennis Hardley). The tartan is Modern Hunting Stewart of Appin.

Index